JOHN ROBERT GODLEY
OF CANTERBURY

JOHN ROBERT GODLEY

JOHN ROBERT GODLEY

OF CANTERBURY

by

C. E. CARRINGTON, M.A.

Christ Church, Oxford

Sans Dieu Rien

LONDON

CAMBRIDGE UNIVERSITY PRESS

AUSTRALIA AND NEW ZEALAND

WHITCOMBE AND TOMBS LIMITED

CAMBRIDGE UNIVERSITY PRESS
Cambridge, New York, Melbourne, Madrid, Cape Town, Singapore, São Paulo

Cambridge University Press
The Edinburgh Building, Cambridge CB2 8RU, UK

Published in the United States of America by Cambridge University Press, New York

www.cambridge.org
Information on this title: www.cambridge.org/9780521045780

© Cambridge University Press 1950

First published 1950
This digitally printed version 2008

A catalogue record for this publication is available from the British Library

ISBN 978-0-521-04578-0 hardback
ISBN 978-0-521-07275-5 paperback

Acknowledgements

My first thanks are due to the members of the Godley family who have placed their archives at my disposal, and especially to Miss F. E. Godley, Lord Kilbracken, General Sir Alexander Godley, and the Hon. John Godley. The Viscount Cobham, with equal generosity, allowed me to search the Lyttelton papers at Hagley Hall. Lord Norton has been most helpful in tracing the papers of C. B. Adderley (the first Lord Norton). I am obliged to Sir James Hight and to Professor W. P. Morrell who helped me, many years ago, in a research into the archives of early Canterbury, in Christchurch and Dunedin; also to the Association of Universities of the British Commonwealth which enabled me to undertake this research; to Mr R. H. Dundas, Christ Church, Oxford; to Dr E. D. Laborde, Harrow School; to Professor A. F. Hattersley, University of Natal, and to Mr C. R. Straubel of Christchurch, New Zealand. Mr H. R. Aldridge of the British Museum has taken a great deal of trouble in investigating the Gladstone Papers for relevant material. The librarian of the Royal Empire Society has been most helpful. For secretarial assistance I am obliged to Mrs L. K. Mills, and Miss F. Short.

A3

Contents

Contents

Contents

Contents

Illustrations

Preface

THE centenary of the Canterbury Settlement in New Zealand is an occasion for drawing attention to an early Victorian whose name is little known to-day outside the narrow circle of those interested in the history of the Dominions. A typical man of his age—earnest, candid, single-minded, deeply religious, and at the same time bold, adventurous and independent—John Robert Godley, the Founder of Canterbury, exhibited qualities of mind which are not so evident among the leaders of the introverted age in which we now live. He was the friend of Gladstone, Thackeray, Tennyson, and other leading figures in Victorian society, but especially he inspired and encouraged a group of young politicians who, between 1847 and 1861, fostered the emergent nationalism of the young Dominions. Godley's short career is associated with a failure and two successes. The tragedy of Ireland in the 1840s first moved his political activity, and posterity may well regret his failure to convert English politicians to his magnanimous way of thinking. Next he founded the model colony, in New Zealand; and, in the last years of his short life, took a great part in rationalizing the defences of the British Empire. Entire self-government, autonomy of the colonial Churches, and in military matters the 'self-reliant policy' were the subjects to which he gave his attention. His views on what came to be known as Dominion Status were far in advance of the common thought of his age, either in England or in the colonies.

Preface

The Canterbury Settlement as the climax of the Colonial Reform movement, and Godley, as the man who achieved his ideal by founding Canterbury, will be found worth the attention of all who wish to know how free nations come to birth.

C.E.C.

Cambridge Dec. 1949

John Robert Godley 1814-1861

1814, May 29 . . .	Born at 33 Merrion Square, Dublin.
1824	To the Rev. E. Ward's school at Iver.
1828, January . .	To Harrow School.
1832, October . . .	To Christ Church, Oxford.
1836, October 7 . .	B.A. Oxon.
1837-38	Travels in France, Germany, Norway, Sweden (dates uncertain).
1839, June 24 . . .	Called to the Irish Bar in Dublin.
1839-41	In practice at the Irish Bar.
1841	Acting for his father at Killegar.
1842	Foreman of the Grand Jury, Co. Leitrim.
1842, July-November .	Travels in U.S.A. and Canada.
1843	High Sheriff of Co. Leitrim.
1844, May (?) . . .	Published *Letters from America*.
1844, July	J.P. and D.L.
1845, January . . .	Gave evidence before Lord Devon's Commission on Ireland.
1846, June	In London. Engaged to be married.
September 29 .	Married Charlotte Wynne at Voelas, North Wales.
December . .	On the working committee of the Irish Landlords' assembly.
1847, March 31 . .	Publication of Godley's Irish Emigration plan.
June 17 . . .	Eldest child, Arthur, born in London.
June 22 . . .	Gave evidence before the House of Lords' Committee on Irish emigration.
August 9-11 .	Election for Co. Leitrim. Defeated.
November . .	Met E. G. Wakefield at Malvern.
December (?) .	Began to reside at 69 Gloucester Place, London.
1848, March . . .	The Canterbury Association founded.
1848-49	Leader-writer for the *Morning Chronicle*.
1849, September . .	Advised to go abroad for his health.
December 13 .	Sailed for New Zealand, from Plymouth.
1850, March 25 . .	At Dunedin, New Zealand.
April 12 . . .	First visit to Canterbury, New Zealand.
April-November	At Wellington, New Zealand.

Chronology

GODLEY OF KILLEGAR, *County Leitrim*

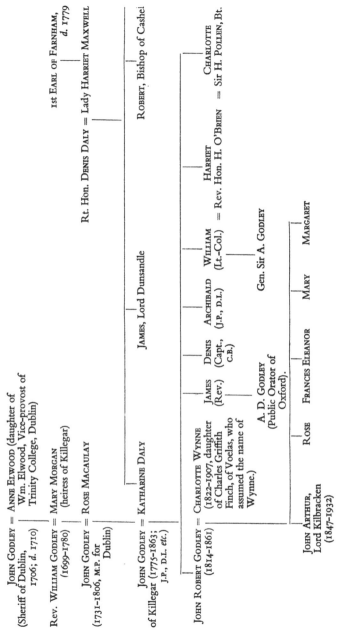

JOHN ROBERT GODLEY
OF CANTERBURY

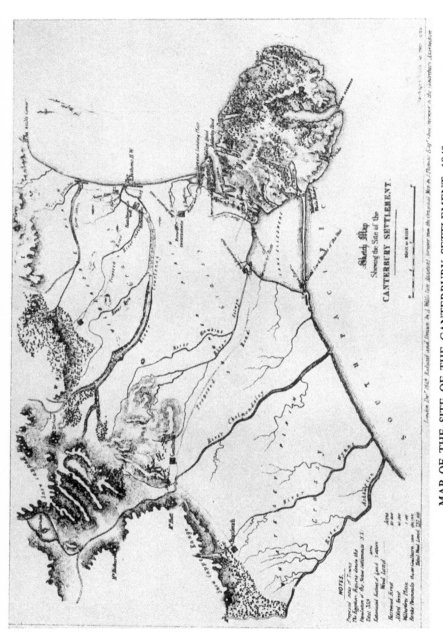

MAP OF THE SITE OF THE CANTERBURY SETTLEMENT, 1849

Based on Captain J. Thomas's first sketch map, and published by the Canterbury Association in December,

CHAPTER I

Education of an Irish Gentleman

FORTNIGHTLY sailings from Liverpool to Halifax and Boston by Samuel Cunard's new steam-ships were first announced in September, 1841; with them began the age of the globe-trotters. In the following year among hundreds of passengers who set out to form their impressions of the New World was Charles Dickens, already celebrated and assured that he would be well paid for whatever he cared to write about America; another passenger, an Irish barrister named John Robert Godley was unknown outside the circle of his family and college friends. Dickens's *American Notes*, published before the end of the year 1842, caused no little stir for their candid comments on private manners and social organisation in the United States, not least for his denunciation of the book-pirates in America, who made free with the author's copyrights. Godley, too, wrote a book, as an afterthought. His friend Charles Adderley persuaded him to work up his long letters home into a compilation which John Murray published, in two small volumes, early in 1844, under the title of *Letters from America.*

Covering the same ground as Dickens's *Notes* it was as different from it as a book could be. Godley resolutely determined to make no personal remarks, to use no satire, and to see the best in American institutions, though he was, by nature and habit, entirely out of sympathy with the

American way of life. A bad mixer, as Americans would
say, rather lonely and diffident, he blamed himself for
indulging in the luxury of travel when so much was to be
done for the public good in his own country of Ireland.
The sight of Irish immigrants prosperously settled across
the Atlantic gave him greater pleasure than any wonders
of the New World. And the discovery that in the United
States there was a flourishing episcopal church, in communion with Canterbury, but self-governing and self-
reliant, gave him more food for thought than any observations of democracy in action. A solemn young man, by
twentieth-century standards, yet he never omitted to notice
a good horse and seized every opportunity of a day's
shooting. The sport, though, was never as good as in
County Leitrim. Perhaps no incident delighted him more
than the tribute paid him by a fellow-passenger when he
brought down a duck with a long shot from the rail of a
river-steamer: 'Well, you're a smarter chap with a piece
than I took you for.'

In a modest way, Godley's *Letters from America*
attracted notice. His college tutor, Roundell Palmer (many
years later Lord Chancellor and Earl of Selborne) helped
to revise the manuscript and, when Godley was in London,
invited him to meet the American ambassador, Mr Everett,
at dinner, (27th May, 1844). They assured him he had
written the best account of America by any Englishman;
and Palmer told him that Mr Gladstone wished to make
his acquaintance. Gladstone at that date was but a rising
politician and a Tory. He was aged thirty-five, that is five
years older than Godley. Time would show that the voyage
to America had supplied Godley with a vocation. The
favourable reception of his book had given him an opening
in public life, which he sorely needed. He was soon required
to give evidence on Irish emigration to Canada before a
Royal Commission on Irish distress, then sitting under the
Presidency of Lord Devon. At thirty he was deeply dissatisfied with the small progress he had made in his career

and confessed his dissatisfaction in many letters to his father.

Old John Godley, born as long ago as 1775, 'a short thick-set man in old-fashioned black clothes', was the kindest of parents but none the less an autocrat in his own house. The son, a scholar brought up at English schools, admitted sadly that he knew little of the family estates; the father managed all. In his youth John Godley had built Killegar House as a country residence on a piece of land inherited from his grandmother, 'a place of the most wild beauty among hills, woods and lakes, bogland and marsh-land and river, remote and almost inaccessible'. He acquired land in County Leitrim and County Meath which he administered as a model landlord, a great organiser of churches and schools. Of a Dublin family, which had pro-duced several members of parliament, John Godley had married Catherine Daly, whose two brothers were the Bishop of Cashel and Lord Dunsandle. Husband and wife were connected with half the Protestant Ascendancy. Good protestant churchmen as the Godleys were, it would never have occurred to them to doubt that loyalty to Church and Crown was the right cause for a trueborn Irishman.

Their eldest son, John Robert, the subject of this memoir, was born on 29th May, 1814, at 33 Merrion Square, the Dublin house of his grandmother, Lady Harriet Daly, who was Lord Farnham's daughter.

Before his tenth birthday young John was sent to Eng-land, a formidable journey in 1824, eighty miles by stage-coach from Killegar to Dublin, then by the new steam-packet to Holyhead, then two hundred miles by coach over the Snowdon range and across the midland plain by Telford's Holyhead Road, one of the wonders of the age. The last stage was made by post-chaise to the Rev. Edward Ward's parsonage at Iver near Uxbridge, where a few boys were prepared for entrance to the public schools. The journey cost £11 or £12, no small sum in the values of those days, and a substantial addition to Mr Ward's high

fees of no less than £ 84 for each half-year. For this sum
he supplied more than mere instruction; he was a kind,
considerate master who took a great liking to the lonely
little boy and wrote, with evident pleasure, to his parents
in Ireland that the tears of his first homesickness were
quickly dried. Mr Ward was able to say of young Godley
in his first half: 'His abilities are good, his diligence considerable, and his moral principles more established than
is usually seen at so early an age'—this at ten years old.
Year by year such commendations were repeated until, in
January, 1828, he was entered at Harrow School of which
the high steeple on its hill could be seen, seven miles away
from Iver, across the fields. His old master, in handing him
over to the new, regretted that so exemplary a pupil was
not to be placed higher in the school. And, in assuring the
parents that their boy might always turn to him if he needed
a friend, he wrote: 'I have rarely parted with a pupil whose
proficiency has been more satisfactory throughout'. The
little boy, however, had not been happy at Iver; his next
school was to please him better.

   That reforming spirit which was to change the whole
character of the English upper and middle classes through
the Public schools had just begun to work, and Godley's
new housemaster, Mr Batten, was in the van of the movement. In that very term he failed, by a narrow margin, to
win the appointment as headmaster of Rugby, and it is
clear from Batten's letters that he was a man of the same
stamp as his celebrated and successful rival, Dr Thomas
Arnold. He, too, assumed that the duty of an English
schoolmaster was to make his charges into Christian gentlemen. As at Iver, so at Harrow, Godley's half-yearly reports
arrived at Killegar with long personal letters of eulogy from
the housemaster. Nothing was ever said against him but
that he was a little too fond of cricket; no warning note was
sounded, except some anxiety about his health. Coughs and
colds, exhaustion after the long journeys, and doctor's bills
appear perhaps too frequently in the letters. Mr Batten

wrote of the earnest seriousness displayed by John Godley at his confirmation, of the excellent reforms and the change of tone in the school inspired by Dr Longley, the new headmaster, and of John's success in his school work. In 1831 he won second place in the scholarship examination, though a year below the usual age, and was offered a Sayer Scholarship at Caius College, Cambridge. On his father's advice he declined it, having noticed that an Irishman born would not be eligible for a fellowship at Caius. Both father and son preferred an attempt for an open scholarship at Oxford in the following year. Godley was captain of the Harrow XI at cricket in 1831, and in March, 1832, won his scholarship. A Harrovian school hero, he carved his name, where it may still be seen among many famous names, on the panelled wall of the celebrated Fourth Form Room. In May he went up to interview Dr Gaisford, the Dean of Christ Church, the greatest Greek scholar of the age and, in September, 1832, was entered as a commoner. To the 'Lyon' scholarship provided by the Governors of Harrow School, he later added an exhibition, on the foundation of Dr Fell, at Christ Church.

At Harrow he had made some friends of whom one or two, notably W. P. Prendergast—afterwards a Dublin lawyer—maintained their friendship through life, and Harrow gave him none but happy memories of boyish success. Oxford was to give him more and to confront him with failure.

It will not be amiss to say a few words about the great House to which Godley was admitted in 1832, and which he was to commemorate in the name of Christchurch, New Zealand. Wolsey's magnificent project:

> though unfinish'd, yet so famous,
> So excellent in art, and still so rising
> That Christendom shall ever speak his virtue,

re-founded by King Henry VIII as a cathedral and a college under a single governing body, the wealthiest and the most extensive foundation in either university, was never more pre-eminent than at the beginning of the nineteenth century, a nursery of statesmen and viceroys. Its most brilliant moment, perhaps, was a year or two before Godley's time when William Ewart Gladstone was the most conspicuous among the undergraduates. So notable was he in his generation that a 'W.E.G. Club' was formed among his contemporaries when he went down from Oxford in 1832. Among his associates at Christ Church had been Roundell Palmer, the future Lord Chancellor, James Ramsay (later Lord Dalhousie) and Charles Canning the future viceroys, and Lord Lincoln (later the 5th Duke of Newcastle) the future Secretary of State for War and the Colonies. Their friends at Oxford, in other colleges, were such men as Henry Manning the future cardinal, Sidney Herbert, Edward Cardwell, Robert Lowe, and James Bruce (later as Lord Elgin the most eminent of Canadian governors). With few exceptions these men were High-Churchmen and, in their youth, high Tories. Gladstone, in particular, was regarded by the party leaders, when they looked to the universities for young men of mark, as the rising hope of the Tory Party. Thirty or forty years on, when the world had changed out of all recognition, through the impulse of the new industrialism, all these young aristocrats had changed with the times. What they had inherited from their families or acquired at Oxford, their strong sense of public duty, their belief in the value of personal endeavour and self-help, their sympathy with the unfortunate, their scepticism about all materialist pedantries and tyrannies—these ingrained habits of mind had led them all towards the left in politics. Enlightened thinking, as the world then was, tended to point that way. They abandoned the old rigid Tory doctrines for a new liberal conservatism or even for the complete liberalism of the late Victorian age. Yet none of them had changed their fundamental belief in a society based upon the principles of the Christian religion, that is to say, upon natural duties, not natural rights.

This was the tradition among the young men at Oxford

when Godley became one of them, at eighteen years old. In his first year an event occurred in Oxford which was to resound through the nineteenth century though it would hardly be noticed in the newspapers if it occurred to-day. The Rev. John Keble preached a sermon in the University Church upon national apostacy, the occasion being the suppression, by the Whig government, of some bishoprics in the Irish Protestant Church. England was then ripe for a religious revival. Evangelicalism, largely spread by the Methodists, had already permeated the nation, giving the age its serious, even sombre, tone. But, while simple Bible Christianity, personal religion, was already prevalent, was even becoming modish, the organization of the national Church was untouched by it. The Church seemed to have parted company with the religion it professed. The movement which John Keble inaugurated at Oxford in July, 1833, and which was propagated by a series of publications called *Tracts for the Times* was designed to carry out a revolution in England, to free the national Church from its subservience to courts and parliaments composed largely of free-thinkers, and to elevate the Church into its true place as a divinely-inspired national organism. It is useless to attempt to understand the politics of nineteenth century England, or the background of Godley's Canterbury Settlement, except in terms of the Evangelical Revival and the Tractarian or Oxford Movement. The tide of religious revival directed the motives of most Englishmen in that age, and all politicians were deeply concerned with the claim of a party in the Church to take a greater share in directing the life of the nation. Gladstone and his set were, in the first instance, Church reformers. The intellectual leader of the Oxford Movement for Church reform was Canon Pusey, of Christ Church, whose followers were known as Pusey-ites. Henry O'Brien, the rector at Killegar who married Godley's sister, was something of a Pusey-ite, and Godley himself did not pass through Oxford untouched by the enthusiasm that was the mark of his generation.

It need not be supposed, however, that aspirations for Church reform and political fame filled the hours of all the undergradutes of Christ Church in the eighteen-thirties. Many years later Godley told his son that he had spent his time at Oxford in riding and not reading, and Christ Church was renowned for its hunting men no less than for its reading men. The young country squires who then engrossed so large a share of places at the universities neglected none of the privileges of rank and wealth. The world was all before them, and all theirs. If they kept their chapels, as indeed they were obliged to do, it was in a pink hunting-coat hastily concealed beneath a surplice; if they halloo-ed their applause of young Gladstone's oratory at the Union Society, it was an entertainment to conclude a wine-party; and their classical studies were the minimum that enabled them to reside in the pleasant Georgian quad-rangles of Christ Church.

Whatever the proportion of his time that Godley allotted to hunting and to cricket, he began his studies assiduously. He read Greek with Roundell Palmer, then a classical tutor at the neighbouring college of Merton and barely three years older than his pupil. Palmer, in his memoirs, wrote with enthusiasm of Godley's 'high intellectual gifts and noble aspirations'; he was 'a born politician'. But these aspirations were not fulfilled at Oxford and when Godley appeared in the schools for his examinations, in 1835, he did not obtain the first-class honours which were necessary to qualify him for a fellowship and an academic career. A chastened lad of twenty-one is not to be taken too literally when writing to his father to confess his failure at the university, and his letter, of 13th November, 1835, is more passionate than it would have been if written after long reflection. 'I have not done so well as I hoped,' he wrote before the end of the examination, 'though I am sure of a second-class. Palmer thought me sure of a first.' He had been unlucky, he said, in the order of his papers, but admitted that he had neglected to prepare one of the subjects. But there was a more serious weakness in his performance. 'The last month,' he wrote, 'I have been more nervous and wretched than I would have conceived possible. I would not endure the misery which I have done, thinking of it all day and dreaming all night, for fifty first-classes. The sooner I lose sight of Oxford the better.' And yet a 'second in Greats' has always been considered a very respectable degree. To conclude this sad tale, it may be mentioned that Gladstone, a year or two before Godley, and Ruskin, a year or two after him, complained of being driven too hard in their studies at Christ Church.

He went back to Ireland a disappointed young man, conscious that he had not cut the figure foretold by his school record and his tutor's confidence. An excuse, if not a consolation, was his uncertain health. A tendency to what his doctor called chronic laryngitis, or more laughingly 'clergyman's sore throat', had interfered with work and play, warning him that his voice might not bear the strain imposed by the public speaking which a political career would require. Even so, his years at Oxford were not time lost. There were influences that never ceased to move him, memories of his hopeful youth when Newman's silvery voice pleaded from St. Mary's pulpit, in phrasing as lucid as it was eloquent, for the historic cause of the national Church; lessons learned from Palmer's precise and lawyerly scholarship; above all the friendship of the young men of his class against whose wits he sharpened his own. They had recognized Godley as the natural leader of their little society, and, some years later, one who was associated with them gave his opinion that 'the young men of Godley's school resemble both in heart and head the nobler spirits of Elizabeth's time'.

Godley took his degree on 7th October, 1836, and nearly three years later, in June, 1839, he was called to the Irish Bar in Dublin. Few records remain of the intervening period, which, it may be supposed, he spent largely at Dublin or at Killegar. Some part of the time, however,

was spent in foreign travel which won for him the description given him in the Harrow School Register, 'Godley, a
great traveller'. A grand tour of France, Switzerland, and
Italy was common enough as a coping-stone to the education of young gentlemen in those days, but Godley's tours
were out of the ordinary. He did not cross the Alps but
turned northward to Germany, even to Norway and
Sweden, which tourists then rarely visited. It is evident, too,
from his later writings, that he became very well acquainted
with French life and literature. The only letter that survives
from these three years was not, however, written from
abroad but from Batt's Hotel, London, on 2nd June, 1837.
He wrote to his father very cheerfully of a journey from
Ireland, using the new Liverpool and London Railway to
Tamworth. Thence he posted to Hams Hall in Warwick-
shire to stay with his college friend, Charles Adderley.
Hams Hall was a splendid mansion amid historic oak trees,
maintained in a style far grander than was customary on
Irish estates, and furnished, Godley thought, rather too
lavishly. The Hall and the royalist tradition of the Adderley
family touched his romantic sensibilities, and honest,
generous, forthright Charles Adderley was to be his lifelong correspondent. From Hams Hall he posted to Oxford
to meet old friends, pay old scores, and 'keep Bachelor's
and Master's terms', as well-pleased at re-visiting his old
college as, two years earlier, he had been at leaving it. He
picked up another Christ Church friend, Charles Wynne,
and posted to town with him for a sight-seeing holiday and
to visit friends, notably Palmer, whom they found established in chambers, as a rising barrister of Lincoln's Inn.

When Godley was called to the Bar he wrote home
dutifully to say that he was determined to devote himself
to his profession; so earnest a declaration was it that he felt
obliged to end the letter by apologizing. It was not a son's
part to preach to his father. He wrote also to Adderley in
another vein. The Irish Bar was disagreeable and offered
little prospect of advancement. Worst of all, there was not

enough to do. He must have occupation for his untiring
energy, food for his ambition. He could never be content
with the life of a briefless barrister in Dublin, having no
taste for general society. Even country sports, the delight
of Irish squires, palled on him at the end of every shooting
season. He applied himself to serious reading—history and
theology—and recorded his observations in long letters to
his friend. Adderley should read Burke, 'get him by heart,
the greatest political writer that we have'. But dilettante
reading was worthless; a man should take a period of
history and master it, draw from it a lesson for his own life
and times. Let Adderley begin with Burke and the French
Revolution.

Godley saw much of his grandmother, Lady Harriet,
who remembered the old world before 1789. She regaled
him with stories of the splendours of Versailles in the days
of *la vieille cour* and never realised that he found the tale
of irresponsible luxury disgusting. If that was the age of
chivalry whose passing was deplored by Burke, it was better
dead. He found in de Tocqueville another picture that
pleased him better, the loyalist province of La Vendée.
Why had the seigneurs, the priests, and the peasants of one
province united to defend their church and their social
system against the materialist excesses of debauched
Parisians? La Vendée had been an integrated society where
men knew and did their duty, whether they were rich or
poor. And its strength lay in a sense of unity felt by all
because class differences were slight. The squires of the
bocage, a broken undulating wooded region, were small
men who lived on their estates and minded their business,
not great nobles wasting their lives at Court. Above all
there was in La Vendée 'a numerous, resident clergy'
devoted to their sacred profession. Was there not a lesson
here for Ireland? And would not Church reform help to
solve the Irish problem? The Irish squires and Protestant
clergy had failed in their duty.

England was then much agitated by the *Tracts for the*

Times which Newman and Pusey were publishing. Godley admitted that they were his 'hobby'. He was called upon to expound them to his friends and family. He wrote at length to his father on the correct use of the words 'catholic' and 'protestant' when applied to the Anglican church, asserting for his own part that he was an Anglo-Catholic. But he deplored the Romanising tendencies of the Tractarians who spoiled their defence of the historic English Church, by sneering at the Protestant reformers. The father became increasingly dependent on his scholarly son for these comments on current affairs.

Early in 1840 Godley was again in London engaged in further legal studies. Just then the political crisis known as the 'Bedchamber Question' took place, when the young Queen, a fervent Whig, refused to admit Tory ladies to her intimate circle of appointments at Court, upon a change of government. After a complicated series of manoeuvres the Whigs returned to office but only with the support of the extreme radicals. Godley thought this affair menacing, and blamed the Queen. Her action might have the disastrous effect of hastening the class-war by strengthening the radicals. 'Property versus numbers' might yet be the issue. It is surprising to modern readers to find that, in the 1840s, the Tories were not the royalist party but rather the contrary, since the Queen had shown her rigorous opposition to their leader, Peel. And when the attachment of the colonies to the mother-country was discussed it did not occur to the Tories that loyalty to the Queen was much in question.

When the summer vacation came, Godley and Adderley made a tour of Ireland, meeting many of their friends, and notably William Sewell, the educational reformer who was engaged in founding St. Columba's, an Irish public school. (He was to be more celebrated as the founder of Radley.) As they were riding past the gate of Derrynane where lived Daniel O'Connell, the 'Liberator', Adderley's horse fell, and, knowing that O'Connell kept open house, they presented themselves. 'I am very much obliged to your horse for falling just where he did', said O'Connell, fully conscious that the two young gentlemen were his political enemies. 'The great man was treated as royalty,' wrote Adderley. 'He sat at dinner with a cap of maintenance on his head. When dinner was over he retired to bed, and a wild Irish revel began and lasted till morning.'

The tour of Ireland, like all Godley's undertakings, was made with a serious purpose—of studying social problems in his native country. He was particularly interested in visiting some districts in the remote west where an energetic clergyman had converted large numbers of his Roman Catholic parishioners to Protestantism. 'There had been nothing like it since the Reformation.' But the climax of the tour was a visit to Killarney. Frequently, thereafter, when writing to Adderley from distant countries, he referred to this holiday. Killarney was more beautiful than any place he saw in his travels and his riding tour to Killarney with his friends, Prendergast, Monsell, Adare, and Adderley, perhaps the pleasantest period of his life.

In the winter he was back at his lodgings in Dublin, buried in his books. He read and meditated deeply on the sanctions of political authority. The fundamental error of the Whigs, he decided, was 'the derivation of power from below', that is to say from the supposed natural rights of man. 'Principles of conduct should be founded upon morality not upon natural rights.' But Whiggish notions of the social contract permeated English thought and even Peel, the Tory leader, was, in Godley's opinion, a Whig at heart. He might have been something worse; 'better an old Whig than a new radical.' The last degradation of political thought was the mere materialism of Franklin and Bentham, basing all the rules of society upon utility. What then was the alternative? It was to found society upon duties not upon rights, and so upon revealed religion. He boldly declared for Divine Right—not the foolish unhistorical subservience to a dynasty, Stewarts or Bourbons, which sentimentalists still maintained, but a strong sense that power is ordained of God. He ventured to say: 'tyranny is more tolerable than mob-rule,' and again, 'I prefer super-stition to scepticism.' There were times when he felt out of tune with the age in which he lived. 'Here among my books,' he wrote, 'when I am alone, I feel as if my greatest happi-ness would be to live a life of contemplation and prayer;' but added, 'when exposed to the amusements and tempta-tions of the world all longing after immortality vanishes'.

Here was a man who had not yet found his vocation, who knew that he was becoming morbid and fanciful. He could not be idle and he would not be submissive. The divine ordinance as revealed to Godley was a call to action not contemplation, to take his place in the world and find out his duty.

Some friends in County Leitrim proposed that John Godley's talented son should stand for Parliament at the election of 1841, but he refused to stand, since he thought there was no chance of election by so corrupt a constituency.

He wrote to his father for more work to do. 'I am in danger of becoming a mere, indolent, dreaming book-worm.' 'I have nothing to do but fill commonplace books with arguments about the Divine Right of Kings.' Would not his father appoint him his agent for some part of the family property, in Louth and Meath, and so give him active employment. Young Prendergast and most of his other friends at the Bar held agencies for landed estates. But to this proposal his father would not at first accede, and Godley remained in his chambers for several months longer, an almost briefless barrister, reading Hooker and Bishop Butler and Adam Smith, and writing to Adderley to say that these logical writers gave him as much pleasure as he got from solving problems in Euclid. At the end of the year 1840 the father was away from home and the son at last attained his wish. For several months he was left in charge at Killegar and tasted real responsibility. In 1842 he was chosen foreman of the Grand Jury of the Shire.

Meanwhile four younger brothers were growing to maturity and the eldest son was consulted about their careers. He had hoped to save his father the cost of a land-agent's salary, an economy which would enable his brother James to go to Oxford, but this plan had not been carried out and James had to be content with Trinity College, Dublin. William obtained a commission in the 56th Regiment. Archibald was sent off to Scotland to learn the principles of estate management. Denis, a gay lively lad, went off to Canada as an ensign in the 74th Regiment, and this, presumably, attracted John Robert towards North America in the summer vacation of 1842.

CHAPTER II

'Letters from America'

THE voyage to America was no pleasure-trip, if only
because Godley was a bad sailor. He wrote from
Liverpool that he never felt more 'blue-devilish' in
his life and knew no one on the ship but Lady Bagot, who
was going out to join her husband, the Governor of Canada.
After a fifteen-day crossing they reached Halifax, not sorry
to see the last of the *Acadia*, a steamship of 1200 tons
which, said Godley, could hardly be a commercial success
since she carried little but her own coal. Halifax was uninspiring, a town with no buildings in the 'modern' (that is
the revived Gothic) taste. The streets were full of runaway
negro slaves from across the border and some Indians could
also be seen. The negroes were treated as domestic animals
and behaved accordingly, the Indians were untamable and
'the most degraded part of the population'.

New York in July and Saratoga Springs in August offered
more for his consideration. First, the inns were so good
and cheap, the best accommodation could be had for 8s. 6d.
a day, with no annoying extras or servile flunkeys
demanding gratuities. All classes sat down to a common
table and it surprised him to notice that, whereas Americans
took no wine at table, they compensated for it by standing
up to take short drinks at a bar. All looked alike and all
conversed freely with strangers, 'but your travelling
acquaintances are likely to be the worst not the best people'.

He made up his mind to consider the Americans gravely
and soberly 'in a high spirit of goodwill and friendly feeling'.
Under no circumstances would he 'wound their pride by
vituperation or bitterness', although he found himself, in
many of his opinions, diametrically opposed to them. 'In
their good and bad qualities,' he wrote, 'the Americans are
an exaggeration of ourselves.' 'In energy, enterprise, per-
severance, sagacity, activity, all the faculties of a material
civilization, they beat us. I never met a stupid American.
Idleness is unfashionable here.' But what a pity that the
colonists of a new world should be so commercial: 'the only
object has been gain'. It was strange and sad to observe
that America had never produced a Gladstone or a Wilberforce.

America in 1842 was in deep financial depression after
a series of banking crises. There was no credit and no cur-
rency. Hundreds of miles of new railways had been laid
down, hastily and badly, with borrowed English money,
and none were paying their way. 'Why have the United
States "gone ahead" faster than Canada? The prosperity
of America is the fruit of English capital, and the capital
has not been repaid. England has sunk forty million pounds
in the States; and it is impossible to avoid reflecting how
profitably and *securely* a great part of that sum might have
been spent in assisting our own countrymen. But Canada
was too slow a coach for speculators. The money was sunk,
the interest due, the profits deficient, and then came the
trial of the people's honesty.' Alas! There America failed.

The restless, contriving spirit of the Americans had been
nowise damped by the bankruptcy of several States, nor
did their indebtedness diminish their dislike of the British.
Only the upper class is friendly, he wrote, but it is 'always
property that constitutes the pacific element of a state.
Democracy and despotism are both warlike'. On every
frontier the Americans were encroaching upon their neighbours. But most astonishing to Godley was their desire to
be industrialised. He visited a model factory where no

worker received less than eighty cents a day and, while wondering at this prosperity, could not understand why anyone should wish to entail upon America the industrial system which was bringing such misery to Lancashire in the hungry 'forties. No high wages could ever justify the demoralising effect of industrialism. The American farmers were the most fortunate of men, if only they knew their own good. Only the growth of a landed interest could form an established, contented, and truly civilized society. But in America, as yet, 'land is an investment, not a home'. The American strength, in Godley's eyes, was their admirable system of land settlement which favoured the genuine settler and discouraged the speculator. It was part of their good fortune that 'their colony, the West, is adjacent to the East, with no Atlantic to be crossed'. Their merit was that native-born Americans were the best farmers, while his own countrymen, the Irish immigrants, were the worst. He noted, too, the curious fact that the Irish who at home are so fundamentally a peasant people, drift into the slums of the towns, as wage-earners, when they go overseas.

Godley did not much like American society. He had many introductions and even dined with the formidable Daniel Webster, 'by far the first man of the day'. At Saratoga Springs he found the summer visitors very dressy and very formal. To his surprise he discovered that they took no exercise and indulged in no outdoor sports. It was thought very strange that he should spend the day duck-shooting when no duck were actually needed for the pot. Consequently, he thought the Americans, especially the women, much inferior to the English in physique. He never saw a man with the figure of a London life-guardsman. The English known to him were still a country-bred people not yet stunted by bad food and housing. The summer visitors had no conversation, that is to say they had nothing to say of literature, politics, or religion, the subjects Godley cared for, but talked only of money and business. He went about, visited schools and colleges, which pleased him better, and

was delighted to find that the boys at a New England
college made a good showing when he questioned them in
Greek. In general, he found Americans deficient in good
taste. Their buildings were 'grotesque', except for one
Gothic church newly built in New York. Though Dickens
in spite of his anti-American prejudices was a favourite
author, their real liking was for pretentious fine writing.
Godley allows his readers one anecdote to illustrate the
fashionable false modesty which other visitors to America
ridiculed so freely. 'I wrote down my name in the Pennsylvania Picture Gallery, and was delighted with the considerate delicacy of an old woman who acted as cicerone
and who, after pointing, with half-averted head, to a copy
of one of Titian's Venuses in a corner, gave me a wand
wherewith to remove the veil, and then blushingly retreated
behind the door while I did it.'

Late in the fall Godley went south to Washington and
Virginia. There was then much sympathy between the land-
owning aristocracy of England and the aristocracy of the
Old South, still, in 1842, based upon negro slavery. In the
British colonies, slavery had been abolished during the
previous decade. Godley was prepared to find some justifi-
cation for a patriarchal system which many wise and good
men defended by quoting Holy Writ. He did not find it. On
his principle of writing nothing 'vituperative' he preferred
to write very little of what he saw in Virginia. It was worse
than he expected. His rule of judging all institutions by
moral and not by material standards set him on the right
side over slavery. The degradation of the slave and the
slave-owner condemned it. 'I do not see any prospect of
emancipation,' he wrote, 'except through the agency of a
foreign invasion or a dissolution of the Union.'

During the summer he spent a month with his brother
Denis, who had got leave from his regiment on the
Canadian frontier. They thought it odd that wherever they
went the innkeepers took it for granted that two brothers
would share a room. A holiday of deer-hunting, duck-

shooting, and bathing in the lakes and rivers of the border
States was pleasant enough, but for the voracious mosquitos;
it provided the two brothers with many observations of
frontier life from the decks of the new river-steamers driven
at high speeds along the water-ways, on English coal, with
not the slightest regard for safety from accident.

The Canadian border was in those days strongly
garrisoned with British regular troops, a consideration
which occupied Godley's mind. Nearly twenty years later
he was to apply his knowledge of these 'imperial posts' to
good effect. He noted with pride the stature and conduct
of the British soldiers, especially of the two cavalry regiments at La Prairie, mounted on American horses from
Vermont, the best troop-horses he had ever seen. After the
defence of Canada he turned next to observing the political
and social scene, especially about Toronto where he made
some lifelong friends, among them Chief-Justice Sir J.
Robinson.

The celebrated Durham Report, the charter of liberties
for the British Dominions, was but three years old in 1842;
and Governor Bagot was engaged in an attempt to carry
out Durham's main recommendation, by introducing the
system of responsible government. He formed his Executive
Council from the leaders of the popular party in the elected
assembly, not from nominees and officials. Godley dined
with Bagot, adopted his views, and defended his policy
stoutly in a long letter published in the *Dublin Evening
Mail*, on 25th January, 1843, after his return to Ireland.
It was the first intimation that Godley, high Tory though
he was, had a deeper understanding of what a grant of self-
government to a colony should really imply than did most
liberals of his day. Sir Charles Bagot was severely criticized
by loyalists in Canada, and by interested statesmen in
Whitehall, for admitting to his Council such men as Robert
Baldwin and Hippolyte Lafontaine who had shown their
sympathy with the Canadian rebels in 1837 and 1838.
But if responsible government was sincerely granted, Bagot

had done right, in bowing to 'the deliberate and permanent sense of the nation, expressed in the constitutional manner through their representatives'. So far, this was the common belief of Lord Durham and his followers, the colonial reformers; but Godley went further, in applying the same principle to Ireland. It was bold indeed for a Tory to say, in the eighteen-forties that the same rule should apply even to Irish agitators. 'I think no reasonable man can doubt,' he said—and that was taking a high view of human common-sense, 'that, if Mr O'Connell himself should unfortunately command a decisive majority in the British House of Commons (a majority which would follow and support no other leader), Her Majesty would commit to his hands the administration of affairs.' The mere suggestion of such authority in the hands of Daniel O'Connell the Liberator, was shocking; and even the reposal of confidence in M. Lafontaine, the French-Canadian nationalist, was too much for the nerves of the Colonial Office. When ill-health obliged Bagot to resign his post, it was made plain that the new Governor was sent to Canada to assert imperial sovereignty, and full responsible government was withheld from Canada for several years.

In Canadian politics, Godley's sympathy lay, not with the Presbyterian reformers of Ontario but with the Catholic *canadiens* of Quebec who resembled in some ways the Irish peasantry of his own home. 'If ever there was a people fitted by nature to be good and loyal subjects of a monarchical government, it is the French population of Lower Canada. It may be too late to conciliate them', he wrote, echoing Lord Durham's words, 'but the experiment is well worth trying.' In Upper Canada what pleased him best was finding Irishmen from his own neighbourhood, settled and prosperous, having acquired land through a regular system of survey, development, and purchase at a fixed price. Here in operation was the systematic colonization associated with the name of Edward Gibbon Wakefield, whose theories were much before the public.

Godley made, as always, a special study of schools and colleges, and of Church endowments. His last, and strongest impression was of the new vitality displayed by the Anglican church in North America, under self-government. Why, he wondered, had the Protestant Episcopal Church (the Anglican church of America) made such slight progress in colonial days? Why did emigrants tend to drift into one of the other Protestant sects? And why in quite recent years had there been a change for the better?

Everyone who cared for serious matters in the New World questioned Godley about the Tractarian Movement at Oxford. Even when he went to West Point to study American military training, he found the place an Episcopalian stronghold where there was keen interest in the *Tracts for the Times*. Godley was perhaps the only man alive who knew and cared about the two unrelated topics of responsible government for the colonies and a new life for the national Church, the only man who was a disciple, on the one hand of Pusey and Newman, on the other of Durham and Wakefield. The weakness of the national Church at home lay in the lack of self-government. Bishops were nominees of the crown, beneficed clergy were freeholders in their benefices, and, although there was much voluntary effort, no means existed by which the whole Church of England, as a divinely-inspired body, could reform its organization, extend its activity, or even manage its own property to the best worldly advantage.

How different was the situation of the American Episcopal church, since it had been set free. 'Everywhere there are signs of a superintending authority; new dioceses are admitted, new parishes formed in proportion to the extension of the demand for them; domestic and foreign missions are maintained and regulated; canons are altered to suit the fluctuating circumstances of the time; coadjutor bishops are appointed where necessary; in short each emergency is met as it arises.' This was the happy situation of a self-governing church, whereas in England where the Church was established—that is to say state-controlled—'if the Minister of the day happens to be a friend of the Church, he consults a bishop or two, and never troubles his head with what the Church thinks of the matter. Why should he? The Church is passive, helpless, dumb'.

In Canada, too, these affairs were managed better than in England. Godley agreed with Lord Durham that the former system of scheduling a proportion of the land as a reserve for endowing the clergy had been a mistake. He noted with approval that his friend Chief Justice Robinson, together with Bishop Strachan of Toronto, had begun a new method by setting up a Trust (and with laymen among the Trustees) to manage a general fund of endowments for the Church. This was something quite new in Anglican church practice.

Godley returned to Liverpool in November, 1842, a very much better-instructed man than he had been. By observation and reading, and by a sustained correspondence with friends in North America, he was now able to master some knotty problems upon which few of his contemporaries were well-informed. Colonial defence, systematic colonization, the extension of Church work overseas were subjects to which he would return. For the present all his attention was focused on Ireland which, in the year 1843, drifted into one of its unhappy phases of abortive revolution.

CHAPTER III

Public Service in Ireland

EIGHTEEN FORTY-THREE was Daniel O'Connell's year in Ireland. He toured the country addressing monster meetings and promising that the year would be marked by the repeal of the Union with Great Britain. In politics a radical, he was always for peaceful methods and, so far as his influence prevailed, there was no disorder. His success lay in detaching the Irish voters from control by their landlords to control by the Roman Catholic clergy. But when the 'uncrowned King of Ireland' failed to bring about repeal, when his meeting at Clontarf (8th October, 1843), was proclaimed unlawful, and when O'Connell submitted to the law, his power over the Irish people began to wane. The secret societies, never absent from the Irish polity, resumed their sway, and a new agitation for the use of physical force as a means to Irish independence broke out.

In this year Godley was High Sheriff of County Leitrim. His duties were largely formal, to attend the Lord Lieutenant's levée at Dublin Castle, which he thought an unreal and unpleasing pageant, and to conduct the Assizes at Carrick-on-Shannon. This done in the early part of the year, he spent his time quietly at Killegar, shooting woodcock, reading hugely, and writing long letters to Adderley on Church and State. In July a series of agrarian outrages broke out in the west. Godley ordered 200 muskets from

Birmingham, armed his father's labourers and tenants and patrolled the country every night. In October, he wrote, 'At three separate times during the last week a stranger has been seen lurking in the woods, twice in ambuscade near the carriage-road, and once, armed with a pistol, close to the farmyard. We cannot avoid coming to the conclusion that his intention was to assassinate either my father or myself, and we are obliged to regulate our proceedings accordingly, by never going out unarmed or alone. To myself it signifies comparatively little; a young man, active, armed, and on his guard, can hardly be considered unable to take care of himself, but with my father the case is different. He is far too plucky to leave the country, and even my mother, though dreadfully frightened, never speaks of that, I am happy to say. But it is a melancholy thing that a man who has spent forty years in doing good to his country and harm to no living thing should have to be guarded about his own place in his old age.'

At the end of the year the county was quieter, and he spent some weeks in London seeing his *Letters from America* through the press. By July, 1844, he was back in Ireland fully occupied with county business, first as foreman of the Grand Jury and then as a county magistrate. The elder Godley resigned from the Commission of the Peace in favour of his son, who now, as deputy-lieutenant and Justice of the Peace, made up his mind, he said, to settle in Ireland and to devote himself to local affairs. The woes of Ireland he attributed to neglect of duty by the landlords, the only educated class. Many were permanent absentees, many more had fled to England in terror of the 'whiteboys', and those who remained were afraid to do their duty. How, then, were the miseries of Ireland to be alleviated? First, of course by good husbandry; there was so much that a landlord could do for his tenants by care, consideration, and improved methods of agriculture. But the population of Ireland had increased far beyond the means of subsistence, so that half of them lived on their potato-grounds, that is at the margin of starvation. For them there could be no remedies, thought Godley, but a new poor-law as in England, sternly if justly administered and charged against the rack-renting landlords; a policy of public works to create employment; and emigration.

But far more alarming to him were the moral symptoms, 'the radically, irreconcilably hostile disposition of the Irish agitators', the utter breakdown of law and order. 'Against a population hostile to law, and determined to avail itself of every possible means of both legal chicane and physical intimidation, our executive appears to be utterly powerless. It is really frightful to compare the list of reported crimes with that of prosecutions, and again that of prosecutions with that of convictions. It cannot be too often repeated that the jury-box is the source of our weakness and their strength.'

In his own county Godley knew what to do. 'The Assizes are going on here,' he wrote to Adderley in July, 1843. 'As we could get no middle-class jurors to act, I persuaded Tenison to summon *gents* upon the petty juries. He acceded, and has excited, I fear, a good deal of odium among our cowardly Grand Jurors, who veil their fears under the mask of pride, and affect to be very indignant at the degradation. I have been on two petty juries to-day, and in both we got convictions. Eleven of our number were magistrates and the twelfth a Grand Juror. I have sworn in a great number of special constables about Killegar, and hitherto have succeeded in keeping the peace pretty well in our parish; so much so, that the magistrates, in memorialising the Lord Lieutenant to proclaim the southern part of the county as in a state of disturbance, specially exempted that parish alone.' His reward for these exertions, in the general opinion, was likely to be a bullet. 'Sometimes I get warnings that I am in danger; at other times they tell me I am popular with the Roman Catholics; and the priest harangued, I am told, strongly in my favour from the altar. I take precautions, of course, never going out unarmed.'

All through the years 1844 and 1845 the remoter Irish counties continued in this disturbed state, and Godley kept the peace in his district of County Leitrim. As a magistrate he gave notice that every disturbed 'townland' would be placed under guard of a night patrol and that a special rate would be levied to pay for it. As an officer of yeomanry he organized and usually led the night patrols, calling out a hundred farmers, 'elderly respectable men', and as a natural leader of men he made his plan succeed. His efforts distinguished him among the Irish landlords and were noticed in the London press. When there was talk in Parliament of coercion bills he showed little sympathy. 'It is the executive of law that matters, not the enlargement of power.'

Coercion bills, which the Tories advocated and which the Whigs denounced with windy talk about political liberty, would make no remedy for Irish ignorance or Irish poverty. Next after security, the need was for a system of poor-rates and a programme of national education. He took part in the controversy over the Irish Education Bill of 1844 in which Peel proposed to give grants in aid of schools whatever their religious denomination. Here Godley broke from his class, the Protestant ascendancy. Religious bigotry ran so high in Ireland that the Protestants denounced a measure which endowed any schools but those of the (Protestant) Church of Ireland. His neighbours were astonished that so good a Churchman as young Mr Godley could be so lax. He welcomed the promise of national education, accepting a grant-in-aid with the consequent state control for the school which his father had founded in their own parish. Old Mr Godley sometimes found it hard to understand his brilliant son who, sound though he was on law and order, yet proposed to burden the landlords with new taxes and to weaken the position of the national Church. Religious questions were much in the public eye in 1845 and John Robert Godley was at cross-purposes with his friends. He was frankly disgusted at the report of Newman's secession to the Church of Rome in November, nor, though he respected Gladstone's scruples, could he agree with his friend's action in resigning from Peel's government over his Irish education policy.

As a devoted student of Adam Smith, Godley was of course a free trader, and welcomed Peel's conversion to the cause. When the government was reconstructed, after the cabinet crisis of December, 1845, it was clear that Peel would make the decisive move by repealing the corn-laws, and it was also clear that disaster was impending in Ireland. A poor-law and an education bill would tell in time, but Ireland, held back from the brink of revolution, was also on the brink of famine. The potato crop had failed. On 25th November Godley wrote anxiously to Adderley to report that a neighbour had been shot at his own front door; that a list had been discovered of 'persons marked for assassination, the first name on which was John Godley'; and that there was danger of a famine. 'The ravages of the [potato] disease have not been on the whole so great as we feared at first, and there is a larger stock of oats in the country than ever was known before. Everything, however, depends upon the manner in which the potatoes stand in the heaps.' When the potatoes were lifted for the winter it was found, throughout Ireland, that the new disease had reduced them to stinking garbage, and it was plain that there would be starvation before the crop of 1846 could be grown.

The loss of one crop, alarming though it was, did not imply that Ireland was to undergo nearly three years of famine. There had been famines before, and the Irish nation, inured to poverty, had survived them. Irish politics, in the early months of 1846, seemed more alarming than Irish economics. However Peel's new Chief Secretary, Lord Lincoln, was authorized to advance loans to local authorities for road-making which would create temporary employment in districts affected by the potato disease, and so enable the destitute to buy food.

Henry Pelham-Clinton, by courtesy Earl of Lincoln and later fifth Duke of Newcastle, had been at Christ Church

in Gladstone's day, that is to say in the university generation before Godley's. It is probable that Godley first met
him when on county business in Dublin, early in 1846.
Thereafter he was Godley's friend and patron. At any rate
Godley's letters, about that time, reveal that he was in close
touch with someone who knew the secrets of high policy.
Lincoln was much occupied in negotiation with Sir Lucius
O'Brien, a friend and distant connexion of the Godley
family, about public works in that part of the country; and
the Godleys, father and son, threw themselves into this new
public activity. There was no actual famine that spring
around Killegar and, supposing that the worst was over,
John Robert Godley crossed over to London, where there
was a counter-attraction.

For about two years past, his college friend, Charles
Wynne, had often figured in Godley's intimate letters. He
came of an ancient Welsh family with a seat at Voelas in
the Snowdon Range; they were close friends of the Glynnes
of Hawarden Castle, into whose family Gladstone had
married. When Godley went to visit Wynne, ostensibly to
study problems of Church and State in Anglesey (which he
found as backward as Ireland), he had another motive,
revealed ingenuously in his letters. 'I have the greatest
horror that I should grow into a club-frequenting and dis-
contented old bachelor, without a career of public utility,
and without resolution and self-denial enough to settle
down at home, and sedulously perform the humble duties
of a country gentleman's life. If I had the life of action I
could do without the domestic interior; if I had the
domestic interior, I could perhaps do without the life of
action; and in either case I might fulfil the vocation of a
useful citizen of the world.' His search for a domestic
interior led him, whenever he was in London, to the
Wynne's town house in Portman Square, and a biographer
with the privilege of reading confidential letters, a hundred
years later, is not surprised to find a sudden change of tune.
After attending his sister's wedding at Killegar in June,

1846, Godley returned to London and announced to his father and his friends that he was engaged to be married to Charlotte, the sister of Charles Wynne. He now proposed to settle in London and to practise as a parliamentary lawyer.

During the wet summer of 1846, while weeks of rain 'washed away the corn-laws', and while the right wing of Peel's conservative majority reacted against his measures for repealing them, Godley was occupied with his private affairs. In writing to his father about his marriage he did not, however, omit to send a subscription of £20, from his very small means, for the relief fund at Killegar. Not every young man would have done that when hard put to it to finance his approaching marriage. Old Mr Wynne, a shy, kindly recluse, proved very stubborn on the score of marriage settlements. He would not allow his daughter to marry unless the bridegroom should have an assured income of £800 a year, and Godley had nothing but his prospects and a voluntary allowance of £500 from his father. Old Mr Godley was not easily persuaded to give his consent, and had difficulty in finding the required endowment. Irish rents had vanished in the famine year and no one was likely to advance money on Irish land at a favourable rate. There were also four younger sons and two daughters whose expectations must be considered. Until the very morning of the marriage it remained uncertain whether Mr Wynne's scruples would be satisfied. The deed of settlement, at last approved by his lawyer in London, arrived only a few hours before the ceremony.

John Robert Godley and Charlotte Wynne, he aged 32 and she aged 24, were married at Voelas on 29th September, 1846. They drove away in sheets of rain, which drenched the triumphal arch and the cheering school-children, to spend a short honeymoon at Cefnamlwch—short because duty was calling Godley back to Ireland. The potato crop had failed again and the country was now starving.

Whatever may be the verdict of history upon the great Irish Famine, the most shocking economic disaster in these islands since the Black Death, there can be little doubt on one point. The British government was deplorably slow in realising the gravity of the situation and in adopting emergency measures. England had just come through a political crisis that had shaken the foundations of the State. Sir Robert Peel's submission to the logic of Free Trade marked the transference of power from the landed to the commercial interest, a fundamental change in the dynamic of English society. His decision to repeal the corn-laws had split his party with the consequence that, in July, 1846, he was obliged to give place to a Whig administration, led by Lord John Russell, and it was uncertain whether Lord John could maintain a working majority in Parliament.

An able group of young politicians (Gladstone, Lincoln, Sidney Herbert, Cardwell, Dalhousie, and others), known as the Peel-ites, or Liberal-Conservatives, followed Sir Robert into opposition but often held the balance of power in the House. The Irish liberals, whose leader, O'Connell, was fast ageing, and who were falling under the influence of the revolutionary Smith O'Brien, played a dangerous game. They sometimes voted against measures for the relief of Irish misery, if these measures were proposed by Peel-ites, since, in general, they preferred to support Russell's administration rather than to restore Peel to power. Irish factiousness and the confusion of English parties weakened the administration, and it was clear that no strong measures could be taken until a new parliament should be elected. Russell held on and did not dissolve Parliament until July, 1847, by which time a million Irish had died of starvation. But this was not the effect of mere callousness. Whigs and Tories alike had been taught by all the most reputed economists in the world and by a generation of propaganda that Free Trade was the best cure for the wretchedness of the poor. Peel had instituted free trade in corn, by repealing the corn-laws, and England now waited agog for the magic to work.

To buy food in bulk, to sell through government agencies, to restrict the activity of merchants, to allot rations were the very activities which they had been taught to abhor. Had not the economists proved by irrefutable logic that restriction created poverty and that only by free trade could plenty be created? A hundred years ago the most enlightened progressive opinion was as convinced of the blessings of free competition, as to-day of the necessity for a planned economy. And men were most unwilling to admit that what was good for England would not be good for Ireland too.

Almost the only action taken by Russell's government before the end of the year was the issue of a letter of instructions by the new Chief Secretary, Henry Labouchere (who had succeeded Lord Lincoln), authorising the local authorities in Ireland to extend the policy of providing employment on public works. He called upon them to prepare schemes for land-development and drainage, that is, for works of direct value, as well as for road-making which would bring in no immediate return. Some depots for reserves of food were also established but the food was not to be released while private stores were still held by traders, or at less than the market price.

Meanwhile the Irish peasantry, who were accustomed to living on their own potatoes, had no money with which to buy other foodstuffs. The resident landlords could not pay their rates because they could not collect their rents, and the Labouchere Letter produced but small effect. Only one-tenth part of the rates levied on County Leitrim could be collected in that year. At Killegar, the Godleys stored oatmeal for their immediate dependents, and John Robert Godley bought five tons of Indian corn in Dublin, the only cheap food available. He was active in following up the Labouchere policy in County Leitrim, where his friend Prendergast became, through his influence, Inspector of

EDWARD GIBBON WAKEFIELD

Painting in oils, by E. J. Collier, in the Canterbury Museum.

Drainage. But how much more remained to be done. 'Things here are tolerably quiet,' he wrote to Adderley on 31st December, 1846, 'but there is dreadful distress, and who dares to contemplate the end? A whole population living upon alms, and a country borrowing more than a year's income to be spent within the year; agriculture neglected; the law a mockery; no rents paid; and, in spite of all, the people starving; a spectacle unprecedented in the history of the world.'

By this time he was deeply involved in national politics also. One of the woes of Ireland was the unsatisfactory land-law which left the tenant at the mercy of the landlord, often an alien Englishman and an absentee. Those resident landlords who accepted their obligations, almost in despair at the complacency of the Government, formed a committee in Dublin, in December, 1846, to concert plans of relief. Their first intention was to combine as a new national Irish party but, since most of them were Protestants, they failed to gain the confidence of the Roman Catholic masses. They were, however, able to agree upon a memorandum which they presented to Parliament, proposing a short-term plan to cope with the famine, and a long-term plan to restore the national economy. Fourteen peers, twenty-six M.P.s and six hundred other landed proprietors met at the Rotunda in Dublin, on 14th January, 1847, to discuss this memorandum, which had been drawn up by a committee of whom Godley was one. At first the committee had included members of all parties, Daniel O'Connell and even Smith O'Brien. It is not easy to distinguish Godley's part in the affair because, at his suggestion, the preliminary proceedings were private. He described in a letter to his father how Smith O'Brien attempted to convert the conference into a political demonstration and how he, with the help of two young friends, Charles Monck and William Monsell, outwitted O'Brien, by rallying a majority who voted for the exclusion of press-reporters. They thus enabled the conference to devote its attention to practical

c

remedies instead of to barren political invective. 'What do you, who think me a radical, think of Smith O'Brien calling me yesterday "the very type of Unionism and Conservatism"?' wrote Godley to his father.*

The memorandum pointed out that the Irish famine was an Imperial disaster which should be relieved by the whole resources of the Empire; that the expense of relief was now being borne by the resident landlords while the rack-renting absentees and mortgagors contributed nothing; that the system of rating failed to provide adequate funds; that food was actually leaving the country in search of a better market since the starving peasants could not afford to buy it; that agriculture was at a standstill; that capital for creating employment on public works was insufficient; that there had been great waste and mismanagement in such public works as had been undertaken; and that the local government of Ireland, largely conducted by the Grand Juries, was quite inadequate. Among the improvements urgently needed, in addition to many measures for improving the standard of life of the poor were, particularly, three —a revised poor-law, a bold programme of railway-building (for these were the days of the first railway boom), and a plan for assisted emigration.

In Parliament, the session of 1847 was largely taken up with debating proposals arising out of this memorandum and Godley spent the spring of the year in London, as honorary Secretary of the new Irish Party until it was wrecked by the secession of Smith O'Brien and his followers. Among the plans brought forward was that of Lord George Bentinck, for a guaranteed loan of £16 millions to be spent at once on Irish railways. It was defeated by the opposition of the Irish extremists in the House, who abstained from voting to score a party advantage. An Irish poor-law authorizing the grant of 'outdoor relief' was

---

* Five years later, when Godley was administering Canterbury Settlement and O'Brien was a felon transported for high treason to Van Diemens Land, O'Brien wrote to Godley offering to serve under him.

indeed passed, but with so stringent a means-test that the memory of it was execrated in Ireland for a generation. The general view of political thinkers at that time was that there should be no outdoor relief if remunerative labour could be found; and the whole intention of the Irish reformers was to set the people at work for good wages. Godley was strongly of that opinion and had printed a pamphlet for the Landlord's Committee in Dublin proposing a liberal system of outdoor relief with a means-test.

A clause was light-heartedly proposed by the young member for Dublin, W. H. Gregory, and was accepted, with the effect that no outdoor relief should be given to any pauper who was in possession of even a quarter of an acre of land. Thus the Irish cottar, with a potato patch but no sound potatoes, was confronted with the alternatives: starve or be evicted. 'Quarter-acre' Gregory was for many years the best-hated man in Ireland, and it was unfortunate for Godley that their names were associated. Gregory had been at school with Godley at Iver, and had followed him to Harrow and Christ Church, but two men could hardly be less alike. Gregory was a careless, sporting squire, a duellist and a great gambler, who took his politics with his other pleasures, and thought it great fun to outface O'Connell the Liberator on a Dublin platform. He was in general a reformer and voted for many liberal measures. His celebrated clause was meant for the best and he defended it gallantly in his racy, amusing autobiography, where he records the significant fact that only two of the Irish members voted against it.*

A few days later came Godley's turn. On 31st March,

---

* Some years later, Gregory's weakness for low company brought him into the clutches of a plausible rogue who got money out of Gregory's friends on false pretences. Gregory wrote abjectly to Godley, who replied characteristically: 'Though I was quite aware of poor O'Flaherty's obvious faults, yet his good nature and sympathy had quite won me over . . . . You must indeed be wretched now. It is hard enough to lose a dear friend, but to have him turn out unworthy is a blow for which there is no consolation to be offered.'

1847, an open letter to Lord John Russell, signed by Godley, Gregory, and another Irish M.P. named M. J. O'Connell (not a relative of the Liberator), appeared in the *Spectator* and several other journals. It proposed a plan for the systematic colonization of Upper Canada with Irishmen. Always described in Parliament and the press as 'Mr Godley's Scheme', it perhaps lost credit from the addition of Gregory's name. R. S. Rintoul, the editor of the *Spectator*, was its most determined adherent and, from this time onward, one of Godley's associates. In Dublin the proposal was supported, though coolly, by the leading daily paper, the *Freeman's Journal*.

The plan had been maturing in Godley's mind since his visit to America. For about thirty years before the famine a stream of emigrants had been passing from Ireland to America. Crossing the sea under conditions of misery, which had been condemned in Lord Durham's report, these Irishmen drifted into the slums of American and Canadian cities where they formed an overflowing reservoir of cheap labour. Politically they had no notions beyond a blind hatred of England which they held responsible for all the real and fancied woes of Ireland. Since few Irish peasants arrived in the New World with any capital, few indeed were the prosperous Irish settlers, like those whom Godley had visited in Upper Canada.

There were hardly two opinions among political economists on one point: Ireland was over-populated and must be relieved of its surplus. Emigration as a palliative for Irish poverty had been recommended by Archbishop Whateley's Commission, which the Whig Government appointed in 1838, and by Lord Devon's Commission, which the succeeding Tory Government appointed a few years later. The reports of these and other Commissions were emphasized by the potato disease and its consequences. The emigration was assuming the character of a panic flight of refugees and the need to regulate it was obvious. Godley did not propose that there should be more emigration than occurred, but that the emigrants should have some opportunity of being comfortable and prosperous. At least a million Irishmen died of starvation, at least a million fled to America in misery, and emigration was, to the Irish Nationalist leaders, a word of horror. For the evicted cottars, the dirt and crowding of the emigrant ships, the friendless arrival in New York, held no glamour. Emigration was exile to a place where wages could be earned and food bought, not to a New Ireland. Godley was almost alone among Irishmen in regarding life in Canada as a splendid opportunity. Smith O'Brien's newspaper, *The Nation*, contemptuously remarked that Godley's alternative was 'Canada or Starve' and seemed unable to realize much advantage in one alternative over the other.

Godley's evidence before Lord Devon's Commission, on 23rd January, 1845, had mostly related to land tenures and agricultural methods in Canada. He had asserted his belief in what was known as the Wakefield system of selling the Crown Lands to settlers at a uniform high price, in order to provide funds for 'churches, schools, roads, bridges, mills, and survey,' and for bringing in more emigrants as labourers. Chief Justice Robinson had suggested to him in Toronto that group settlements on this plan might be usefully attempted, on a small scale, and for his part he thought something might be done by Government, on a large scale. The report of the Devon Commission had commended Godley's scheme to the notice of Government and, two years later, at the height of the famine, he now brought it forward again.

In the letter to Lord John Russell, Godley and his friends made four points: that there was a necessity for the state-aided colonization of Canada with Irishmen on a very large scale, that the actual work of land settlement should be conducted by private enterprise, that a religious provision should be made for the colonists, and that an income tax should be levied upon Ireland to finance the scheme. He supported his proposal with a wealth of statistical and historical information. Ireland was over-populated and, either there must be a great influx of capital which clearly would not happen, or there must be a great outflow of labour. Since the latter was inevitable, was in fact taking place, the Imperial Government should guarantee loans which would enable the emigrants to settle on the land, in a British colony. 'If 1,500,000 should emigrate in three years the sum required would be about £3 millions annually.' The interest and sinking-fund should be raised by an income tax and a property tax by which the loan would be paid off in twenty years at the rate of £195,000 a year, 'a great relief to the Irish poor-rate'.

Since the scheme never came to birth, it will not be necessary to recapitulate its details, except one which astonished the Protestants. Godley proposed that the Roman Catholic Church should be invited to patronize the scheme, that it should be a Catholic emigration like that to seventeenth-century Maryland, and that a religious endowment for a priest should be created in every settlement. The reason, said Godley, why Irishmen in America lingered in the towns and did not settle in the country was that the practice of their religion was possible only in the towns. So liberal an attitude to the religion of Rome in the eighteen-forties was a revelation. And Godley's proposal was endorsed by the Protestant Archbishop of Dublin (Whateley) as Chairman of the last Whig Commission on Ireland, by the Earl of Devon as chairman of the last Tory Commission, by twenty-seven Irish Peers, by twenty-one M.P.s, and by other members of the Landlords' Committee, nearly all Protestants.

Godley obtained interviews with Sir Robert Peel, the leader of the opposition, who 'almost promised' to support him, and also with three members of the Cabinet. In an undated letter to his father he reported that he had met Lord John Russell, Lord Lansdowne, and Lord Grey, but that they declined to adopt systematic colonization as a government measure. This seems to have been the first occasion on which Godley met Henry, third Earl Grey, who will reappear in later chapters of this book. Appealing from the Whig ministers to the Peel-ite opposition, he briefed Lord Lincoln to raise the question in the House, on 5th June, when there was a hot debate. Gregory answered many objections. Peel came forward so far as to speak in generous terms of Godley's intention, but he did not force the issue. He admitted that he thought the plan far too audacious. Perhaps 300,000 emigrants might be settled in Canada over a term of years. Russell was hostile and facetious, but brought forward a serious criticism. Several Canadian statesmen had written anxiously to ask whether it was true that they were to be flooded with Irish paupers. The decisive speech was that of Benjamin Hawes, the Under-Secretary for the Colonies, who confessed himself 'staggered' at Mr Godley's plan, a proposal 'that the country should be taxed £9 millions in order that two millions of the able-bodied people of Ireland should be exported to North America—and that as a means of benefiting Ireland!' This was the classic point of view of the Colonial Office, which poured cold water on every ambitious project. It was echoed in the House of Lords by Lord Grey who dismissed the whole scheme as moonshine. 'Let it slumber,' he said, 'on dusty shelves in the limbo to which such visionary and impracticable projects are, as the poet tells us, confined.' The precise limbo in which it slumbered was a House of Lords Committee, with Lord Monteagle in the chair, and a last word of blessing by Lord Grey to the effect that the committee would 'disabuse men's minds of the dangerous error as to the extent to which emigration might be carried'.

While the committee sat considering these limitations, one-sixth of the people of Ireland died, and one-sixth fled to America in poverty and degradation, while the taxpayers of England were shamed into spending more than £9 millions to keep the rest alive.

In truth any decision on so gigantic a scheme was out of the question in the last days of life of a parliament.

Men's minds were already fixed upon the approaching dissolution, which came on 23rd July, 1847. In the ensuing
election Godley stood as a candidate for the county of
Leitrim. Before discussing the election, it will be convenient
to see the last of the abortive plan for an Irish colonization
of Canada. Monteagle's Committee met on 22nd June to
hear evidence from Godley. To what he had already stated
in writing, he added remarks upon what he had seen in
America, and observations on the state of Ireland. Since
only one-eighth of the normal potato crop had been sown
it was to be expected that 1848 would be worse than 1847.
Emigration on a large scale was therefore a question of
emergency and not of cautious prudence.

When the new parliament met in September, Monteagle's
Committee met again and sat intermittently for many
months. Since it was plain that the Whigs had no intention
of proceeding with the Irish colonization scheme, the committee occupied itself with collecting evidence on problems
of emigration from an eminent list of witnesses, all of whom
expressed a general sympathy with Godley's scheme in
principle, while they doubted the possibility of putting it
into practice. Sir Thomas Mitchell the explorer of Victoria,
Father Matthew the Irish philanthropist, Mrs Caroline Chis-
holm of the Family Colonization Society, and Edward
Wakefield senior, were among those called before the committee. Sir Samuel Cunard of Nova Scotia and John Macarthur of New South Wales, perhaps the two most celebrated
living colonists, concurred in stating that an Irish emigration on a large scale was possible and desirable; but that a
policy of railway-building with a loan guaranteed in London
was the best means of financing it. This was the policy
approved by the Colonial Office, the policy by which, in
fact, Canada was peopled, but which did nothing to allay
the miseries of Ireland in that awful crisis. And two colonists
from New Zealand, Mr Edmund Halswell, Q.C. and Captain Joseph Thomas drew attention to the possibilities of
colonizing the empty southern island of New Zealand.

Nothing was done except that some members of Parliament were somewhat better informed about the colonies. Lord Monteagle became a friend of Godley's, and a supporter of his later schemes.

*   *   *   *   *

While the Irish Colonization Scheme was before Parliament, Godley wrote several times to his father in a tone of excitement. There was a chance that Lord Leitrim, the Whig magnate of that part of the country, would not put up a candidate and, in that case, he might get into Parliament for the County, unopposed. He sounded several Irish gentlemen who happened to be in London, to get their interest. In this he was not altogether successful, and it was an annoyance when Lord Leitrim decided to bring forward his son, the Hon. C. Clements, as a Whig candidate. However, on 21st June Godley was able to tell his father that a friend (perhaps Lord Stavordale) had advanced £200 for his expenses and given a guarantee of a further £500. Godley was at the moment a man of mark in the public eye and the subject of acrimonious discussion. He stood as a Conservative but without specifying a detailed policy in his election address.

An Irish county election, a hundred years ago, did not much resemble a modern election under universal suffrage. The franchise was restricted to the more substantial farmers who were expected, in their own interest, to vote, and, from feudal feeling were generally willing to vote, with their landlord. By making interest with the landlords a candidate could thus forecast how many votes he was likely to poll. The incalculable factor was the influence of the priests who might divert some votes from the temporal to the spiritual power. All voting was in public, by open declaration at the hustings, and the poll was kept open for several days. Influence was used, as of right, but not direct corruption, at least not when Godley was a candidate. The utmost he would do was to provide carriages to bring in voters from

the wild hills of western Leitrim and to provide these supporters with refreshments. He refused indignantly to help
one constituent, though he knew the man well, with a
temporary loan just before polling-day. Things were different in Dublin where, at the previous election, Gregory had
been obliged, as a matter of ordinary propriety, to lay out
£4,500 in gratuities to voters at £3 a head.

The modern reader may well wonder why so enlightened
a man as Godley opposed the enlargement of the franchise.
On this subject he had expressed his opinion to Adderley,
four years previously, in no uncertain terms. 'I have long
thought that the age of equality is coming upon us, and
that our business is not so much to struggle against it, as
to retard its progress, and to modify its effects; at present
we are not ready for it. I think no man can look upon the
state of our working classes, their ignorance in all which
it is important for them to know . . . their widespread
indifference to religious obligations, without trembling at
the thought of their obtaining political power. . . Nation-
ally and individually, Church and State, landlord and
capitalist, all should join heart and hand in this great work,
preparing the way for a safe democracy.'

The nominations were made in the court-house at
Carrick-on-Shannon, the county town of Leitrim thirty Irish
miles from Killegar, on 9th August, before 200 electors
and a mob of their voteless clients. After the three candidates, Clements, Godley, and Tenison, had been formally
proposed, a well-known Catholic politician, Father Thomas
Maguire, took the platform. He said that the priests might
have put forward an extremist as their candidate but they
preferred to trust Lord Leitrim. Their man was Clements
because the Clements family were the true local aristocracy
and Lady Louisa Clements the friend of the famine-stricken
people; 'she did not shun contact with the poor'. But who
was Mr Godley? Admitted that he was 'a gentleman in
every respect and a most hard-working man', he was not
known to the people of Carrick-on-Shannon. No matter

how great his 'book-learning' he was not fit to represent the county. Was he not the son of John Godley, the enemy of the Roman Catholic Church, 'not only their political and religious foe but the personal enemy of the people?' And what were Mr Godley's politics? He was a 'perfect sphinx'. Would he vote for enlarging the franchise? 'No, I will not,' said Godley.

Speaking on his own behalf, Godley was received with 'some cheers and loud expressions of disapprobation'. He began by saying that he 'gloried in the accusation of being his father's son'. His father had spent forty years of his life discharging his public and private duty in County Leitrim. He indignantly denied that his father had ever been an enemy of the Roman Catholics. He stood as a Conservative, preferring Peel's administration to Russell's, but as a Liberal Conservative, which was too fine a distinction for his hearers. Before that audience and under the scornful heckling of Father Maguire, he appealed in vain for an independent non-party vote, for a united Irish Party 'in the awful tumult when a deluge of calamity has swept over the land'. Taunted with the phrase 'Canada or the grave', he replied that 'if Canada was better than the grave he would be for Canada'. But it was plain that the meeting was against him, and more so when he turned on Maguire, denouncing him for bringing 'a mob to howl at his heels'. This was not the way to win an Irish election.

After the combat between Godley and Maguire, the speeches of the other two candidates were tame and, when a vote was taken by show of hands, the qualified electors, voting on party lines, were evenly divided. Godley demanded a poll and on the second day was leading. On the third day, 11th August at 3 p.m., 'no voter having presented himself during the last half-hour,' he withdrew his candidature. Since the votes were openly counted as they were given, he knew that he was beaten.

At the final count, the voting stood:

K. Tenison (Whig) 385

Hon. C. Clements (Whig) 354
J. R. Godley (Conservative) 319

and thus ended Godley's one parliamentary venture. He had failed because the Roman Catholic Church rejected his colonization scheme. Godley was the man who wished to 'transport' the people and he was the associate of 'quarter-acre' Gregory. He wrote to Adderley, 'I was beat by the priests, who for no reason in the world except that the gentry took me up, determined to oppose me with their whole might. Even the priest of my own parish, who had not only promised me his vote, but actually canvassed with and for me, turned right round, voted against me, and carried with him all those of his flock whom he was able to influence.' A London newspaper, the *Morning Chronicle* gave another explanation of Godley's defeat. 'The ultra-church party have raised a cry against Mr Godley on the ground that he had propounded the "popish colonization scheme" as they term the project.' With the Roman Catholic clergy, the extreme Protestants, and the local grandee—Lord Leitrim—against him, it is remarkable that he mustered nearly 30 per cent of the votes in an Irish election. A typically Irish comment was made by Father Maguire to one of Godley's friends: 'It would never do to have the county represented from Killegar, but Mr Godley is an able and a rising man, and we will get him in some day for a borough.'

Lord John Russell was returned to power with a majority of one, and precariously remained in office for five years. Godley's friend, Monsell, who had concentrated on public works rather than emigration for Irish relief, won a signal victory at the poll, standing as a Whig. Gregory lost his seat for Dublin, as did 47 out of 120 Peel-ite candidates.

Soon after the election Godley left Ireland, out of heart with Irish politics. What he had seen of electioneering in that country disgusted him and still his efforts to make a mark in the world were frustrated. Furthermore he was short of funds and obliged to earn his living. He was now free to follow his old bent for the law and journalism in London, where Rintoul was pressing him to write for the *Spectator*. In the long affectionate correspondence between John Robert Godley and his old father there is but one moment of ill-humour between them, and that short-lived. In August, 1847, there was a disagreement about settlements of money, soon resolved with mutual protestations of goodwill. A son, Arthur (afterwards Lord Kilbracken), had been born to Charlotte Godley, in June, at her father's house in London and at the end of 1847 the Godleys took a house of their own in Gloucester Place, a few doors away. Godley never again lived at Killegar and, as events turned out, visited it rarely. His younger brother Archibald stepped into his place as factotum to old John Godley.

When he left Ireland the famine was past its climax. Such potatoes as had been planted were found to be free from disease in 1847 and the wheat harvest throughout Europe was bountiful. Yet the effects of the previous shortage were then most powerfully felt in Ireland. Half the nation was living on poor-relief or on charitable funds from overseas. British charity subscribed one and a half million pounds. America sent a hundred thousand tons of food, even the Sultan of Turkey made a donation. At last unstinted relief was allowed and free food was distributed from soup-kitchens. Many months yet passed before the famine was allayed and during those months epidemics raged, sparing the rich no more than the poor in those insanitary days. Gregory's father died of fever during the election, as did Godley's uncle, Lord Dunsandle, and nowhere did scarcity and disease prevail more than in Carrick-on-Shannon. Godley fought his election in a land where unburied corpses lying by the roadside caused no scandal, in a town where fifty patients died of fever each week at the public hospital. At Killegar, thirty miles away, there were no such horrors. 'No one died of want on Mr Godley's property,' said an old servant many years later, and that was a remarkable fact in famine-stricken Ireland.

Remarkable, too, that in Godley's district there were no crimes of violence.

'My father has nearly ninety men at work every day,' he wrote to Adderley at the end of the year. 'So I hope, for their own interest, they won't shoot him.'

CHAPTER IV

The Colonial Reformers

D URING the autumn of 1847, five long weekly letters from Godley's pen appeared in the *Spectator*. Ostensibly they were published as accounts of the social state of Ireland, seen by a land-owner in Leitrim. The poor-rate could not be collected, the school was half-empty, the people dying around him. 'Who would invest money on public works in Ireland now?' Among the remedies proposed, 'repeal [of the Union], or abolition of the landlords, or the payment of priests may possibly make Ireland a very pleasant place ten or twenty years hence, but it is not so now'. On the other hand, everyone of enterprise in Ireland talked of emigration, the only remedy for the immediate crisis, and while the flight from Ireland increased in volume the Colonial Office did nothing at all.

Emigration was opposed by two parties only, the nationalists 'who dislike any measure calculated to diminish the raw material of rebels, and the tenants of the Colonial Office who feel themselves already incapable of doing the ordinary business of their department and want no further trouble'. When the celebrated Sir James Stephen, who had managed the Colonial Office for many years, retired in November, Godley fired a parting shot in his Irish letter for the week. Under Stephen's rule the colonies had reached a stage where Australian squatters were importing cannibals from the Islands to work for them while a House of Lords

Committee was solemnly inquiring how to dispose of the starving Irish. 'This empire,' he wrote, 'is distinguished by containing the largest amount of waste territory and the largest number of unemployed, destitute labourers.' He lamented the decay of the art of colonization as it had been practised by the ancient Greeks—a favourite theme with Godley—and by the seventeenth-century English. 'To transplant a perfect type of the parent society with its various classes and institutions, and to remove in this way sufficient numbers for the relief of the mother-country—the art has apparently not descended to us.'

Although he came to it by independent study of the Irish problem, Godley had now embraced the whole doctrine of the group known as the Colonial Reformers, whose leader was Gibbon Wakefield, and whose organ was the *Spectator*. It is therefore not surprising that, in the last week of November, 1847, Godley and Wakefield met, at Malvern, where Wakefield was taking a cure, convalescing after a paralytic stroke.

The man whom Wakefield met at Malvern, in November, 1847, was thirty-three years old, tall and sparely-built, with a broad, high domed forehead, scanty brown hair, pale blue eyes set very wide apart, a straight firm mouth, and a serious expression. He read and wrote much but spoke little, sparing his throat which he had strained by twelve months of politics. In manner he was courteous but reserved, often abstracted, absorbed in his own thoughts. Those who knew him well agreed already that he was no ordinary man. As a philosopher he was guide and tutor to several of his political friends, as a man of action he had proved himself in the Irish troubles, but most remarkable was the restless energy with which he brought men of mark together, organized committees, drafted reports, and got things done. No man in Ireland had done more to overcome English complacency about the famine than Godley, behind the scenes. But no man could cut a figure in Irish politics without arousing opposition, and there were some who thought Godley a dangerous man, a hasty, impetuous visionary.

The man whom Godley met was older and more conspicuous. Edward Gibbon Wakefield was an invalid of fifty-one, but still a florid, John-Bull figure, a middle-sized, stoutish man with the air of a prosperous farmer. He went about with a pack of well-bred dogs at his heels. In any company he was hail-fellow-well-met. Infinitely plausible, the most lucid, outspoken of men in conversation or correspondence, he never quite inspired confidence among men of the world. He would be all things to all men and, sooner or later, it was noticed that he would. A novelist should be a judge of character, and Thackeray wrote to a friend, after lunching with Wakefield, 'a rogue if ever there was one. I am sure by his face and the sound of his voice'.

Between Godley, loved and trusted by all who knew him, and Wakefield, whom the world abused, there sprang up an instant partnership. Their hobby—colonization—and their views upon it were identical, their talents were complementary. Though they were never intimate friends, the student may search the voluminous letters of Godley in vain for a single unkind allusion to his disreputable acquaintance. Godley never talked or wrote scandal.

In 1847, Wakefield was nearing the end of his career. Twenty years had passed since his abduction of an heiress had led to the trial and sentence of imprisonment which ruined his reputation and deprived him of all hopes of public advancement. In those twenty years he had made himself master of the problems of colonization to such a degree that his advice was indispensable. Always a centre of controversy; always suspect by the strait-laced; over-bearing, quarrelsome, jealous though he was; nothing could be done in the field of colonial reform without taking him into account. Colonial statesmen were for or against the Wakefield system, they could not ignore it. Rarely did his name come before the public; it was his function, he said, to 'work like the mole in out-of-sight obscurity', and in the background his astonishing talents were most effective. He had unbounded energy and enthusiasm, an easy mastery of facts and figures, a powerful and lucid style, and a persuasive skill in conversation that deserved the name of genius. His method was to conceal himself behind a stalking-horse, to inspire some rising young politician, who enjoyed an unspotted reputation, with the pure Wakefield theory and to use him as the public champion of the Wakefield schemes. Sooner or later, his young men escaped from tutelage and were then in danger of being violently abused, for Wakefield was a good hater. Godley was to be the last of the series.

Twenty years earlier the British Empire had presented an uninspiring picture. Excluding India which was still ruled by the East India Company, it had consisted chiefly of military and naval stations, most of which had been captured in the wars from the French, the Spanish, or the Dutch. Reasonably enough as things stood, these colonies were ruled by military governors under the direct control of a Secretary of State for War and the Colonies, two branches of the administration that went naturally together.

Several of these colonies were served in Parliament by pressure-groups of M.P.s with interests in particular lines of commerce, and these groups, in turn, were sometimes supported by the Navy. Thus the West Indian sugar trade, the Newfoundland fisheries, the Nova Scotian timber trade were influential branches of the system, but the shippers and the importing merchants, not the colonists, were the wielders of influence. A remarkable feature of nineteenth-century England was the emergence of the new philanthropic pressure-group of the missionary societies which, in the 1830s and 1840s, were actively opposed to white settlement among aboriginal races. Their great triumph in abolishing slavery gave them a commanding position in Parliament and, for many years, they swayed the policy of the Colonial Office.

As for the white settlers of British origin, they were only to be found in some parts of Canada where, as yet, the one staple they provided for the English market was the softwood from the Maritime Provinces; and in the Australian settlements, known collectively to the English as 'Botany Bay'. It is a strange comment upon human vagaries that the transportation of convicts to Botany Bay was a part of the philanthropic movement. While the free settlers in the colonies withstood the influx of convicts, and while the Colonial Reformers protested against it in Parliament, Home Secretary after Home Secretary, when reducing the number of crimes punishable by death or corporal punishment, found that he could not provide for convicts by any other means than transporting them overseas.

Meanwhile the population of the British Isles grew at an unprecedented rate. The opening of new continents and new lines of communication offered an outlet, and the surplus population of the British Isles began to flock overseas, in numbers which increased from 0.5 per cent of the population in the year 1832 to 1.3 per cent in 1852. In this great phase of emigration the Secretary for War and the Colonies took but a small part. More than half of the migrants left British soil for the United States, where they were made welcome, and no English statesman of the first rank appeared to regret their departure; for those who went to a British colony no provision was made by the Colonial Office. On the other hand the impression given by a series of Colonial Secretaries was that they preferred to placate the Home Office (always on the look-out for new convict settlements) or the missionary societies (always anxious to protect their converts from white exploitation). The great migration entirely changed the character of the British Empire, a fact of which the British governing classes seemed quite unaware. It was the task of Wakefield and his friends to compel the Colonial Office to take notice of this fact and provide for it.

Wakefield formed his first group of Colonial Reformers on the extreme Left in politics, among the radicals, and his first experiments in colonization were tinged with the materialist philosophy of that school. When the Whigs were in office in the eighteen-thirties his radical friends were often able to affect the colonial policy of Whig Governments and, between 1834 and 1839, they achieved a great deal. They persuaded the Colonial Office to adopt, in part, his principle that Crown lands in the colonies should be sold to intending settlers at a uniform fixed price; they put a stop to the indiscriminate transportation of convicts; they initiated the plan upon which Adelaide, the first of his model colonies, was founded. Wakefield was one of the contributors to Lord Durham's Report on Canada, the foundation charter of colonial self-government; he founded the New Zealand Company, and in 1839, by sending settlers to New Zealand, he compelled the Government to proclaim it a British colony. The return of the Tories to power under Sir Robert Peel, in 1841, was regarded as a set-back by the Colonial Reformers and, during the next five years, their influence in public affairs was slight. Convict transportation to Australia was resumed, and a long series of disputes dragged on between the New Zealand Company and the Colonial Office.

After the death of Lord Durham, Wakefield had associated himself with a rising young politician of the Left, named Charles Buller, who became the leader of the Colonial Reformers in the House of Commons. He, too, had accompanied Lord Durham to Canada, and the extension of responsible government to all the settlement colonies was his main interest. Buller was a witty and effective critic of Peel's administration on many grounds, especially on the deplorable state of affairs in New Zealand, which reached a climax in 1845.

The New Zealand Company had founded three settlements, at Wellington, Nelson, and New Plymouth, on land acquired from the natives by its chief agent, one of Wakefield's brothers. Meanwhile a Lieutenant Governor, commissioned by the Colonial Office, had arrived and had taken up his residence in the far north of New Zealand, hundreds of miles away, where white settlers were few, but Maoris numerous. With the help of the Anglican missionaries, the Governor was able to negotiate the Treaty of Waitangi, to which a large number of the principal chiefs adhered. It secured them in the possession of their tribal lands, and sowed seeds of doubt in their minds about the validity of the Wakefield land-purchases. Several years passed before any satisfactory allotment of land titles was made at the settlements of the New Zealand Company and, during this time of uncertainty, friction between settlers and natives often produced bloodshed. In 1843, Arthur, the youngest of the Wakefield brothers, was killed in the Wairau Massacre near Nelson and, in 1845, there was petty warfare at several points in the North Island. Though the Colonial Office was disposed to blame the settlers for these disorders, and to accept the vindication of the native case put forward by the missionaries, they had accepted responsibility for public security in New Zealand. Their solution of the problem was to send Captain (later Sir) George Grey as Governor, with adequate resources to restore law and order.

Grey was a young, active official who proved to have those natural qualities of leadership which at once impressed the Maoris; to them he was always 'Good Governor Grey'. But his previous appointment had been at Adelaide where it had been his task to restore the chaotic finances of the first Wakefield colony. Though an advanced liberal who favoured colonial self-government in principle, he arrived in New Zealand with a strong prejudice against the Wakefield system.

Meanwhile, in England, the prospects of the Colonial Reformers had improved. In the last few months of Peel's administration, before his majority disintegrated, Gladstone was at the Colonial Office, and on his future the Colonial Reformers were beginning to base their hopes. Then came the break, described in the last chapter, when Peel gave place to Russell and the Whigs. The election of 1847 (when Godley stood for County Leitrim) established Russell in power with a very small majority.

During this critical year Wakefield was absent from the scene. He had a paralytic stroke in August 1846 and returned to his subterranean activities in 1847, a changed man. He never regained his physical energy, nor were his natural faults of temper improved by his illness. His jealous, irritable impatience of opposition grew more pronounced, not least because his influence with the Whig government proved to be less than he expected. The new Colonial Secretary was Henry, 3rd Earl Grey, a statesman whose services to the Commonwealth have perhaps been under-estimated. Formerly one of Wakefield's associates, in the earliest days of Colonial Reform, he was one of those numerous people who could never work with Wakefield in person. High-minded and head-strong, a liberal aristocrat, son and successor to Lord Grey of the Reform Bill, he resented criticism and resisted advice. Though formerly, in the early utilitarian days of the movement, he had been a Colonial Reformer and had promoted the Wakefield high-price system, he detested and despised Wakefield the man. When Charles Buller endeavoured to bring them together, shortly after Lord Grey became Colonial Secretary, the meeting ended in a violent quarrel, of which Wakefield and Grey recorded conflicting accounts. The six years (1846-1852) during which Lord Grey ruled the colonies saw the establishment of the Otago and Canterbury settlements, the repeal of the navigation laws, the first grants of responsible government, the enabling Act which gave constitutions to the Australian States, and the end of convict transportation in colonies where convicts were unwelcome. The colonies, in these years, were set free, but hardly a word of gratitude was spoken to Lord Grey. All that he did was done ungraciously, he made concessions as a superior to his inferiors, he did for the colonies what he, not what they, thought best for them, and he made it clear that residual sovereignty remained in Whitehall.

In Wakefield's eyes, Lord Grey's greatest offence was that he won over Charles Buller, who accepted a minor post under Government. Buller was thus responsible for a settlement of outstanding differences between the Colonial Office and the New Zealand Company in May, 1847. The Treasury advanced a sum of £236,000, partly as a loan and partly in compensation for colonizing expenses already undertaken by the Company, and placed the Company in possession of most of the land it claimed to have acquired in New Zealand. The life of the Company was extended for three years, during which it was to renew its efforts to colonize. Wakefield's summary of the proceedings was that 'the Directors sold the honour of the Company and the interests of the Colony for money . . . and with this purchase-money Lord Grey bought exemption from the obligations of rectitude and honour.' It deprived the Company, as Wakefield supposed, of its high political function and reduced it to a mere speculation in land. Worse news was to follow. Lord Grey had carried through Parliament a bill for providing the colony of New Zealand with a liberal constitution. It was repudiated by the Governor, Sir George Grey,* on the grounds that it would subordinate the interests of the natives to those of the settlers though, at that date, they out-numbered the settlers many times over. To the general surprise, Lord Grey accepted this rebuke from his own subordinate and allowed the constitution to lie dormant.

Wakefield was now quite out of patience with Lord Grey and began to cast about for another political combination. The Whigs held office by a narrow margin of votes which they had won because of the split in the Tory Party. Of the two Tory factions, the Derby-ites were of no use to Wakefield; their leader, Lord Derby (actually known as Lord Stanley until 1851), had been the very unsympathetic Colonial Secretary in the last administration. The Peel-ites held the key position. Gladstone, the rising man of the group, was already too big a fish to be caught on any line

---

* The reader must be accustomed to distinguishing between the two Greys who take so large a part in the history of New Zealand. They came of two unrelated families.

that Wakefield could throw. There was, however, a young man in Gladstone's circle of friends, a travelled man who had seen colonial life, an expert in problems of emigration, above all a Churchman of high personal character, whose ecclesiastical connections might be used to overcome the hostility of the missionary societies. Godley was to be the *jeune premier* for Wakefield's next performance.

The essence of the Wakefield system of colonization was that it should be undertaken by formed groups of emigrants, selected in due proportion of age and sex, and provided with a supply of working capital proportionate to the number of agricultural settlers. His intention was to prevent their rapid dispersal over a wider area of land than they could use, to keep them concentrated so that they would have the two economic advantages, of public works and a home market for their products, and the moral advantage of an organized social life. 'Concentration is Civilization' was the phrase he most strongly emphasized in his published works. The sort of colonization which was most repugnant to him was that in which a sparse population of scattered farmers became the tenants or hired servants of absentee proprietors or mortgagees. The fault of his system, and it was a fault shared with all the economists of his generation, was the presumption that a new colony must be an agricultural society. On this presumption and in accordance with enlightened economic theory as it was then accepted, he based his fundamental principle of the Sufficient Price. The misfortunes of earlier colonies, he said, had been caused by the granting away of great estates to the first comers, with the result that later emigrants were forced to disperse into the wilderness. Land, labour, and capital were thus thrown into the wrong proportion, and thus progress had been exceedingly slow, for example in New South Wales, in the Maritime Provinces of Canada, and more recently in Western Australia. The solution to the problem was simple, to sell land, after survey, at a uniform price which should be sufficiently high to raise funds for paying the passages of more immigrants. Men of substance would be attracted to the new colony by the assurance that there would be no shortage of labour, and each colony would be systematically developed from a single centre. This was the method used in the United States, which progressed so much more rapidly than Canada where land was given away.

The Sufficient Price was imposed, though never to Wakefield's satisfaction, at several Australian settlements, and its effects have, on the whole, been condemned by Australian economists. But Wakefield's critics have generally neglected the other aspects of his plan. His influence may be detected in many colonizing experiments. He was directly responsible for six settlements (Adelaide, Wellington, Nelson, New Plymouth, Otago, Canterbury), but only in the Canterbury Settlement of 1850 was his plan completed with all the features he thought essential, and it is by the character of Canterbury that his work must be judged. The Sufficient Price was the means; the end was to take a cutting from the old English oak and to transplant it in a new field. He was concerned, like the Elizabethans who went to Virginia, in founding new 'commonwealths', not in disposing of the English and Irish unemployed. From the first he was a student of seventeenth-century colonization and never tired of drawing a contrast between the 'thirteen colonies' in North America which enjoyed complete self-government from their first day, and the new colonies which were directly administered from Whitehall. Lord Grey, in particular was addicted to the method of granting self-government by slow stages, as if Englishmen who went abroad were no longer fit to enjoy the liberties they had exercised at home, but must be taught to govern themselves, step by step, like primitive barbarians. No wonder, said Wakefield, that the English upper classes did not emigrate. Would Penn and Baltimore have gone to found Pennsylvania and Maryland if they were to act there on instructions from a clerk in Downing Street?

The fight for responsible government was won with

continual reference to the seventeenth-century colonies and, inevitably, the attention of the Reformers was drawn to the religious character of these settlements. Massachusetts, Pennsylvania, Maryland were sectarian colonies and their moral unity was the secret of their strength. The eighteen-forties were years of deep religious fervour, and to organize colonists in groups with a religious affiliation was a natural step to take. As early as 1843 Wakefield was discussing with his fellow-directors of the New Zealand Company, the possibility of planning Anglican, Scottish Presbyterian, Irish Catholic, and Zionist settlements. Of these nebulous proposals, the first to take shape was the Scottish Colony, precipitated by the disruption of the Scottish Church. A body of Edinburgh Free-churchmen was got together under the leadership of Captain Cargill and the Rev. Thomas Burns. In 1848 they founded the settlement of Otago and were established when, two years later, the Canterbury settlement was formed, two hundred miles away. The Scottish colony lies outside the scope of this book, and it will be sufficient to say that the commencement was on a very small scale—no great fault, perhaps, in colonization. The emergence of Otago to the leading position it enjoyed in New Zealand, a generation later, was due largely to the sterling quality of the settlers, an essential of the Wakefield plan; but that emergence belongs to another phase in New Zealand's short history, when the goldfields had stimulated development.

The most authoritative account of the origins of the Canterbury Settlement is given in *The Founders of Canterbury,* a selection from the correspondence of Gibbon Wakefield edited by his son, Edward Jerningham Wakefield. With pardonable family pride, the son set himself the task of establishing his father's claim to be the founder, or at least the co-founder, in opposition to the claim of Godley's friends, who gave all the credit to him. It seems reasonable to share the honour between these two men whose talents, interests, and connections were so happily complementary.

According to Jerningham Wakefield, his father, who had been considering Church colonization for two or three years, sent him, in October, 1845, to Dublin to confer with Dr S. Hinds, Archbishop Whately's chaplain, and the author of a thoughtful pamphlet on the subject. Hinds, whose name was afterwards given in commemoration to a New Zealand river. has some claim to be the first exponent of a practicable scheme. At that time Godley was already studying Irish emigration and was not unknown to the Archbishop, but it does not appear that Hinds and Godley collaborated. The Wakefields, at that time, were more disposed to look to Daniel O'Connell and Smith O'Brien for support. When Godley's grand plan for Irish colonization was published, Gibbon Wakefield was incapacitated by illness. He claimed, however, to have watched it with attention and to have recommended it to Rintoul of the *Spectator*. No record has survived of the first contacts between Wakefield and Godley but there can be little doubt that Rintoul was the link between the two Colonial Reformers. Godley's weekly articles on the state of Ireland appeared in the *Spectator* in October and November, 1847, and when, on 27th November, Wakefield invited Godley to meet him at Malvern he addressed him as 'My dear Godley', a form of address which implies a fair degree of intimacy. They met and, in forty-eight hours, Wakefield's persuasive tongue engaged Godley in the cause of an Anglican church settlement.

Three days later, on 30th November, Wakefield wrote to John Abel Smith, the banker, his confidant among the directors of the New Zealand Company, announcing that the scheme was launched.

'I find that my notion of a distinct settlement in New Zealand, under the patronage of a powerful body in this country, desirous of spreading the Church of England, stands a good chance of being realized sooner than we expected. The subject has been fully considered, and at length something like practical conclusions have been arrived at. Mr Godley left me this morning for Ireland.'

'We adhere to the old plan of a settlement, to consist of 300,000 acres (with right of pasturage attached), to be purchased from the [New Zealand] Company for 10s. per acre or £150,000 . . . . The purchasers, whether colonists or absentees, to pay to the Company, as a trustee for them, £2 10s. per acre in addition to the price of 10s.; and the amount, being in all £750,000, to be laid out by the Company on behalf of the purchasers, in public objects, such as emigration, roads, and church and school endowments.'

'The plan of the colony . . . to be carried out, by a society outside of the Company, consisting of bishops and clergymen, peers, members of parliament, and intending colonists of the higher class.'

'In all this there is nothing new to many of the Directors. But now comes the all-important practical question. By whose exertions in particular is the whole scheme to be realized? I have succeeded in persuading Godley to think of devoting himself to the work . . . . He ought to become a Director of the Company.'

Wakefield's correspondence during the next few weeks was typical of his method of working. He wrote frequently to Godley assuring him that he might safely begin to draw his friends together into a colonizing association, promising him a directorship, a salary of £500 a year, and a loan of £500 for buying the block of shares which constituted a director's qualification. Simultaneously he lobbied the other directors with assurances that Godley would come into line and must be remunerated. On 13th December he was able to tell Godley that the Company would guarantee preliminary expenses. 'The next step, therefore, is to form the Society and this is wholly *your* work.'

On 22nd January, 1848, he wrote again to say that the directorship and salary were settled. Godley, however, insisted on buying his own shares with his first year's salary. Matters were so far advanced by 29th February that the Company sent a despatch to its agent in New Zealand giving him general notice of the proposed Church colony.

The names of several of its distinguished promoters were mentioned and among them that of Mr J. R. Godley, 'so well-known for his exertions on behalf of Irish emigration'. The first meeting of the Canterbury Association was held on 27th March, 1848, but, before we proceed with its history, something must be said of Godley's private affairs.

CHAPTER V

Godley and the Canterbury Association

THE new Church Colony was to be Godley's dominant interest but it did not, at first, provide his profession or his livelihood. He settled in London, at Gloucester Place, in December, 1847, with the intention of living by the law and journalism, and allowed himself a Christmas holiday, for a start, with his wife's relative, Colonel Hildyard, at Stokesley in Durham. Here is a picture of England a hundred years ago:

January 1st 1848.

Manor House, Stokesley. New Year's Day.

MY DEAR FATHER,

I must begin by wishing you and my mother many happy New Years, happier than circumstances over which you have had no control, and which therefore (if I may say so without disrespect) you ought not to think so much of as you do, have, I fear, made this one. We arrived here safely last night at 6.30 having had a good passage, and wife and child quite well—no adventure of any kind, and we came just in time for a great ball and supper down stairs for the servants and tenantry—to dance in the New Year. About 70 or 80 sat down to a splendid supper, and there were card-rooms for the old people, and a room where they might smoke their pipes, and nothing could possibly go off more brilliantly. I danced a country-dance with the infant-school mistress (a characteristic partner, Charlotte said) and the Col. with the wife of the 'one policeman' who keeps the peace at Stokesley. The Squire sat up to bow them out at 3 a.m. This is a quaint old house at the end of a good-sized country town, from which it is only separated by a courtyard and wall. The present owner has added largely to it, and it is a most queer looking affair, half modern façade, half ivy-grown manor-house—but so large and comfortable—and the whole establishment redolent of wealth and ease. He hardly ever leaves it, except to go for a month or so to a shooting-lodge in Durham, and generally has it full of neighbours. A maiden sister lives with him, and keeps house, a sort of *passée* Di-Vernon, tall and handsome, and who used to drive a phaeton and ride to hounds better than most men. On the whole, I cannot fancy a more charming *milieu* for an idle sportsman, and even I, who am not that, am very sorry that I can't stay longer. I suppose I shall hunt every day next week, to lay in a stock of exercise before 6 months of London. Both Uncle and Aunt are devoted to Charlotte, so I can afford to let her stay here for a month without me, knowing that she will be taken good care of. I shall hope to hear that the apprehensions excited by Graves will be removed when he shall have received Predington's letter about licencing, and that no harm will ensue. If there should still be a difficulty, those whom he will not licence might leave their arms with you or Henry O'Brien, or any two Magistrates may swear them in as special constables, who are nominally excepted from the operation of the Act. I did not see Guinness, who was out of town. In fact I had no business with him, except to say that I wish him, whenever he has wherewithal, to pay my annuity to Cocks & Biddulph and this you can tell him.

Love, your affectionate son,
J.R.G.

From these junketings he returned to London and to work. Letters between the Godleys, father and son, for the next two years, relate almost exclusively to business. John Godley had lost money in the banking crisis that followed the bursting of the railway 'boom' in 1847; he lost more by the defalcation of an agent; and rents in Ireland could not be collected, even though he reduced them by 15 per cent, to help the tenants in those troubled times. Meanwhile the poor-rate was at 7s. 6d. in the pound and must be paid to feed the starving country. One of the letters deals with a further misfortune. John Godley's luggage—'plate, port-manteau, pistols, and carpet-bag, books and papers'—was stolen at Paddington Station. Luckily his son was able to write later that the thief was taken on another charge and had confessed his crime in Newgate. Most of the lost goods were recovered from a pawnshop.

While writing week by week to advise his father on financial problems, great and small, Godley was able to assure him that his own finances were sound; he was earning £700 or £800 a year with his pen. In February, 1848, Godley's friends, Lord Lincoln and Sidney Herbert, acquired the ownership of a newspaper, the *Morning Chronicle,* as an organ for the Peel-ite party. An old-established daily, it had lost ground in recent years to *The Times* which, under the management of Delane was just then assuming a commanding position among English newspapers. For a few years, the *Chronicle* was able to make headway under the able editorship of J. D. Cook, and for two of those years, 1848-9, Godley was a regular leader-writer in the 'liberal-conservative' interest. After he had gone to New Zealand the *Chronicle* languished, not through any fault of management but because of the gradual disin-tegration of the Peel-ite group. Lincoln and Herbert sold out in 1854, having lost a great deal of money, and the *Chronicle* was eventually absorbed into the *Daily Telegraph.*

Godley was a good journalist with a style that can be easily recognized in the columns of the *Chronicle* or the *Spectator*. It is the style of a scholarly, liberal-minded lawyer, lucid, plain, and unadorned except for an occa-sional tag in lawyer's Latin or an illustration from the French classics. A living to earn, family troubles, political journalism, contracts with the Peel-ite leaders (Gladstone, Palmer, Herbert, Lincoln), were the background of Godley's efforts to found the Canterbury Settlement.

Nor did he at first abandon the plan for an Irish Catholic

PORT LYTTELTON AND THE CANTERBURY PLAINS, 1849
From the Illustrated London News *of 18 May, 1850.*

colony. When Wakefield published his *Art of Colonization* early in 1849, he mentioned, among other 'asides' in that remarkable book, that he, Charles Buller, and Godley had worked at such a plan during the previous winter. It seems to have lapsed after Buller's death in December, 1848. But, even when Godley was fully engaged in work for Canterbury, he never ceased to be one of the Colonial Reformers, concerned with all the problems of the Empire in general.

*   *   *   *   *

In forming the Canterbury Association Godley first turned to his old friend Adderley, who made the following entry in his reminiscences. 'Canterbury Colony was now set on foot by Godley, Gibbon Wakefield, Gladstone, Lord Lyttelton, Sewell, several others, and myself', but of these five names only three appeared in the printed list of members of the Association. Sewell, a solicitor from the Isle of Wight, did not subscribe his name until 1850, Wakefield—as was his custom—remained in the background, and Gladstone, though a good friend to Canterbury, was too shrewd a politician to commit himself too deeply with a project of this sort. He made it a rule throughout life not to take up any cause outside Parliament which he could more effectively help by parliamentary action and, throughout the history of the Canterbury Association, an undercurrent of party politics can be detected.

The fifty members* who subscribed their names to the prospectus, early in 1848, were by far the most distinguished body of supporters to any colonizing plan since John Locke devised the Utopian constitution of Carolina in 1668. The Archbishop of Canterbury (Dr J. B. Sumner, who was promoted to Lambeth only in February, 1848) was President of the Association, and was supported by Archbishop Whately, seven other bishops, two deans, the chaplain-

---

* A list, with biographical notes, is given in Appendix B. The membership of the Association changed considerably during the four years of its existence.

general, several other beneficed clergymen, and the Secretary to the Society for the Propagation of the Gospel. Next in importance were several of the higher nobility who were known to take an interest in philanthropic projects. The two names remembered by posterity are those of Lord Ashley (afterwards the great Earl of Shaftesbury) and Lord John Manners who had founded the 'Young England' party with the intention of reviving the true traditions of Old England under the circumstances of the new age. Lord Lyttelton was introduced to Godley by Charles Wynne, in January, 1848, and thought long and prudently before committing himself. Then came a large number of active politicians, all of them Conservatives, and most of them members of the Peel-ite group. The most distinguished was Henry Goulburn who had been Peel's Chancellor of the Exchequer, at this date an elderly man, near the end of his career. Lord Lincoln and Sidney Herbert had already held minor ΄office and were marked for political promotion. Sir W. Farquhar, Sir W. James, C. B. Adderley, the Hon. F. Charteris, John Simeon, T. Somers Cocks (Godley's banker and Mrs Godley's brother-in-law), were Godley's contemporaries at Christ Church Oxford, and all were members of Parliament at some time in their career. Wakefield had brought in several of his friends, choosing them with care. There were none of his radical utilitarian cronies, not even Sir William Molesworth, who was generally regarded as the leader of the Colonial Reformers after the death of Charles Buller, and no directors of the New Zealand Company save those who were safe Tories. Perhaps the most influential family in early-Victorian England were the Barings, a banking family widely intermarried with the aristocracy. William Baring, Lord Ashburton, was a member of the Canterbury Association, a Conservative but a Derby-ite, and therefore useful as a link with the other wing of the Opposition. Adderley was on the whole a Derby-ite, though always independent, and another was Augustus Stafford, one of the most active members of the Association. The list was made up with three or four men having colonial experience. In addition to Godley himself there was Jerningham Wakefield who had been in New Zealand with his uncle, there was the barrister Edmund Halswell who had visited the unoccupied plains of the South Island, and there was Gibbon Wakefield's last champion, John Hutt, recently returned from governing Western Australia. Almost all the members were graduates of Oxford or Cambridge, and sixteen out of the fifty were members of Christ Church, Oxford. Summarized, the list may be arranged into clergy, and philanthropists, Peel-ite politicians, Godley's Oxford friends, and the more respectably Conservative friends of Gibbon Wakefield, with not a single representative of the Whig and Liberal majority in Parliament.

But Lord John Russell's administration was weakly supported and was likely to be overthrown by some new grouping of parties. His two strong men, Lord Grey at the Colonial Office and Lord Palmerston at the Foreign Office, were bitter rivals. Lord Grey was intensely unpopular throughout the colonies and was the target of attack for Colonial Reformers in all parts of the House; Lord Palmerston was rapidly becoming the most popular man in England. If the government should break, what was the most prudent action for the Peel-ites, a middle party of ambitious young politicians with more talent than voting-power? They must consider very carefully the moment at which to act and the issue on which to challenge the government. Some of them thought that Colonial Reform, the vendetta against Lord Grey, would make a good battle-ground, but not so thought Sir Robert Peel and not so thought Gladstone, nor Roundell Palmer. Above all, the Canterbury Association was a dangerous connection. England was working up to one of its periodical 'no-popery' panics, which became acute in 1850, and there was some alarm that Godley and his friends were Tractarians—'popishly' inclined. In his letters to Godley, Wakefield repeatedly begs him to stick to 'safe' men, like the Bishop of Oxford, and to avoid the Tractarian

high-churchmen. Was a Tractarian colony one to which
Gladstone, High-Churchman though he was, thought it wise
to attach the Peel-ite party? And as dangerous as Trac-
tarianism was the stigma attaching to the name of Wakefield.
Was this notorious person wisely chosen as the focus about
which a parliamentary battle should rage? Gladstone preferred to give Canterbury his advice and countenance, but
to leave its management to his wife's brother-in-law, Lord
Lyttelton, and to his friends Adderley, Godley, and Sir
Walter James. The future Lord Chancellor also stood aside.
Godley wrote enthusiastically to Palmer asking his support
for a colony 'stamped with a definite religious character,
formed not in order to get rich but to live under congenial
civil institutions'. Palmer drily replied that he did not share
Godley's confidence in Gibbon Wakefield.

It was not to be expected that fifty busy public men
could give sustained attention to the administrative detail
of founding a colony. Most of the members lent their names,
which were later affixed to lakes, rivers, and mountains in
Canterbury, and, when the Association was hard-pressed,
advanced large sums of money on very doubtful security. It
was their readiness to pay that astonished Wakefield.
Godley's friends, he said, were friends indeed. The business
of the Association was carried on by a small managing committee which first met, in the Association's rooms at 41
Charing Cross, on 27th March, 1848. Those present were
the Bishop of Oxford (in the chair), Lord Courtenay, Lord
Lyttelton, Sir W. Farquhar, the Hon. F. Charteris, the Hon.
R. Cavendish, the Rev. E. Hawkins, the Rev. G. R. Gleig,
Somers Cocks (of the firm of Cocks and Biddulph, bankers
to the Association), John Hutt, Adderley, Halswell, and
Godley. The committee had power to co-opt and used it
freely, at their later meetings. After the first meeting, since
the Bishop was not often in town, Lord Lyttelton usually
took the chair, until the dissolution of Parliament when
he went down to his country house, Hagley Hall in
Worcestershire. Wakefield then persuaded the committee to

select John Hutt as their permanent chairman (which proved to be an error). It was typical of Wakefield that he manipulated the committee though he was not even a member of the Canterbury Association. Similarly he manipulated the Board of the New Zealand Company though he rarely attended as a director. In December, 1848, he resigned from the Board, feeling, quite rightly that his presence was an embarrassment to his colleagues. The Company and the Association were then engaged in intricate negotiations with Lord Grey, who hated and distrusted him. Wakefield's resignation enabled him to publish his masterpiece, *The Art of Colonization,* which contains bitter personal attacks on Lord Grey. It did not prevent Wakefield from managing the Association and the Company from the background. Both societies found him indispensable.

At the first meeting of the committee it was resolved 'that the proposed settlement be Canterbury and the name of the chief town be Christchurch'. Since there has been some controversy over the origin of the name it may be said, at once, that Godley wrote to his father in February, 1851, 'I hope that my old College is grateful to me for naming the future capital of New Zealand after it'.

A week later they met again to consider a draft prospectus which Godley had prepared, and agreed to distribute it widely. The next step was to make formal application for a site, to the directors of the New Zealand Company, who of course were kept fully aware of these deliberations by Wakefield and Godley. They asked for three hundred thousand acres of land at ten shillings an acre with the proviso that settlers would be obliged to pay an additional sum, four times as great, for subsidising immigration, and for an ecclesiastical and educational endowment which would be administered by the Society for the Propagation of the Gospel. There followed much correspondence between the New Zealand Company and the Colonial Office, neither party being aware that a step had been taken in New Zealand, which would change the nature of the plan.

The first intention of the Association was to plant the settlement in the North Island of New Zealand not far from Wellington, perhaps on the Wairarapa plains. The South Island was, at that date, largely unexplored, and uninhabited but for the two infant settlements at Nelson and Otago, a few whaling-stations and some Maori villages along the eastern coast.

At the very time of these conversations in London the agent of the Company at Wellington was negotiating with the scattered Maori inhabitants for a general purchase of the whole central section of the South Island, between Nelson and Otago. On 12th June, 1848, the Governor, Sir George Grey, wrote to the Colonial Office to report that the purchase had been concluded for a sum of £2,000. These proceedings, of course, could not be known in London until three or four months later. When the dispatch came it was accompanied by a formal protest from Governor Grey's subordinate at Wellington, Lieutenant-governor Eyre, who complained, first that it was absurd to credit a few hundred Maoris of the Ngaitahu tribe with ownership of an area as large as Scotland, and secondly that it was unjust to buy out such rights as they possessed for cash, without providing native reserves. However, the great plains of the South Island were now available for settlement.

Still unaware of the negotiations for the Ngaitahu purchase, the Company and the Association agreed in May to send Captain Joseph Thomas to New Zealand to survey 300,000 acres of land for the settlement at an estimated cost of £15,000. Godley at once intervened to say that this sum was not nearly large enough. He persuaded the Company to advance £20,000 with, as yet, no security, because the Association was not yet legally incorporated and owned no funds. Captain Thomas sailed for New Zealand in July as an agent of the New Zealand Company charged with authority to select the site of the Canterbury settlement, subject to the approval of the Governor and the Bishop of New Zealand. He was a Worcestershire man, known to Lord Lyttelton, and an experienced surveyor; after serving in the Army he had sent in his papers and had emigrated to Wellington at the beginning of 1840. After surveying at Wanganui and exploring the Wairarapa coast, he spent more than a year on the Otago surveys. On his return to England in 1847 he gave evidence about the South Island of New Zealand before Lord Monteagle's Committee on Irish Emigration.

While Thomas and his two assistants, one of them a nephew of Wakefield, were at sea, the Canterbury Association negotiated with Lord Grey. On 9th May Lyttelton wrote formally to ask for authority to acquire a million acres of land in New Zealand, on behalf of 'a body of gentlemen who have constituted themselves an Association for establishing a settlement composed of members of the Church of England'. Lord Grey replied most cordially and, on 17th May, received a deputation consisting of Lyttelton and Godley. In conversation they found him less effusive. When they asked for a colonizing charter on the lines of those granted in the seventeenth century he demurred. The most that he would promise was that, when the suspended constitution was established in New Zealand, he would consider setting up a distinct provincial government in Canterbury. He could hardly do more since Canterbury was not yet located on the map. He had however given general approval to the scheme and wrote to Governor Grey to say so. 'I take a great interest in the success of their enterprise . . . . All depends on news from their agent that land with good title has been found.' Nothing more could be done for many months until news should come, and in those months the Association languished. There were some resignations and, in the autumn, some faint-hearted talk of what should be done if enough land was not sold to meet their liability to the Company. One of those who lost faith was the Duke of Buccleuch; he despatched forty tenants from his Hampshire estates to Natal at his own expense, despairing, it seems, at the long delay in founding Canterbury.

Wakefield spent the winter in France writing his book, Godley in London writing for the *Morning Chronicle*. Early in 1849 they resumed operations, with Hutt in the chair and H. F. Alston as secretary to the Association, at £150 a year.

But the tone of their proceedings had changed, and for the reason we must consult the state of world politics. Eighteen-forty-eight, the Year of Revolutions, was the worst moment in the nineteenth century for launching a great enterprise. The Irish famine had precipitated a financial crisis, the worst of that generation and a grave discouragement to investors. Then, in February, revolution in Paris had blazed the way for a series of outbreaks until class warfare raged in almost every European capital. Smith O'Brien's futile tumult seemed to fulfil the worst forebodings of the Irish loyalists, and even in London revolution was expected. The Chartist meeting on Kennington Common, when the Duke of Wellington was called from retirement to garrison vital points and organize special constables, took place in April while decorous correspondence was passing between the Canterbury Association, the New Zealand Company, and the Colonial Office. Though reactionary governments were restoring order in Europe, another outburst flared up in 1849, and, in March, Godley wrote gloomily to his father on the European situation. A would-be assassin, that month, fired a shot at the Queen.

From this general unrest the colonies were not free. There were political riots at Montreal, in April, 1849, for which the Colonial Reformers, rather unjustly, blamed Lord Grey. There was unrest in New Zealand, at the Cape, in New South Wales, colonies to which he was slow in granting constitutions. There was rebellion in Ceylon. He chose this moment to resume the transportation to the colonies of convicts, many of them political offenders. From every colony clamours of protest arose and the history of the Empire in 1849 is largely a history of refusals to accept the convicts he sent. Protests from Sydney, Melbourne and

Capetown were followed by obstructive action; the colonists would not allow his convict-ships to disembark their passengers, and passed them on to some other more compliant port. The New Zealand settlers redoubled their complaints against Governor Grey when he accepted a shipload of juvenile delinquents at Auckland, the official capital and the only New Zealand settlement which was not a Wakefield colony. A military post among the Maori tribes, it was being settled by Army reservists, pensioned off as 'military settlers'.

Because Lord Grey seemed unwilling to grant New Zealand a constitution, or Canterbury a charter, since the only colonization he actively supported was the export of convicts and pensioners, the Colonial Reformers broke with him. The publication of Wakefield's book in January, 1849, was a declaration of hostility and, in the parliamentary session of 1849, Godley's friends fought him on several fronts. In March Godley persuaded Adderley to take up the South African question in the House, and in that session Adderley stepped into the front rank of parliamentarians. He made himself the champion of the constitutional party at the Cape, supported their demands, and defended their action in rejecting convicts. His name is still commemorated in Adderley Street, the main street of Capetown. Molesworth was anxious to combine the forces of the Reformers for a general vote of censure on Grey's colonial policy. He moved a resolution but failed to carry it. Gladstone and the Peel-ites preferred to concentrate on particulars. They fought Lord Grey over Ceylon, over his Canadian policy, and over Vancouver Island, which was then first organized as a colony. Gladstone took up the case of Vancouver, attacking the Hudson's Bay Company which, he said, obstructed colonization under pretence of colonizing. This brought a new champion into the field, a young Irishman named James Edward FitzGerald who came from Godley's circle of acquaintances. He was first cousin to Godley's brother-in-law, O'Brien. FitzGerald was a Cambridge man and held the post of assistant-curator at the British Museum. An ardent, ambitious Celt, who sighed for a more adventurous life, he had taken to political pamphleteering. An attack by FitzGerald on the Hudson's Bay Company caught Gladstone's attention and, for more than forty years, Gladstone and FitzGerald were occasional correspondents. In 1849 FitzGerald thought of emigrating to Vancouver Island, until Gladstone commended his attention to Canterbury.

In July, as the session drew to a close, Godley, Adderley, and Wakefield seem to have been chiefly concerned with preparing plans for a parliamentary campaign against Lord Grey in the following session. They held a public dinner at which all the Reformers met and began to organize a Society for the Reform of Colonial Government, which should include representatives of all political parties. Throughout the summer rumours grew stronger of a new political combination; perhaps the Peel-ites and Derby-ites might compose their feud to form a more effective government. Wakefield, with his deep political insight, did not think so. He judged correctly that, when the Whig administration collapsed, a weak protectionist government under Lord Derby would come into office for a short time. Meanwhile he had another card to play: the ecclesiastical pressure of the Canterbury Association should be invoked. If Canterbury settlement could be formed into a diocese, with a bishop of its own, there would be another form of influence to use against the low church missionary influence at the Colonial Office. He began to search for a colonial bishop, an inquiry rather outside the scope of his normal interests.

As well as a bishop, Canterbury would need a civil officer. Each of the seventeenth-century colonies had been founded by a 'leader', what the Greeks called a 'legislator', who set the tone and framed the social system. Penn and Baltimore were never far from his thoughts; but who was to play the part of Lord Baltimore at New Canterbury? He allowed his fancy to roam over the unlikely prospect of finding some rich and cultured gentleman ready to transfer himself, his family, and his capital to New Zealand where he would be accepted as the natural leader of society. Might not such a man be appointed by the Crown as governor for life, or even as hereditary governor of the colony? Several years later, Wakefield still fancied that Lord Lyttelton might emigrate with that intention. In 1849, he had hopes of Lord Mandeville, then of a Suffolk baronet, Sir William Bellairs. Influence alone would secure the liberties of Canterbury against Lord Grey and his fellow-Whigs. He must find a bishop and a titled aristocrat.

The affairs of Canterbury were brought to a crisis by a first report from Governor Grey on the site for the settlement; it reached the Colonial Office in July, 1849, a full year after Captain Thomas's departure, and announced that Thomas favoured the plains of the South Island. Wakefield now applied himself to the problem of translating theory into practice. How should he overcome the frustration that beset every colonial enterprise in 1849? Suddenly the problem was resolved, and he instantly decided upon the method by which Canterbury must be brought to birth. Wakefield was a valetudinarian, in bad health, and interested in medical prescription. Since January, 1849, he had noticed that Godley's throat was troubling him again. He recommended *hydropathy*, the fashionable fad, and persuaded Godley to consult a practitioner, Dr Walshe. He would cure Godley's chronic laryngitis with cold water and fresh air, a truly heroic expedient, as men lived a hundred years ago. But Godley's throat grew worse and, in September, Dr Walshe ordered him to spend the winter in a milder climate, at Madeira or Naples. At first this seemed to mean death to the Canterbury Association even if it meant life to Godley. But Wakefield saw his chance. As, two years ago, he had persuaded Godley to form the Association, a task which no other of his acquaintance could have undertaken, now again he persuaded Godley to go to New Zealand as the Association's agent. If Godley went to the site of Canterbury his energy and resolution would bring the settlement into being. Though he had neither rank nor wealth he had all the qualities of heart and head that the leader of a new society required; and his friends in high places at home might be trusted to back him up. He even made a move to petition the Queen for a baronetcy to be conferred on Godley but got no support. Such an honour was not to be expected for a Tory, while the Whigs were in office.

Until September, 1849, the idea of emigration had never crossed Godley's mind. When he devoted his energies to systematic migration, the despatch, not the reception, of colonists was his concern. He regarded himself as an Irish squire whose duty lay in County Leitrim. While his father was alive he must earn his living and prepare himself for his duties as a landowner. When his father should die he might enter Parliament—if his health permitted. The suggestion that he should personally found a colony was quite new, and he accepted it because idleness in Naples was utterly repugnant to him. Two objections arose in his mind: he would not undertake to go until his father approved it as he did—generously—and he must wait a few weeks because his wife was expecting her confinement.

Since the Association had as yet no charter, and therefore no legal status, it could not give Godley a secure appointment. Wakefield had some difficulty in persuading the other members of the Committee to take the step. They were too much accustomed to acting on Godley's initiative—he was too proud and sensitive to propose his own appointment. By working on Godley's friends, Wakefield, as usual, got his way.

On 10th October the managing committee of the Association recorded their approval of Godley's agreement to go to New Zealand as Resident Chief Agent, and, with that fortifying achievement behind them, decided at once to proceed with organizing and despatching the settlers. Parliament was not sitting and no distracting political event disconcerted their councils. Having resolved to act, they found the obstacles in their path not so formidable as they had supposed; and Lord Grey proved to be reasonable. At the end of October came a despatch from New Zealand announcing that Thomas, having made his final decision, was beginning to survey the district about 'Port Cooper' in the South Island. The Governor, though he still preferred the Wairarapa site, had given his consent, and so had the Bishop.

Among the members of the Association were three members of the Coleridge family, often alluded to by Wakefield as if they spoke in unison; and 'the Coleridges' watched the interests of the Bishop of New Zealand. George Augustus Selwyn, one of the greatest of the Victorians, had placed his episcopal see at Auckland since 1842, and was regarded as a friend to the native and missionary interest, that is to say as a foe to the Wakefield colonists. An indefatigable and courageous traveller, he had passed through New Zealand, on foot and alone, and was well-acquainted with the 'Port Cooper Plains'. He wrote to his friend, the Rev. E. Coleridge of Eton, commending them, and offering a great deal of gratuitous advice that did not at all suit the plans of the Association. To placate Bishop Selwyn was one of Godley's most important assignments. In his farewell letter to Godley, Gladstone made this the crucial issue. 'You are the man,' he wrote, 'to put colonizing operations into harmony with the Bishop.' But Wakefield and Godley were determined to have a bishop of their own, whose first concern would be with the pastoral care of the Canterbury settlers, not with converting the heathen, a diocesan not a missionary bishop, and his appointment would mean the partition of Selwyn's diocese.

The reader to-day may well wonder at the depth of political feeling about the appointment of colonial bishops a hundred years ago. It was a constitutional rather than a religious question. When Englishmen founded a colony of settlement, it was assumed by the lawyers that they 'carried

the common-law of England with them', and in the same
sense they carried with them the Established Church. Such
clergy as there were in the colonies were often provided with
endowments or even with salaries from the public funds, a
form of patronage and an expense against which the settlers
often objected, all the more as the proportion of Presbyterian Scotsmen and Roman Catholic Irishmen increased
in the colonies. The alternative, in that very religious age,
was for the clergy to be subsidised by the missionary
societies, as in parts of North America by the Society for
the Propagation of the Gospel, as in the North Island of
New Zealand by the Church Missionary Society. In neither
case did the Church-people of the colonies have any direct
interest in the temporal affairs of their Church. The parson
was either a government official, jobbed into a good position
with a salary, or he was a missionary to the heathen.
Godley's visit to Canada had taught him a lesson in church
government. A self-reliant episcopal church in communion
with the Church of England was being organized there, and
such a church establishment was to be an essential of the
Canterbury scheme.

But this was not all. The only bishops known to the
lawyers were functionaries appointed by the Crown and
endowed with judicial powers according to Canon Law.
For a local branch of the Church of England to provide
itself with a bishop and to get him consecrated, without the
royal letters-patent, might, as they supposed, make all those
concerned liable to the terrific 'penalties of *Praemunire*'.*
A bishop, in short, was a royal official under the old Erastian
system. Radicals in the colonies objected on rationalist
grounds, while High-Churchmen of the new Tractarian
school objected no less on grounds of ethics and catholic
tradition. How, then, was Canterbury to get a bishop of the
right sort, constitutionally, canonically, and with Bishop

---

* All these suppositions were swept away in 1865 by the judgment of the
  Privy Council in the case of Bishop Colenso. The establishment of the
  colonial churches was shown to be a fiction.

Selwyn's goodwill? The Colonial Office, as a rule, insisted that there should be a sure endowment of £10,000 available and, on that consideration, was usually prepared to advise the Crown that letters-patent ought to be issued.

The committee of the Canterbury Association invoked the aid of their titular president. Lord Courtenay and Godley went down to ask Archbishop Sumner at Addington, his country-house, whether he would use his influence with Lord Grey, and armed with a cautiously worded recommendation from the Archbishop, Lord Courtenay bearded Lord Grey at his country-house. Provisional approval for another bishopric to be carved out of Selwyn's diocese, so soon as the endowment fund was guaranteed, was enough. The Association made up its mind to launch the Canterbury Settlement. The final decision was made by Godley and Wakefield at Reigate, on 24th October, 1849.

All the vital problems drew to a head in the two months between Godley's decision to go and his departure. Lord Grey's approval made the choice of a suitable clergyman for the bishopric an urgent question, since it was agreed that the bishop should lead his flock to the new settlement. The official despatch from New Zealand, confirming the selection of a site for Canterbury reached the Colonial Office on 20th October. The charter, drafted by the managing committee six months earlier, passed the Great Seal on 13th November. Now the regulations for land-sales must be prepared and issued; a campaign of advertisement must be opened; salaried officers must be appointed to arrange for land-sales, shipping, assisted emigration; and, at the last moment, a new project was brought forward.

Land was to be sold in lots of 50 acres at £3 an acre, with the addition of a town section, and a right of pasturage, on favourable terms outside the occupied freehold land, to every original purchaser. The purchase-money realized at this high price was to be applied in a fixed proportion, prescribed in the charter, to certain approved expenses: ten shillings to recompensing the New Zealand Company for its land, ten shillings for survey and public works, one pound for assisted emigration, and one pound for the provision of the churches and schools which were to distinguish Canterbury from every other colony. The first suggestion had been that the Ecclesiastical and Educational Fund should be administered by the Society for the Propagation of the Gospel, but, as the plan developed, the name of Christchurch and the influence of the Christ Church men inevitably pointed to a foundation which, like Christ Church, Oxford, should embrace a cathedral and a college. One of the reasons, said J. E. FitzGerald in April, 1850, for calling the settlement Christchurch was that it was intended from the beginning that it should contain a large college.

In September, 1849, when Wakefield and Godley were in daily correspondence, one of the topics they discussed was the co-option of Mr F. A. McGeachy, a Conservative M.P. and Adderley's brother-in-law, to the managing committee. He was invited down to Wakefield's cottage at Reigate for the week-end of 30th September, and there the three men agreed upon a new branch of the plan. Wakefield found McGeachy sensible and prompt and, as he had been brought forward on the express grounds that he 'laid the foundation of the new Church of England College Schools, such as Marlborough', there can be little doubt that the subject they discussed was the college at Canterbury.

About the same time, another group of Wakefield's friends were busy with a similar scheme. The Hon. Francis Baring (Lord Ashburton's brother and successor in the title) suggested that an educational foundation in the colonies should be endowed as a memorial to Charles Buller, the leader among the Colonial Reformers who had died twelve months previously. Godley and Baring met at the Travellers' Club, on 24th November, to discuss the matter. Suddenly all the members of the group began to talk of founding a 'Buller College' in New Zealand and, before Godley sailed, it was generally agreed that it should be a feature of the Canterbury Settlement. Baring clinched the matter by subscribing £600 as a nucleus about which the endowment of the college grew. Few subjects can cause more bitter disputes among friends than the best disposition of a memorial fund, and there were those among Buller's radical friends who disliked the Church and Tory flavour of Buller College.

The subscribers split and, while some contributed to the college at Canterbury, others preferred to commemorate their friend with a tablet in Westminster Abbey. Eventually the Oxford men asserted their control over the college, which they proposed to endow principally from the land-fund, though they gratefully accepted contributions from Baring and some others.

The Buller College was not the first of the schemes to extend the English Public School system to the colonies. In an age of reform this was a matter of interest in every established settlement; it was only the proposal to found a college at the very foundation of the colony that was new. The plan derived something from Sir John Franklin's plan, drawn up upon the advice of Arnold of Rugby, for the foundation of Christ College in Tasmania. Unfortunately it could never be brought into being except on a much reduced scale. When Franklin was governor at Hobart his chaplain (and son-in-law), the Rev. J. P. Gell was named as the first principal of Christ College, Tasmania. Later Gell was a friend of Lyttelton who urged him to accept the bishopric at Canterbury settlement. Gell's influence may be traced through much of the Canterbury correspondence.

Godley sailed from Plymouth on 12th December, 1849, and, with his departure, there was grave danger of the heart going out of the Association. It was during the next nine months, until reports came back from Godley in New Zealand, that the genius of Wakefield showed its amazing fertility and variety. From his cottage at Reigate, in the grounds of the White Hart Inn, he conducted a prodigious correspondence, with directors of the New Zealand Company and committee-men of the Canterbury Association, with bankers and shippers in the City, with radical and Peel-ite M.P.s, with the editors of the *Chronicle* and the *Spectator,* with clergymen who might be induced to accept the Canterbury bishopric. To each of these diverse correspondents he wrote in appropriate style and with discreetly adjusted emphasis. With no formal authority to act in any of these capacities, he manipulated the Association, the Company, and the new Colonial Reform Society. When his health permitted he was a frequent visitor at the Company's office in Broad Street, the Association's office at Charing Cross, and the rooms fitted up in the Adelphi for the reception of intending settlers; and he boasted that thirty-six members of Parliament came down to Reigate to consult him in one week-end. In the words of Dr Garnett, his first biographer: 'We see the sanguine, enthusiastic projector, fertile, inventive, creative, his head an arsenal of expedients, and every failure pregnant with a remedy; imperious or suasive, as suits his turn; terrible in wrath, and exuberant in affection; commanding, exhorting, entreating, permitting, as, like an eminent personage of old, he

> With head, hands, wings or feet, pursues his way,
> And swims, or sinks, or wades, or creeps, or flies.'

His particular interest was to maintain the Church and Tory connection that Godley had built up. He persuaded Godley to give him an introduction to the editor of the *Chronicle,* and to write on his behalf to Adderley and Lyttelton. Could not Adderley be persuaded to come to Reigate and make friends with him? How could he work closely with these men if he was not on easy terms with them? Adderley was slow in losing his distrust for Wakefield: 'the most amazing genius I ever knew,' he said, but 'sulky', 'satanic', 'machiavellian'.

CHAPTER VI

The 'Canterbury Pilgrims'

HAVING received a friendly letter from Gladstone, bidding him farewell, Godley had seized the opportunity of replying at length, with an appeal for colonial reform, which was published in several newspapers.* His departure thus attracted some attention in the press, notably from *The Times* which was, on the whole, hostile to the Colonial Reformers and suspicious of colonizing schemes. Its leading article on 19th December expressed its surprise that the much puffed undertaking of the Canterbury Association had led to any practical result. However, 'the prominent part taken by Mr Godley, a man of great colonial information, gave some assurance that it was not a mere pious utopia'.

Wakefield was not the man to miss a chance of working up publicity. He inspired the campaign for getting settlers of the right sort, and he produced the managers for the various departments. The Canterbury Association moved its office to larger premises in Cockspur Street, and before long Wakefield decided that a more active set of officers was needed. By some unfathomable intrigue he induced his own nominee, John Hutt, to resign in favour of Lord Lyttelton who resumed the chair. For about two years and a half, from April, 1850, to September, 1852, Lyttelton was effectively the manager of the Canterbury Association and,

* See Appendix A.

as events turned out, its financial mainstay. But Wakefield was dissatisfied also with the Secretary, Alston, an easy-going elderly man, and succeeded in supplanting him by placing over his head a salaried deputy-chairman who supervised the office routine when Lyttelton was not available. This was Henry Sewell, a lawyer, introduced by John Simeon, and further recommended as the brother of William Sewell who was one of Godley's oldest friends. The administrative history of the Canterbury Association was thereafter the tale of Sewell's activities. These arrangements, and many others, were effected by a simple device. Wakefield could count on whipping up a majority for his clandestine proposals by appealing to Godley's friends, Adderley, Simeon, Cocks, and McGeachy, and he strengthened the group by bringing in one or two more, notably Godley's brother-in-law Charles Wynne.

Wakefield was a consummate nepotist. Two of the New Zealand settlements had been founded by his brothers, William and Arthur; a third brother was a judge in New Zealand; his nephew had gone to New Zealand with Captain Thomas, his only son with Godley; he still had a brother to provide for, Felix Wakefield, a surveyor and engineer who had been in Tasmania. Felix, known to his friends as Felix Van Diemen, was as fruitful in schemes as his elder brother. His system of land-surveying was adopted by the Association, with the result that Captain Thomas laid out the site of Canterbury more rapidly and more accurately than had ever been known in any new country. He was a sportsman and a naturalist, a great acclimatiser of English flora and fauna in the colonies. He wanted occupation and he wanted money. He was put in charge of land-sales, on commission, and made an exceedingly good thing of it.

The management of shipping contracts was put in the hands of William Bowler, a self-made man who was said to have begun in life as door-keeper to the New Zealand Company. He, too, worked on commission and cleared £2,500. It was well-earned; his reports were full and business-like, and no body of emigrants ever left the British Isles in greater comfort than the emigrants whom the world was beginning to call the 'Canterbury Pilgrims'. But there were bitter complaints of his extravagance. He was unlikely to be parsimonious while he drew a commission on the total expenses of his department.

Land-sales to settlers with money to invest began early. The choice of labourers to whom assisted passages were to be given was left rather late, and was committed to J. E. FitzGerald, who decided in March, 1850, to emigrate to Canterbury. Every emigrant claiming assistance was required to produce a certificate of good health and vaccination, a certificate of good conduct signed by the vicar of his parish, and counter-signed by a Justice of the Peace. The original intention had been to restrict the settlement entirely to members of the Church of England, had not Lord Grey firmly 'drawn his pen through that clause of the charter'. The Association was content with less rigid regulations which would ensure a Church of England majority. No land-purchaser was likely to pay £1 an acre for the Ecclesiastical Fund if he were not a churchman, and land-purchasers' nominations were preferred in selecting the assisted emigrants.

Felix Wakefield toured about the country in search of land-purchasers. His efforts were supported by a series of public meetings convened in the provinces by the keener members of the Association. In several counties committees were formed among the clergy to promote the Canterbury settlement. Lyttelton and Adderley conducted a meeting at Birmingham, Simeon in the Isle of Wight, Bishop Wilberforce at Reading, Bishop Hinds at Ipswich, and a distinguished company of clergy and gentry appeared on the platform at the London meeting in St Martin's Hall. Birmingham was a dull meeting, Ipswich a theatrical success, St Martin's Hall a crowded controversial meeting. After the Bishop of Norwich, Simeon, and Herbert had expounded the Canterbury plan, an outsider, a Mr S. Sidney, stood up in the body of the hall and made a bitter attack upon the Wakefield system. He had seen it, at its worst, in South Australia. He called upon the audience not to be suborned and got some applause from the back of the hall. It fell to the Bishop of Oxford to overwhelm this heretic with eloquence on the subject of Church colonization. Resolutions in favour of the Canterbury plan were carried with acclamation. Mr Sidney remained unconvinced and was still denouncing the Association in the press, three years later.

The Ipswich meeting was remarkable for the appearance of the 'Bishop-designate' of Canterbury whose adventures were to provide an element of comedy in a serious story. Wakefield had great difficulty in finding a candidate for the bishopric. After two candidates had been sounded, and had withdrawn, Hawkins of the Society for the Propagation of the Gospel suggested the name of the Rev. Thomas Jackson, a good classical scholar from Oxford who was principal (until its demise from mismanagement) of the Battersea Training College and a prebendary of St Paul's. At first he seemed the very man, at least in the eyes of Wakefield who, perhaps, was not a good judge of bishops. Jackson was said to be the best platform orator in England. His notions of episcopacy were rather of the old High Church of the eighteenth century than of the new high church of Godley and Selwyn. A palace, a carriage and pair, lawn sleeves, and lordship were the essentials, rather than the art of swimming a flooded river or steering a whaleboat in a sou'wester, in his notion of his duties. But it would be unjust to underrate his peculiar talents or the services he rendered to Canterbury. He had his counterpart among the other Canterbury Pilgrims;

> He was in church a noble ecclesiast
> Well could he read a lesson or a story
> But all the best he sang an offertory;
> Full well he wistè when that song was sung,
> He mustè preach, and well affyle his tongue,
> To winnè silver as he full well could.

The Canterbury publicity was wonderfully enlivened by his fervid oratory, his protested devotion to the cause of Canterbury 'and his high ideals. At Ipswich Jackson won the honours of the evening by his appeal for a new spirit in colonization. 'In Canterbury,' he said, 'the wines may be scanty, but Homer and Milton may be invited to the board.' Canterbury will not be a colony 'where slang will be substituted for conversation . . . where the English language has lost its nerve and purity . . . where men drink and do not dress for dinner'. He appealed for a college to be founded in the settlement; not merely schools but 'that venerable collegiate discipline and training, which has raised generation after generation of English gentlemen'. So far, so good. His admirable sentiments, expressed with power, drew from the good people of Ipswich a voluntary subscription of £385. With this he withdrew to London, omitting to make any arrangements for the hire of the Town Hall or the other expenses of the meeting.

> There was no man nowhere so virtuous
> He was the bestest beggar in his house
> For though a widow haddè not a shoe
> So pleasant was his *In Principio*
> Yet would he have a farthing ere he went.

Before June was ended Wakefield was repenting of his choice.

A façade of publicity could not, for long, conceal the fact that land-purchasers were not coming forward in sufficient numbers. Some respectable heads of families, men of the type that was required, put down their names and paid their deposit, but not one-fourth as many as had been hoped for. It required a considerable act of faith to buy land, unseen, at the end of the world for £3 an acre when it could be bought in other distant provinces for ten shillings, even if the £3 conveyed a hypothetical right to survey, roads, and bridges, churches and schools. The great speculative collapse of 1847 was not yet forgotten and no bubble companies were more fragile than colonizing companies.

Only a few months earlier a speculative company for colonizing Natal had come to grief. The only difference, so far as would-be emigrants could judge, was the distinguished list of names on the prospectus.

The Association had contracted to sell 100,000 acres of land by 16th April, 1850, and to sell as much in each succeeding year. This should provide, as a first charge, £50,000 for repayment to the New Zealand Company and £50,000 for preliminary expenses at the settlement. When the day came, no such sum was available. The directors of the Company grew restive, the weaker members of the Association lost heart. Again it was Wakefield who devised a way out of the difficulty. He first persuaded his friends among the directors to accept a postponement of the settling-day, then a second postponement, and finally offered a guarantee for the deficiency. By working on the sympathy of Godley's friends—this was the only way to save 'poor Godley's scheme'—he induced three wealthy men among them, Lord Lyttelton, John Simeon, and the Hon. Richard Cavendish, to make themselves responsible for the deficiency, a sum of £15,000, giving his own name as a fourth guarantor. The guarantee of 1850 was the first of a series of financial aids given to Canterbury by Godley's friends. In each of the two following years advances were required to supply the stipulated expenditure and, in addition, voluntary contributions were collected from the members of the Association for the Cathedral and the College. To distinguish gifts from loans, and loans from guarantees, in the Association's books is no easy task and it may be supposed that the reluctance of the Association to publish its accounts is partly due to this uncertainty. Suffice it to say that the settlement drew on the benevolence of members of the Association to the amount of £29,000 in three years, and that Lyttelton was by far the largest contributor. Without these advances the Canterbury settlement would never have come to birth.

The first guarantee of £15,000, added to the sum received from land-sales, made up the required £50,000 which placed the Association in possession of the Canterbury block. It was just in time. The New Zealand Company was moribund. Since its final reconstruction in 1847 it had lived only to acquire land for the Otago and Canterbury settlements. It now surrendered its charter and expired, on 7th May, 1850. But, since the Canterbury Association was a sort of subsidiary, it was left in the air. It was Sewell's task to prepare and rush through Parliament before the end of the session a Bill to legalize the proceedings. The Canterbury Settlement Land Act was enacted on 14th August, 1850.* Preparations could then be pushed on for despatching the first fleet of ships. Rather ruefully, the committee reduced the scale of their operations and prepared to despatch four ships instead of the twelve that had been planned for. FitzGerald found the time short for collecting emigrants of the working-class and was soon at odds with the Wakefield brothers. Gibbon Wakefield in London attempted to transfer the business of selecting emigrants to his brother Felix and, long before the sailing of the first ships, realized that FitzGerald was his adversary. He tried to persuade FitzGerald to withdraw, on various excuses, and belittled him in correspondence. He drew a distinction between Godley, 'the only Irishman he ever knew who was not in the least Irish', and FitzGerald, almost a stage Irishman, 'wild enough to hunt his own sheep'. Then according to his custom, he formed another cabal at the Colonists' Rooms in the Adelphi, where the Canterbury Settlers met to exchange information and concert plans. But FitzGerald was not to be put down. He was Godley's loyal friend among the settlers and was beginning to picture himself as Godley's successor, the future leader in the settlement. A healthy rivalry, the germ of that two-party system which is the safeguard of political liberty, had appeared, before

* 13 & 14 Vict., cap. 70.

the settlers left England. There were the rudiments of a Godley party, led by FitzGerald, and a Wakefield party, led by a settler named W. G. Brittan.

Wakefield arranged for the publication of a series of pamphlets during the summer, containing copies of the prospectus, the charter, and the Act of Parliament, accounts of public meetings, extracts from favourable articles in the newspapers, letters from New Zealand, regulations for sales and shipping, and advice to emigrants. In the number for July, 1850, there appeared a valedictory poem by Martin Tupper, the popular poetaster of the day—and a Christ Church man. Hailing the colonists as a new body of 'Canterbury Pilgrims', he gave wide publicity to the venture. The Pilgrims, like the Pilgrim Fathers of New England, were a formed body before they sailed, already a civil society. Their first social act was to collect a library at the rooms in the Adelphi, and the Bishop-designate was importunate in his demand for subscriptions. At the rooms the colonists eagerly debated self-government; the college prospectus, agricultural methods, acclimatization of plants, place-names in Canterbury, and devoured information about colonial life, which Felix Wakefield was always ready to supply. Some of the richer men among the Pilgrims made preparations for importing bloodstock, pre-fabricated houses in sections, furniture and ornaments; and took passages for their domestic servants. Among the cargo of the first fleet was an organ, a church bell, a quantity of Jacobean oak-panelling for church furniture, scientific apparatus for the college, a printing-press, and the library.

On 30th July a public banquet for the gentry among the Pilgrims and their friends was held on board one of the ships moored in the river at Blackwall. It was fully reported in the press where editors noted with astonishment that these prosperous, well-dressed, happy breakfasters—a mid-day function was in those days called a breakfast—were actual emigrants. Did not the word emigration suggest a dreary procession of ragged, feckless paupers? But here were a large body of respectable persons, with actually a Lord's son among them, and all paying their own way.

'The entertainment took place on board the *Randolph*, in the East India Docks, Blackwall, one of four exceedingly fine ships, chartered for the voyage, and giving in their appearance and equipment every reason to anticipate a safe and prosperous passage. The names of the vessels were the *Sir George Seymour*, the *Cressy*, the *Charlotte Jane*, and the *Randolph*; the day appointed for sailing being the 29th of August. They lay close together in dock, and were dressed with flags in honour of the occasion. On the lower deck of the *Randolph* four tables were laid, occupying the whole length of the ship, and covered with an elegant *déjeuner à la fourchette* for 340 persons. Of the company which assembled at two o'clock, and occupied every seat a little after three, about 160 reckoning ladies and children, consisted of actual colonists, whose passages are taken in the ships . . . . A large proportion of these colonists belong to the gentry class at home; and inquiry has satisfied us that they are distinguished from the mass of emigrating colonists no less by high personal character, than by their social position at home; that they are not driven from the mother-country, as too commonly happens, by the pressure of adverse circumstances, but are attracted to the colony by the prospects which its singular organization holds out.'

It had been Wakefield's task to whip up a gathering of eminent guests. He had hoped for Lord John Russell and Lord Grey, but 30th July, 1850, was a critical day in Parliament, near the end of session, with a hot debate on Jewish Disabilities coming on, so that few politicians attended the banquet, even among members of the Association. Lord Grey, whose supposed hostility to Canterbury shrinks, the more closely it is examined, was represented by his countess. The guests included Earl Nelson, the admiral's great-nephew, Miss Burdett-Coutts the millionairess who founded four bishoprics, and those indefatigable diners-out, Mr Thackeray and Mr Monckton Milnes. Wakefield's name did not appear among the guests and was not mentioned in the speeches.

Lord Lyttelton, proposing the health of the Royal
Family, looked forward to the day when a royal prince
might be viceroy in the Antipodes. The Rev. William Sewell
brought the good wishes of 'the members of the University
of Oxford, in their individual capacity at least'. The Bishop
of Norwich proclaimed it 'a grand day for England and the
English Church'. Lord John Manners read a message of
goodwill from the American Ambassador, and enlivened his
speech with references to Lord Baltimore and the 'twenty
gentlemen of good estate with 300 labourers of good
character' who founded Maryland. FitzGerald proposed the
health of Lyttelton, to whose exertions 'they principally
owed the position they then occupied', and Simeon pronounced a panegyric upon the absent founder. Godley's
whole life, said Simeon, speaking of their long unclouded
friendship,

'tended to the point on which he was now engaged. From his
early youth, at school, and afterwards at college, his mind had
been drawn especially to historical research, and had been
gathering the materials on which his views of colonizing were
subsequently founded. His more leisure life was spent in Ireland,
a country where, more than in any other, he was able to see
the evils arising from an undue pressure of population upon
the means of subsistence, and was led to look to emigration as
a corrective of this great social evil. His visit to America, a
journey mainly undertaken for the purpose of inspecting the
condition of some of those who had left their fatherland, placed
him in the presence of the worst evils which attend upon the
careless and unconsidered expatriation of masses of men, and
of the ills which arise from dispersed and un-systematic colonization; while, on the other hand, he saw in French Canada,
beautiful even in its ruins, the result of the colonization of old
times, carried on upon true and high principles, and strongly
marked by the religious element. The result of these investiga-
tions was the formation of the Canterbury Association and Mr
Godley's best reward and encouragement would be to behold
the unrivalled body of Colonists whom he (Mr Simeon) had the
honour to see assembled there that day.'

'It was from no idea of gratifying ambition, or acquiring gain, that Mr Godley placed himself in the position which enabled him to carry out the cherished object of his life; and when his health failed him under the pressure of intellectual labour, and a change of scene and climate was necessary, he did not betake himself to the sunny shores of France or Italy, but to that distant Island whither the Colonists were hastening, and where he was then engaged in making preparations for their arrival, more complete and satisfactory than had ever before been made for the founders of a new people. Under these circumstances, he (Mr Simeon) was justified in attributing the whole scheme, with its present prosperity and its future success, with all that he would characterize as its unselfish reality, to the influence upon kindred spirits of the master mind of John Robert Godley.'

'It had been said that the test of the highest quality of judgment was to be able to distinguish between the difficult and the impossible. This faculty Mr Godley possessed in a remarkable degree.'

The report in *The Times* then continues:

'The toast of "Success to Canterbury" having been acknowledged by W. G. Brittan, chairman of the Colonists, the company broke up, many of them proceeding to the deck, and joining in the mazy dance, to the music of the band of the Coldstream Guards, which, throughout the day, had enlivened the proceedings by playing several favourite and national pieces.'

A banquet for the gentry came first because the land-purchasers were already an organic society. The 'labourers', who were to receive assisted passages, had not yet been assembled. Their turn came a month later. When the ships' companies were made up at the end of August, a valedictory service for the whole body of Pilgrims was held in St Paul's Cathedral in the presence of a large congregation. The Pilgrims received communion together and heard a sermon by the Archbishop of Canterbury, their patron, a purely evangelical sermon* with no references that need be quoted here. The date was Sunday, 1st September, and two days later, Lord Lyttelton presided at a dinner to 600 of the 'labourers', now ensconced aboard the ships which had moved down the river to Gravesend.

The First Four Ships then set sail for Plymouth where the cabin passengers mostly came aboard, and took their final departure on 7th and 8th September, 1850. The largest was a ship of 850 tons and the others not much smaller. They carried 127 cabin passengers at £42 a berth, 85 intermediate passengers at £25 a berth, and 534 steerage passengers at £15 a berth. Passage-money, in the case of land-purchasers, was offset by the proportion of their payment allotted to the emigration fund. The labourers were required to pay what they could before the deficiency was made up from the emigration fund. Each ship carried a chaplain, a surgeon, and a schoolmaster at the expense of the Association.

It will be noticed that the whole of the first settlement did not set sail in September. Two further ships were to follow, a few weeks later, and with them the Bishop-designate would sail.

Only a few days before the sailing of the ships was the first despatch received from Godley in New Zealand, and it is now time to return to his story.

---

* By comparison it may be noted that the Bishop of Oxford preached before the second body of Canterbury settlers, nine months later, in Westminster Abbey, a robust discourse upon the text: 'Now the Lord had said unto Abram, Get thee out of thy country, and from thy kindred, and from thy father's house, unto a land that I will show thee.' At the farewell banquet to the second body of settlers, on 8th May, 1851, the Duke of Newcastle was the principal speaker. Proposing the health of his friend Godley, he remarked that his actual health had been restored by his voyage to New Zealand. The occasion was fully reported in a number of the *Illustrated London News* which contained little else but the opening of the Great Exhibition.

CHAPTER VII

The Godleys in New Zealand

BUSY as they were together, Wakefield had been anxious to get Godley away in 1849, before the worst of the winter should incapacitate him. Godley lingered for the sake of his wife's health. Her second child was still-born. As soon as she was again fit to travel they went down to Plymouth, to a friend's house, and set sail, on 13th December, in the *Lady Nugent*. In a passage of 97 days until they saw the southern extremity of New Zealand they made no landfall.

It is hardly necessary to recount the details of an uneventful voyage a hundred years ago, the letters of good wishes from their friends, the presents that made Charlotte Godley feel as if it were another honeymoon, the search for Charlotte's disused side-saddle and the 'mackintosh life-saver' that John had worn seven years ago in Canada; the delays when the *Lady Nugent* could not clear Plymouth Sound; the sea-sickness; for all three of them were bad sailors; the shipboard theatricals, the young gentleman who abandoned shaving, wore dirty trousers and preferred the company of the foc'sle hands; the other young gentleman (Jerningham Wakefield) who flirted with a lady although she wore an engagement ring; the lectures on improving subjects which Godley wrote and someone else read to spare his throat, the meetings at which he was inevitably asked to take the chair; the emigrant family of Scottish crofters whom Charlotte thought the best company on board; the interest taken by passengers and crew in little Arthur Godley, aged two and a half. Such details and many more are recorded in the lively letters which Charlotte Godley wrote to her mother, and which have been published under the title of *Letters from Early New Zealand.*

Life in the colonies has generally been recorded as if it were a masculine monopoly, and one of the demerits which the Reformers denounced in the old colonial system was the absence of feminine refinement in the settlements. It was one of their axioms that systematic colonization should mean colonization by decent, young, married or marriageable persons. Charlotte Godley was a young lady of fashion. It was doubtful, said her grand-daughter, whether she had ever done her own hair, unaided, before she went to New Zealand, and those who met her, years later in London Society, as a charming and dignified matron or widow, found it hard to believe that she had washed shirts for Maori tribesmen in a clear stream flowing through the New Zealand bush—and seemed to have enjoyed it. She had a natural gaiety of spirit that enabled her to enjoy anything, and with it a serious purpose that won the respect of all she met in any company or clime. Her influence over the settlers was no less profound than that of her husband and she added to it a spark of kindliness and good-humour that he sometimes seemed to lack. John Robert Godley could be hasty and autocratic, though he was quick to make amends if he was shown to have injured anyone. He had few, if any, personal enemies, but she treated all she met as her friends.

The household consisted of husband and wife, the boy Arthur who was two and a half years old when they set sail, William Stormont as groom and valet, and Mary Powles as lady's maid and nurse. William proved something of a disappointment; though he had formerly been a footman at the Wynne's house in Portman Square, he seemed, in New Zealand, to care only for the horses and waited at table in

PILGRIMS' LUGGAGE BEING LANDED AT LYTTELTON, JANUARY, 1851

Water-colour painting by Sir William Fox, in the Hocken Library, Dunedin.

perfunctory style, rather dirty, and wearing an old blue frock-coat which had once been his master's. The prescient Wakefield had warned Godley against him, offering to let Godley take away his own valet instead, a feudal method of procedure that sounds strangely in our ears to-day. But William stayed the course and remained behind in Sydney, a city which seemed to suit his tastes, when, three years later, the Godleys returned to London. Powles was the mainstay of the family and her account of the Canterbury settlement would have been worth hearing. When Godley was ordered to the Mediterranean his wife had doubts whether Powles could be persuaded to go, and she was unaccustomed to moving a step without her. Powles merely wondered how the master could get on with nothing at all to do. 'What a pity they could not make him Governor of Naples!' For her part she would go with her mistress to the end of the world. A few days later came the decision that the end of the world it was to be, and to a task quite as exacting as the governorship of Naples. She went, which Godley thought 'plucky in a London lady's maid'; never relaxed her standards; and returned to be for many years an honoured inmate of the house in Gloucester Place.

*   *   *   *   *

The scene shifts to the southern hemisphere where, after rounding the Snares before a sou'westerly gale, the *Lady Nugent* drove along the east coast of the South Island of New Zealand. On 25th March she entered the winding harbour of Otago, to put her passengers ashore at the new Scottish settlement of Dunedin. The Godleys stayed a day or two with Captain Cargill, the old soldier who was resident agent of the Scottish Association. He reminded them of some resolute covenanting farmer out of the Waverley Novels, and it was pleasant to discover that he had fought at Badajos, before either of them was born, in the Highland Regiment of which Denis Godley was now an officer. They liked him and they liked their first view of the country, but

E.

noted rather sadly that it was Easter Day. At New Edinburgh there was no Anglican church in which they could make their Easter Communion. Godley was shocked to discover, also, that so small an area of ground was yet under plough, a full year after the landing of the first settlers. As soon as they might, they made sail for Port Cooper, two hundred miles up the coast.

All that had been done on the site of Canterbury was the work of Captain Thomas, a big, burly man with much driving-force and resolution. Having left England in the earliest days of the Association, he knew nothing of its later doubts and difficulties. Assuming that the optimistic intentions of the prospectus would be carried out in a short time, he began his operations on the greatest scale. If this was to be the best prepared settlement in the history of the Empire, he was the man to do the work. He knew what he was about, as he had seen colonization at its worst, in Texas, where, he said, 'the state of society is about the lowest you can possibly find for white people'.

His predilection for the South Island had been confirmed by others who had seen the 'Port Cooper Plains' and notably by the only European settlers who had previously made a home on them. The rugged indented mass of Banks Peninsula, which reminded several visitors of the Snowdon range, was pierced by four deep-water inlets, all of which were already well-known to the whaling crews. At one of them, Akaroa, a tiny French colony of about 20 households had been settled for eight years; their lands were excluded from the Canterbury block. In Pigeon Bay two families of Scottish crofters had settled in the hope of ultimately obtaining title to their holdings by virtue of their Wellington land orders. Nearest the plains were two harbours which had been named after the proprietors of the Sydney whaling and trading firm of Cooper and Levy, one of whose captains had been trading for flax there twenty years earlier.

The rumour—whether unfounded or not—that these spacious harbours bore the names of two transported convicts seemed so scandalous to the Canterbury Association that Captain Thomas was instructed to re-name them Ports Victoria and Albert. The old names clung, however, and Port Levy is known by that name still. Port Cooper was Thomas's first choice for the metropolis of Canterbury. He proposed to lay out his town on the rolling hills at the head of the harbour. He changed his mind, however, and placed the capital on the plains, laying out his port town on a narrow shelving site, beneath a rugged mountain side and overlooking a fair anchorage. He called the town Lyttelton, and the name has also attached itself to the harbour. The promontories on either side of the harbour-mouth he called Godley Head and Adderley Head, and, in accordance with his instructions, he provisionally allotted many place-names to rivers, mountains, and districts on the plains, long before word came from England that the scheme was going forward. On some early maps the name of Wakefield was given to the Snowy Range of mountains, but to-day they are exclusively known as the Southern Alps. Place-names in Canterbury were given much attention by the Association which, at an early date, showed a disposition to send minute instructions to Thomas on matters which that masterful man understood much better than they did, and on problems which he had settled for himself long before the instructions arrived.

Naturally enough, he depended upon reports given him by the handful of squatters, especially upon the occupiers of two homesteads. On the plain itself two brothers from Scotland, John and William Deans, had settled as early as 1843 beside one of the rare patches of tall timber. They called their homestead Riccarton, and the clear stream that flowed past it into a wide marshy estuary, they called Avon after the Avon that takes its rise in their native Ayrshire. Their cattle grazed over the site of Christchurch and across the open plains. With no legal title, other than an agreement with the nearest Maori clan 10 miles away, they had brought a large area of land under cultivation and had enclosed a

400-acre homestead block. Like the Pigeon Bay settlers
they held land orders from the New Zealand Company's
other settlements, and even before Thomas's arrival had
begun negotiations with the New Zealand Company to
exchange them for a grant of land around their homestead
on the plains. William Deans had been appointed Justice of
the Peace and occasionally rode to the river-mouth and
sailed away to sit with his nearest colleague, at Akaroa, if
there was call for their services among the seamen of
visiting ships. Though alone, with one family of Scottish
farm-servants, separated by a pathless range of hills from
any other Europeans, they were happy and prosperous.
When rare mails reached them, they watched with interest
the plans of the Canterbury Association and sent, by return,
accounts of life at Riccarton which were received with
enthusiasm, months later, at the Colonists' Rooms in
Adelphi Terrace. On the shores of Port Cooper, and held
under lease from the Maoris, was a sheep and cattle station
managed by George Rhodes for his brother and senior
partner, W. B. Rhodes, who had first visited the bay as
master of a whaler in 1836, and who had established a
cattle station at Akaroa as early as 1839. Rhodes was
invaluable since, like Deans, he could supply meat for
Thomas's labourers. Thomas gave squatters' licences to
Rhodes and Deans in August, 1849, and surveyed the four
hundred acres at Riccarton so that the Deans's holding could
be preserved for their use. When Godley sailed he was
expressly instructed to respect the claims of Rhodes and
Deans, two names which are still held in honour in
Canterbury.

Between August, 1849, and March, 1850, Thomas
worked wonders. He had three distinct tasks to do. The
first was to make a trigonometrical survey and a map of the
whole Canterbury block—'all that tract of waste and unappropriated land situated in the Middle Island of New Zealand, being bounded by the Snowy Range of hills from
Double Corner to the River Ashburton . . . and by the sea

. . . and estimated to contain 2,500,000 acres, more or less, with the exception of certain buildings and the land marked out as appurtenant thereto, situate on Banks Peninsula, and purchased by the New Zealand Company from the Nanto-Bordelaise Company [*i.e.,* the French settlement at Akaroa. *Ed.*]'. The second task was to lay out town sites: as early as September, 1849, Thomas had decided upon the position of the town on the plains, to which the name of Christchurch was eventually fixed, and by March, 1850, he was able to despatch a map of the site to the Association. It is an interesting town-plan, though not so distinguished as one or two others—Melbourne for example—which date from the same generation. Christchurch was laid out on a gridiron plan one mile square, all the streets being of an even width of one chain, with a central space, in which it was intended that the Cathedral and College should arise, and a wide 'town belt' of park-land outside the square mile. Its position was fixed by the navigable limit for whaleboats on the little river Avon, about five miles from the seashore and two or three miles downstream from the homestead at Riccarton. It required imagination and an eye of faith to place the quadrangle of streets diagonally across the course of the river which meanders through the town between grassy boulevards. Until many street-bridges were built it must have been an awkward obstacle. The surveyor of Christchurch was Edward Jollie, Thomas's assistant, and it is recorded that he would have preferred a more spacious street-plan.

In addition to Lyttelton and Christchurch, Thomas decided to lay out a third township on the seashore, near the estuary through which the Avon finds its way to the sea over a dangerous surf-beaten sand-bar. He called it Sumner after the Archbishop. The public domain at Christchurch he called Hagley Park, and the domain at Sumner he called Killegar Park.

Confusion continued about place-names. Thomas in New Zealand and the Association in London were at odds about the relative importance of the townships. Should the metropolis of Canterbury be at the port or on the plains and, consequently, which of the two should be called Christchurch? The issue was confused by a certain shyness on the part of the intending settlers in the use of the sacred name. They petitioned the Association to re-name the capital as Lyttelton, to which the Association replied, on 1st August, 1850, that they had no objection, so long as the college in the metropolis should be called Christchurch. However, Thomas in New Zealand, whose own view was that the metropolis should be Lyttelton, the Port, had his way and gave the name of Christchurch to the city on the plains. According to orders he allotted as street-names in his three townships the names of all the bishoprics in the Anglican communion. 'Thomas, with his gold spectacles on and a Peerage in his hand, read out a name that he fancied' —so Jollie told the tale—'and if he thought it sounded well and I also thought so, it was written on the map. The Lyttelton map was the first that was finished; and Sumner followed.' After that he had few names left for Christchurch except those of colonial and Irish dioceses, with the result that the busiest streets in Christchurch to-day are called Cashel and Colombo Streets.

The Admiralty had a surveying ship, H.M.S. *Acheron,* on the coast that season. Her captain said he had never seen quicker or more accurate work than Thomas's survey. But the third task, preparing for the reception of the first settlers with the amenities he thought proper, was far beyond his financial resources. He had £20,000, advanced to him in cash by the agent of the New Zealand Company in Wellington, according to the agreement negotiated by Godley between the Company and the Association in London; and when this sum was exhausted he borrowed more, in the confident expectation that land-sales in England would bring in a much larger sum. He imported an architect, a team of carpenters, and large supplies of building-timber, the one requisite in which Canterbury was deficient, from

Van Diemens Land; built wooden barracks as temporary shelter for immigrants, an agent's house for Godley, a jetty at the port, a custom-house; and began to plan extensive engineering works. One was essential; there must be a road over the rocky spine of hills between the port and the plains. He laid out the line of a road with a gradient of one in twenty over a rocky pass eight hundred feet high to Sumner, and thence to Christchurch. This was no small undertaking. He arranged to bring down from the North Island a gang of 120 half-civilized Maoris to work on the road for half-a-crown a day, quite ignoring the warning of old Port Cooper hands that there was a blood-feud between these North Islanders and the local tribe. It proved to be the white labourers not the Maoris who made trouble.

All these activities attracted attention throughout the southern colonies. The rumour of a great experiment in colonization attracted speculators hoping to buy land. An old soldier called Major Hornbrook arrived at Lyttelton, opened a saloon which he called appropriately the Mitre Hotel, and announced that he would pay £500 for the site if the Canterbury Association would let him keep it. When an emigrant ship bound for Auckland put in at Akaroa early in 1850, forty of the emigrants decided to stay. Godley arrived, on 12th April, to find Lyttelton already a busy place, Thomas deep in debt, and the Sumner Road not half-finished.

He wrote to Adderley:

'At six we weighed anchor, the wind being fair, though light, and passed up the bay. None of us, I believe, were prepared for the beauty of the scenery. It took us more by surprise than even at Otago, for the sketches which we had seen in England were far from inviting. . . . The hills are very bold, both in face and in outline; bare for the most part—that is, with only small patches of wood at the bottom of the glens—but with much of that sublimity which is produced by extent of view and rugged wildness. . . . Halfway up the harbour we passed a whale-boat, which informed us that we might go up and anchor opposite "the town". At that time we had seen no sign of civilization, except the line of a road in process of formation, along the face and over the top of the hill on the northern shore, and no human habitation, except some Maori huts close to the beach; but we held on, and presently another whale-boat, with Captain Thomas, the Chief Surveyor of the Association, on board, shot from behind a bluff on the northern shore and boarded us. . . . my wife and I went ashore with Thomas.

'On rounding the bluff . . . I was perfectly astounded with what I saw. One might have supposed that the country had been colonized for years, so settled and busy was the look of its port. In the first place, there is what the Yankees would call a "splendid" jetty; from thence a wide, beaten-looking road leads up the hill, and turns off through a deep cutting to the Eastward. On each side of the road there are houses scattered to the number of about twenty-five, including two "hotels" and a custom-house! (In the shape of a small weather-boarded hut certainly, but still a custom-house.) In a square, railed off close to the jetty, are four excellent houses, intended for emigrants' barracks, with a cook-house in the centre. Next to this square comes a small house, which Thomas now inhabits himself, and which he destined for an agent's office. Behind this, divided from it by a plot of ground intended for a garden, stands a stately edifice, which was introduced in due form to us as "our house". It is weather-boarded, has six very good-sized rooms and a verandah; in short, after seeing it, we could not help laughing at our own anticipations of a shed on the bare beach, with a fire at the door. . . . In order to get a general idea of the country, I asked Thomas to have a couple of horses taken from the carts and saddled for us; upon these we started to cross the hills into the plain. The track lies up the side of what may fairly be termed a mountain. In fact it can hardly be called a track at all, and it requires some habit and nerve to keep the saddle. Near the top, we both dismounted, and scrambled up the rocks on foot leading our horses. . . . From the top of the hill there is a perfect view of the whole district. . . .

'There is an amphitheatre of mountains, not snow covered, but snow sprinkled, and a vast grassy plain without the smallest apparent inequality on its surface, stretching between them and the sea; absolutely no other feature whatever, except a large lake close to the sea, on the south-west corner of Banks's Peninsula . . . and several streams which, from flowing in very deep channels, make a small show at a distance. The promontory itself must contain exceedingly beautiful scenery, as its whole surface consists of hills covered with forest, broken and diversified in outline, and indented by bays, reminding me of the "fields and fiords" of Norway. The hills immediately around Port Cooper alone appear comparatively bare; their character resembles very much that of the mountains which form the "Ogwen Pass" near Bangor, or perhaps still more that of the "Bosom of Fann" on Lough Swilly; for while the Welsh Mountain is higher and grander than ours, it would, on the other hand, be very unjust to compare our beautiful dark blue bay to such a paltry lake as Ogwen. The first view of these plains, as of all others that I have seen in New Zealand, is rather disappointing to an English eye: that is, one misses the greenness and luxuriousness which the growth of grass in a country long cultivated and grazed over exhibits . . . but after making allowance for this, I am sure that until it shall have been either broken up or grazed over, no part of it will produce grass to be compared with a soil of equal quality in old countries. There is no difference of opinion, however, so far as I can learn, among those who know the country, as to the land in the Canterbury Plains being of fully average quality, capable of fattening sheep and cattle, as well as of giving good crops of all kinds. When we arrived at Mr Deans's farm we had proof of this; for his garden, which never saw or heard of manure, is producing luxuriantly every kind of vegetables and fruit. I never saw a finer show of them—apples, pears, peaches. Everything in short flourishes. I wish I could send home a specimen of the apples; they look like wax-work. . . .

'On our return to the port we found our passengers and crew scattered about, loud in their praises of the progress which had been made in so short a time, as well as of the prospects held out by the Settlement. They forget that Thomas has had the spending of a larger sum of money on a given spot than any other pioneer of settlement in this country has had, so that the superiority of his operations is not to be laid altogether to the account of his merits. However, certainly, no body of settlers ever found so much done to smooth their path for them as ours will find.

'The first settlers must fence with banks and ditches, and plant gorse and quicks upon them; and they must also make up their minds to pay a high price for their fuel. This is the one drawback to what would otherwise be an incomparable district for settlement; and its existence should be known and published to prevent deception and disappointment. There are quantities of wild pigs on the plain, and quail and wild ducks innumerable; I wish I had a good pointer and retriever. Probably the Indian sport of boar-hunting with the spear on horseback will be introduced, as the country is specially fitted for it. I cannot bring myself to wish for foxes; but deer and hares we must positively have, as well as partridges and pheasants. There are a pair of partridges at Dunedin, which, after being imported with much difficulty, turned out to be both cocks: so, as I cannot hear of any others in the colony, I fear the unfortunate animals are doomed to spend the rest of their lives in cheerless celibacy. . . .

'On Sunday morning we sailed from Port Cooper with a light southerly breeze . . . and only anchored in Wellington harbour this morning between midnight and one o'clock.'

While his impressions of the place seemed so lighthearted, he was deeply anxious about finances. He thought Thomas's preparations at Lyttelton too sumptuous for what were not the first necessities of a colony, and his accounts unsatisfactory. Thomas had persuaded William Fox, the Company's agent at Wellington, to advance a sum of £4,000, over and above the agreed £20,000, a liability for which there was no security, since they did not yet know that the settlement was going forward. There had been some gross extravagances, such as the employment of an architect, for building temporary sheds. Thomas had to admit that he had ordered an expensive pile-driver for building the jetty but had not been able to get the machine ashore until the jetty was built. Godley gave him a peremptory order to complete essential work and to close down for the season. The native labourers must, in any case, be sent home during the winter months, by the terms of their contract, and nothing more could be done on a great scale until funds arrived from England. He called on Thomas for an estimate of the cost of making the Sumner road passable and was given the figure of £7,260, which in fact proved an extreme under-estimate. At any rate, there was nothing more to be done until £7,260 could be produced. Godley and his family then set sail for Wellington, where they could live in comfort and where they might expect the first news from England, leaving the unfortunate Captain Thomas a sadly disappointed man.

From April to November, 1850, the Godleys lived at ease in a furnished house which they rented at Wellington. It was the oldest and the largest of the New Zealand settlements, though not, at that date, the capital of the country, a pleasant little town with 4,000 or 5,000 inhabitants scattered along the shore of its land-locked harbour. There were some pretensions to genteel society. Sir George Grey had so far made concession to the wishes of the southern settlers as to post a Lieutenant-Governor, Mr E. J. Eyre (the Australian explorer, afterwards famous for his severities in Jamaica) to Wellington, and though he consistently snubbed this Lieutenant-Governor and allowed him no share of responsibility, there, at least, was Government House with all it implied. There was also a detachment of the 65th Regiment whose music and parade enlivened the town. Frequently there was a naval vessel in the bay, and there was an Anglican church. Charlotte Godley liked Wellington very well* and it suited the little boy. It was not so satisfactory for her husband, to whom inactivity was miserable. He first devoted his time to taking a cure which was so effective that his weight increased in a year from ten stone eight to eleven stone twelve. By the end of the year for the first time since boyhood Godley was a healthy man, and ascribed it to *hydropathy* at Wellington.

* In the year 1850, Charlotte Godley quoted the saying, already a 'chestnut', that a Wellington man may be recognized by the way he clutches at his hat to save it from the wind.

'My husband has fairly engaged in it now,' wrote Charlotte to her mother, 'under Dr Fitzgerald, and had his first *packing* on May 4th. He now gets up, at an unmitigated 6 a.m., into a wet sheet, and then lies, packed, mummy-fashion, till 6.45, when he has a wet sheet rubbing, in a great bath of cold water, and then tossing on a few clothes walks off to a renowned spring, from which he brings a can of superfine water for home consumption, and then comes dressing, etc., and breakfast at eight, if not before; at twelve another wet sheet rubbing, another walk or ride, and dinner at two; then *another* walk which lasts till dark, and then tea at 6.45; and about ten or sooner, a warm hip-bath for thirty minutes; and then bed.'

During this course of treatment he read all the books he had brought for his whole sojourn abroad, among them Lamartine, Mme. de Sévigné, Ruskin's *Modern Painters*, Tennyson's new poems, and the works of his friend Aubrey de Vere. He and Charlotte waited anxiously for *Pendennis* and the next volume of Macaulay's *History*. He had promised himself to study applied mathematics but found himself too restless to settle to it. He bought a horse, for thirty pounds, and a brace of pointers, and went up-country shooting quail. The closest friend he made in Wellington, or in New Zealand, was Archdeacon Hadfield, the veteran missionary who lived among the Maoris, along the coast at Otaki. Twice he visited Hadfield, on horseback, once taking with him the whole family. They slept rough in the bush and Charlotte, nervous as she was with horses, went off with him on a shooting expedition in high spirits, while Powles remained alone with little Arthur in the house of a Maori whose father had been a notorious cannibal chief.

This was killing time because there was no news of the Canterbury Association. He knew nothing of the failure to sell sufficient land, of Wakefield's struggle for time or of the guarantee given by Lyttelton and his friends. In August came a cheerful letter from Wakefield, but no official despatch. Australian newspapers that found their way to

Wellington brought news of Adderley's Parliamentary struggles, but nothing about Canterbury. It was a notice in a Sydney newspaper that brought him word that the First Four Ships had sailed. Long before then he had thrown himself into New Zealand politics.

In the little world of the Colonial Reformers Godley was already a celebrity whose arrival in a new settlement was an event of note. Every mail that came in brought news of the struggle going on in Parliament where Godley's friends were now challenging Lord Grey over the Australian Constitution Bill. Gladstone, Molesworth, Lyttelton, and Adderley fought it step by step throughout the session of 1850, denouncing it as a petty, inadequate measure of self-government, and forcing Lord Grey to accept amendment after amendment. Much of the news that reached Wellington came by way of Sydney where the Bill was a matter of lively interest. And with this news came six-months' old copies of *The Times* and the *Chronicle* commenting on Godley's letter to Gladstone, the most advanced expression of colonial claims for self-government that had yet been made. It was rather too advanced to win the approval of *The Times,* which nevertheless gave it a leading article.

At Wellington there was, as yet, no organ of self-government, since Sir George Grey had suppressed the constitution of 1846. There was however a Constitutional Association of private citizens who agitated for self-government. In August, 1850, when they elected Godley to their committee, he refused to serve on the grounds that he was 'merely a sojourner for a short period at Wellington'. Later in the year, a constitutional crisis arose, affecting the whole of New Zealand and, into this, Godley threw himself with enthusiasm, instantly assuming the leadership of the Wellington colonists. Sir George Grey had made a cautious step forward by creating a nominated council with restricted powers, for 'New Munster', the name then given to the central and southern settlements of New Zealand. Long before the Ordinance came into effect it had been denounced in London by the Colonial Reformers. It was Godley's part to persuade the Wellington settlers to combine in the endeavours of their friends in London.

On 15th November, 1850, he attended a public meeting at Wellington and it is evidence of the improvement in his health that he made a long speech, moving the first resolution, which was carried by acclamation, 'that the constitutional measure which Sir George Grey . . . has published in the shape of a draft Ordinance, does not deserve their approval or acceptance, inasmuch as it does not confer upon them an effectual control over the management of their own affairs'.

His speech was a denunciation of the general policy of the Colonial Office, in granting self-government by instalments. He admitted that Sir George Grey's Ordinance did 'in measure and after a sort' grant 'representative institutions' but denied that representative institutions were the real goal of the Colonial Reformers. 'We have representative institutions enough already, and can make as many more as we like; this meeting is a representative institution, as soon as we have elected a chairman; but the next question is, what can we do with them when we have them? There is no magic in the word "representative", no people was ever redeemed or regenerated by the mere election of delegates. No, Sir, the object which the colonists have given their energies to obtain, and which they will obtain, if they be true to themselves, is something very different from the mere form of a constitution; it is the substance which all such forms are but methods of exercising; in a word it is *political power;* the power of virtually administering their own affairs, appointing their own officers, disposing of their own revenues, and governing their own country.'

While speaking with scorn of Sir George Grey's Ordinance, 'a measure for constituting provincial debating-clubs', he took pains to exempt Sir George Grey from blame. 'I believe that he is anxious to make every possible concession . . . but he has not the power of giving you a good constitution, if he were ever so well disposed; he is fettered by Acts of Parliament and Instructions, which only fresh Acts and fresh Instructions can revoke. Never forget that the battle of our Constitution must be fought in London; it is by the influence which we can exercise, or the trouble we can give there alone, that we can hope to obtain our local independence.'

Six months later, the Colonial Reform Society was preparing the final onslaught which, according to *The Times,* brought down Lord John Russell's administration and swept away Lord Grey. Their minutes show that Charles Clifford and William Fox (a close friend of Godley), attended meetings with reports from New Zealand.

Sir George Grey's nominated councils were still-born, as he could persuade no prominent settlers to join them. William Deans of Riccarton, a canny Scot if ever there was one, was among those who declined the honour. This contest could hardly be expected to endear Godley to the Governor. It is one of the minor misfortunes of New Zealand history that Grey and Godley should have been at cross-purposes. Both were gentlemen, Churchmen, and scholars; both were liberal imperialists; both were young and enthusiastic. With these common tastes and external likenesses there was a deep temperamental cleavage between the two men. Governor Grey had all the arts of the demagogue, he was eloquent and affable, very skilful in that form of social condescension which is called the 'royal manner'. Simple people, and people who were not too close in affairs with the Governor, adored him. In a general sense he was perhaps the most popular colonial governor of the century. A radical autocrat, the least show of opposition aroused his jealous hostility. He was a good hater and was capable of very dubious intrigue if it was a question of scoring off an enemy. There were also some laxities about his private life that must have offended the strait-laced Godley.

Whatever the reason, Godley came as near to personal hatred of Grey, as so generous a man could come. His own reserved, straightforward, serious, and single-minded temper found no sympathetic response in the Governor's fine words and gestures; he thought the Governor a humbug. Charlotte Godley, too, took something of a dislike to Grey and could not get on easy terms with his cold, handsome, neglected wife.

They had met in Wellington a few days before the political meeting. Having heard from Sydney that the First Four Ships were about to sail, he applied to the Governor for an advance of £7,000 in monthly instalments with which to complete the Sumner Road. Grey went so far as to advance £2,400 on his own responsibility, the sole contribution made by Government to the Canterbury settlement. Even for this he was obliged to ask an indemnity from the Colonial Office and, a year later, received a grudging letter of approval, with a warning not to make such irregular conduct a precedent. Godley, however, wanted no grant-in-aid nor guaranteed loan; he would have been very well content with self-government, so that the Canterbury settlers could raise and spend their own revenue.

Meanwhile he must make haste to Lyttelton in some anxiety lest the First Four Ships should arrive unwelcomed. On 28th November, the Godleys took passage south in H.M.S. *Acheron* which was setting out on another surveying cruise; she carried auxiliary steam and could be sure of putting them ashore next day, at Port Cooper. Sixty wooden huts and storehouses had, by this time, sprung up. Godley now took possession of the agent's house and office, and instructed Captain Thomas to proceed with the work as far as £2,400 would carry him. To complete the Sumner Road was out of the question. Thomas was then ordered to make a temporary bridle-track over the crest behind the town so that the settlers could walk or ride to the Plains, while sending their heavy baggage round by sea in small craft, over Sumner bar and up the river estuary to a point not far from the site of Christchurch. The first obstacle was a strike on the part of the white labourers who required a higher rate of wages than the Maoris. That was quickly settled; Godley told them shortly that if they did not return to work in 24 hours he would replace them all by Maoris, and heard no more of it. The bridle-track was quickly finished, at a cost of £400, and Captain Thomas, having done his duty with the utmost reluctance, proceeded to resign his appointment. He was not the kind of man to knuckle under to Godley, nor did he accept the imputation of extravagance. He had, in fact, prepared the site of the settlement at a cost of £23,958. He departed a few weeks later, leaving his assistant, Thomas Cass, to continue his work on the reduced scale. It is pleasant to remember that, many years later, Thomas called on Godley at the War Office in London to apologize for his hasty action; he admitted that Godley had been right.

Sir George Grey paid a visit of state to Lyttelton on 13th December, in H.M.S. *Fly*. He and his lady were in their most gracious mood and it was a coincidence that pleased everyone that the first shipload of Canterbury Pilgrims was welcomed by the Governor. At ten o'clock on the morning of 16th December, 1850, a full-rigged ship was signalled at the harbour-mouth. She was the *Charlotte Jane*, 100 days out from Plymouth and still in front of the official notification that she was to sail. Hurrying down to the shore, Godley was met by James Edward FitzGerald, 'so altered by a sailor's dress, an immense straw hat, very hollow cheeks, a ferocious moustache, and a lame leg that at first I scarcely knew him'. That long-legged Irishman, though he had hurt his knee playing at deck games, got himself into the leading boat and with a leap was the first of the Pilgrims to land in Canterbury. There was very little about him now that smacked of the British Museum. 'He was so overcome as hardly to know whether to laugh or to cry, and I believe ended by doing both.'

CHAPTER VIII

The Founding of Canterbury

A LL was ready for one shipload, but it was an embarrassment when six hours later the *Randolph* was signalled and came to anchor beside the *Charlotte Jane*, and worse when next morning there appeared the *Sir George Seymour*. The ships had all parted company on the voyage and now came in together by accident. Three-quarters of the Pilgrims, or five hundred and eighty persons had thus to be provided for at once, and quite without notice, a strain upon the accommodation that could not have been foreseen. The fourth ship, *Cressy*, did not cast anchor until 27th December. The weather was fine and warm, so that those who could not get places in the immigration barracks or the two 'hotels' were, on the whole, content to remain aboard until they could raise tents or huts on the hillside. 'Who that was then at Lyttelton,' wrote one of them, 'can ever forget that delightful and exciting time? Those long cloudless summer days when we first began to build sod cottages, to carry boards upon our shoulders, when we first had to *rough it*, when we grumbled and laughed in a breath, and really did a great deal of work. We managed our own affairs as far as we were allowed, and so far we managed them successfully.'

The Governor remained discreetly in the background. Having seen three ships arrive, and having waived the right to import duties which he might have levied on the Pilgrims' stores and baggage, he appointed some officials and set sail, on the 17th. Godley was made Resident Magistrate and Commissioner of Crown Lands, FitzGerald sub-inspector of police. The chief officers of the Association, subordinates to Godley in his capacity as resident agent, were FitzGerald as immigration officer and Brittan as land officer.

A demand for self-government was registered on the second day. Those of the Colonists' Council who had arrived in the three ships met at Lyttelton, constituted themselves as a 'Land-purchasers' Society', with the Hon. J. Stuart-Wortley as their secretary, and appealed to Godley for recognition. They were the actual proprietors of the settlement; their money was being spent on its development: they and neither the Association nor the Government had the right to administer it. Godley replied:

'I consider myself placed here, not merely to act on behalf of the Association as I may think best for the interests of the colonists, but to do so subordinately to their expressed wishes . . . . As a general rule, it is for you and not for me, to determine how those common interests may best be consulted; while I am ready therefore to bear the full weight of responsibility which properly devolves upon me as an executive officer . . . as a general rule . . . . I shall guide myself by your directions, *so long as I shall be satisfied that your body does really and adequately represent the land-purchasers* of the Settlement . . . . I shall therefore, habitually consult the Colonists' Council whose money I am administering, and they shall have access to the accounts.'

On this principle was Canterbury governed during its first two years.

Some dreamers were disappointed that neither church nor college had yet arisen at Lyttelton. Christmas was celebrated, in great heat, with unseasonable plum-puddings and with church services in a loft hung with evergreens, over a warehouse. On New Year's day Bishop Selwyn arrived in his yacht, the *Undine*, which, the whalers said, he managed better than any man in the South Seas. The absence of a church or school-house among the first erections, after all that had been promised in London, grieved and annoyed him. Nor had the 'Bishop-designate of Lyttelton' come out with the first party of settlers. Selwyn instantly struck up a friendship with Godley and was businessman enough to understand—no man better—how Godley was hampered for lack of funds. Though the Association had placed a credit of £10,000 at his disposal, the Union Bank at Wellington, having some insight into the Association's finances, was unwilling to release it. A beginning must be made with what resources there were. The Bishop held a synod of the four clergymen who had come with the four ships, and was present at the commencement of a school in one of the immigration barracks, the modest beginnings of the 'Christchurch College'.

In their ambitious days the Association had flown very high with plans for the college; it was to be much more than the governing body of a system of schools. Wakefield's soaring imagination inflated it into a university, 'the nursing-mother of intelligence and manners for the southern world'. He had almost persuaded Dr Moberly to forsake the head-mastership of Winchester in order to inaugurate his college, and did persuade the head master of the new public school at Lancing to emigrate to Canterbury. Among the clergy who met Bishop Selwyn, in academic cap and gown, was the Rev. Henry Jacobs of Queen's College, Oxford, who had taken this bold step. Instead of becoming classical professor at a university college, he found himself engaged in organizing a small grammar school, much smaller, at first, than Lancing, but the immediate need of the new community. A body of emigrants, however polite and lettered were not likely to take with them, in their first endeavours, any large number of young men desiring academic honours. The ideal was not, however, lost to sight and Mr Jacobs always tutored a few pupils of maturer years, who wore academic dress.

Law and order, a representative council, a church, a school, all were established in some rudimentary form in the first three weeks. The next social organism to arise was a free press. On 11th January, 1851, appeared the first number of the *Lyttelton Times,* edited by the exuberant FitzGerald, and it is through the *Lyttelton Times* that the progress of Canterbury became known to the world. The first number was the subject of a long, amusing, and complimentary leading article in *The Times* of London, on 5th July.

'A slice of England cut from top to bottom was despatched to the Antipodes last September. A complete sample of Christian civilization, weary of the difficult fight for breath within the compass of these narrow isles, took ship at Gravesend in search of less crowded markets . . . a deliberate, long-considered, solemn and devoted pilgrimage to a temple erected by nature for the good of all comers.

'At the head of the pilgrims stood an actual bishop, behind him were working clergy, working schoolmasters, working landlords, working labourers, workers every one. Between deck and keel were the elements of a college, the contents of a public library, the machinery for a bank, yea, the constituent parts of a constitutional government. The adventurers stepped on board British subjects with British failings, British associations, and British habits and, let them be drowned or disembarked where they might, they would carry to the bottom or any other landing-place the British character, as emphatically expressed upon their persons as the effigy of Britannia on their familiar halfpence.

'It is superfluous to add that the enterprising voyagers took on board with them type, a press, an editor, a reporter, pens, ink and paper, and a determined resolution to start a journal for the enlightened public of New Zealand, at the very earliest opportunity. No English traveller is rash enough to deposit himself, even in a railway carriage, without his newspaper. John Bull could scarcely be said to be represented at the Antipodes unless, with his day's work done, he could be shown, with a pipe in his mouth and his feet under a table, deliciously absorbed in the latest news, and the exciting conflict of his local politics.'

The Times went on to praise its antipodean rival for the excellence of its production and the moderation of its views.

This was the most favourable account of the Canterbury settlement given by any quite independent journal, excluding those in journals which might be expected to show favour, as recognized organs of the Colonial Reformers. Under the actual circumstances the Canterbury plan had already failed in two respects. It was being attempted on about one quarter of the intended scale, so that the funds were insufficient for the estimated outlay, and an 'actual bishop' did not in fact stand at the head of the Pilgrims.

Rumours had already reached Godley that the Bishop-designate was not quite the paragon he had first seemed, and Mrs Godley felt sure that he would never take the place in their hearts of their 'dear Bishop Selwyn', who reminded her of the portrait of St Carlo Borromeo. The letters that came with the First Four Ships brought dire confirmation of these rumours. Wakefield wrote candidly to say that Mr Jackson was quite irresponsible in money matters. From various letters it came to light that he had been unwilling, or unable, to render accounts of the large sums he had raised by his eloquent appeals. The managing committee had demanded explanations, in vain. Worse than this, they had felt obliged to avoid a public scandal, which would have ruined their undertaking, by allowing his unauthorized expenses and even by meeting a cheque for £300 which he had overdrawn on his private banking-account. It was said that bailiffs had pursued him to his ship at Plymouth. No one suggested that he was deliberately dishonest, he was by nature casual in managing money and profuse in spending it. The dignity of his new appointment, which he inflated with a vivid imagination, quite swept him off his balance, so that the very factors which made him invaluable as a publicity agent in London, quite disqualified him for the harsh realities of a colonial bishop's life.

Among the numerous and verbose despatches which

Godley received from the Association—they had formerly sent him no word and now sent him far too many—was a letter on Church organization which, in decently veiled terms, proposed to exclude the Bishop-designate from any executive control of the temporal property of the Church in Canterbury. In the hurly-burly of the first weeks at Lyttelton, with new settlers coming ashore daily to pursue Godley, the sole source of authority, with never-ending demands and complaints, the coming of the Bishop-designate was a new oppression, and not the relief it should have been.

It was, perhaps, a comfort that, in the first instance, he was coming for a temporary visit, to bless the beginnings of his diocese. A legal flaw, of extraordinary complexity, appeared in his letters of appointment. When Lord Grey in London advised the Queen to create a bishopric in the southern part of New Zealand, the Law Officers had intervened with the observation that his action was *ultra vires*. The Queen could not divide Bishop Selwyn's diocese without his consent, and, as there was no agreement over the limits of the new diocese, it would be necessary to discuss the matter in detail with Bishop Selwyn. The difficulty in dealing with Lord Grey was his habit of digging in his heels and standing fast on just such points of detail. He had approved a bishopric but, for his own reasons, utterly declined to make it co-terminous with Canterbury; it must be a bishopric for the southern half of New Zealand. When, at last, Bishop Selwyn was consulted, he made it clear that he regarded the Canterbury Association as impudent meddlers in spiritual affairs. Not only had they failed at the proper time to consult him about the new bishopric but they were already making clerical appointments in his diocese before the partition had been authorized. He was prepared to treat with the Bishop-designate who was bringing his commission from the Crown, but not with the Association which had no standing in clerical matters. Selwyn's own plan was one for dividing New Zealand into three bishoprics, based upon the ecclesiastical requirements of the country of which he alone was a good judge. These constitutional and clerical complications took long to unravel, and were not finally unravelled until Selwyn was able to visit England, four years later. Meanwhile, here was the Bishop-designate on his way to Lyttelton, with an imperfect commission and a shabby reputation, a contrast in every way to the Pilgrims' ideal.

The dreaded day of the Bishop-designate's arrival proved worse than the Godleys feared. The *Castle Eden* came into port, on 6th February, 1851, with a new body of settlers and with the Rev. Thomas Jackson, his lady, and two ill-brought-up boys. All were entertained as guests by Charlotte Godley in her six-roomed wooden cottage. She was horrified to find him vulgar, fussy, pretentious and apparently concerned only with the material aspects of his profession. When she asked him in all seriousness which of his clergy he intended to prefer to the parish of Lyttelton he answered with a smirk that he would appoint the parson she liked best. He never knew how deeply she was shocked by this flippancy. Mrs Jackson landed in silks and ostrich-feathers, as became a prelate's wife, and was taken aback when confronted with the genteel Mr Godley in a blue jersey and moleskin trousers. She, however, improved on acquaintance.

It was plain from the first that the Jacksons lost interest in Canterbury as soon as they realized that a palace, a cathedral, and even a road on which to use the carriage-and-pair they had brought with them, existed only in the future. While that heroic pioneer, Bishop Selwyn, seems to have made a little mild fun of the Jacksons and their social pretensions, he received Jackson with enthusiasm, begging him to complete the formalities and take up his residence in Canterbury as soon as possible. They conferred together in Lyttelton on the day when all the settlers were away at the land-selection, at Christchurch. A month later, however, Jackson and his family set sail again for England, to the great relief of Charlotte Godley's housekeeping, and were seen no more in Canterbury. The managing committee in London were now as troubled over getting rid of the Bishop-designate as they had been over finding him. Sewell put out what he thought a discreet inquiry whether Jackson might not be found suitable for the third bishopric in New Zealand, to the general relief of Canterbury. This brought down the whole weight of Bishop Selwyn's wrath. He declined to receive any further communication from the Canterbury Association, even from his old friend, Lord Lyttelton. To Godley, however, he wrote with affection: 'I am ready to sink or swim with you.' The great fiasco of the Bishop-designate, long remembered as a joke in New Zealand, was a fatal blow to the Canterbury Association in London. Without a bishop the settlement could never be what its promoters had intended.

In all new colonies from Captain John Smith's Virginia to Sir Charles Eliòt's Kenya, the fundamental problem has been to get the settlers on to the land. A smooth and regular solution of this problem was the essence of Wakefield's system but only at Canterbury in 1851 was the system operated perfectly. Lord Grey, indeed, had almost prevented it by a stubborn, unreasoned objection to Wakefield's proposal that the first settlers should ballot for choice of sections. He had, however, been satisfied with the alternative (having exactly the same effect) that the officers of the Association should issue land-orders to purchasers in the order in which letters of application should happen to be opened at the Association's office. What was a ballot under another name was thus taken behind his back. One hundred and fifty-four sections of land were sold before the list was closed, and to the holders of these original land-orders, the actual proprietors of the first settlement, certain advantages were given in respect of town-sections and rights of pasturage. They, too, constituted the Council on whose advice Godley promised to rely. In all earlier colonies, absentee proprietors were numerous; it was Wakefield's pride that at Canterbury nine-tenths of the original land-purchasers were working settlers. The few absentees were mostly members of the Association or other well-wishers, several of whom sent sons or other relatives to work their land in Canterbury. FitzGerald, in addition to his other occupations, held a land-order as agent for his friend, H. S. Selfe, an active member of the Association. Godley bought no land in the first instance, keeping himself clear of any imputation of desiring profit from Canterbury. Later, when he had ceased to be an officer of the Association, he bought a little land which increased in value.

December, 1850, was spent in receiving and unloading the ships, January, 1851, in organizing the port and town of Lyttelton. The Land-purchasers' Council had quickly come to the conclusion that Christchurch, not Lyttelton, must be their metropolis. Those settlers who came ashore early and made themselves roughly comfortable were growing restive at the end of six weeks of cloudless summer weather. Lyttelton was a cramped dusty hollow in the hills with no amenity except the blue harbour, and nothing to do but watch the ships or gape at the tattooed, blanketed Maoris from their village at Rapaki. When the bridle-track was ready the Pilgrims soon grew weary of scrambling to its summit to view the promised land on the plains.

Social progress had gone so far by the beginning of February that the Godleys gave a ball at Lyttelton to about a hundred of the leading colonists, by way of leave-taking before they dispersed to their selections on the plains. Long and serious were the discussions as to who should be invited, and, while Charlotte pretended it was 'rather a bore', it is evident that she found the planning of this entertainment highly amusing. All was done that could be done with 'pink calico, ships' flags, and "patent composite" candles.' 'Powles, in severe grandeur, presided over a very great amount of tea, coffee, and cakes; and William over some huge joints of meat, ham, chicken, pie, etc. and sherry'; while all hands behind the scenes washed cups and spoons, of which there were far too few in Canterbury. The four long rooms of one of the immigration barracks contained the party and seemed luxurious until, at three o'clock in the morning, there arose one of the dust-storms for which Canterbury was then famous. The candles blew out; the unlined weather-boarded walls admitted clouds of dust which filled every crease and fold of the ladies' ball-dresses; and the party decamped, tired, disordered, and still in the best of spirits. Charlotte was obliged to admit that the costumes of some of the guests were astonishing. She had been in New Zealand a year longer and had fallen quite behind the fashion.

When William Deans of Riccarton came to tea, a day or two later, his comment was that they must expect that kind of weather two or three times a summer until they planted the hillsides with English grass-seed. Tea with the Godleys was the hub of social life at Lyttelton on ordinary days. The little house was crowded every evening with guests looking for boxes to sit on and cups to drink from, hoping that the talented FitzGeralds would join the party to provide some music.

The allotment of sections according to the serial numbering of the land-orders took place at the site of Christchurch on 17th and 18th February, 1851.

On the rough grass in a bend of the river Avon, carpenters were at work upon the land office, a wooden shed in which sat Godley and Brittan with the surveyors to receive selections in due order, and to enter them on the map. In a marquee nearby an enterprising caterer from Lyttelton served substantial meals of beef and mutton. The scene must have resembled a country agricultural show, but for the empty landscape. In the western sky, the long range of the Southern Alps, lightly tipped with snow, faded at midday into the heat-haze. To southward, five or six miles away rose the sudden, humped, volcanic hills that stood around the port. Otherwise the plain lay bare, showing no vegetation but the coarse straw-coloured, tussock-grass. Along the river banks there grew some tufts of the New Zealand flax which, in the eyes of the Pilgrims, resembled a giant bulrush; and in the distance a plume of smoke arose from the homestead at Riccarton, the only finished house to be seen in a hundred miles of visibility. A few huts and tents showed up like gypsy encampments along the river.

Section Number One had been drawn for one of the few absentees, Mrs Maria Somes, who bought it for the College, and in memory of her late husband, Joseph Somes, a Member of Parliament and a Governor of the New Zealand Company. Godley and Brittan had already selected a quarter-acre section on the frontage at Lyttelton with this land-order and had let it to a hotel-keeper for £100 a year. The rural section for this land order was chosen on the hill slopes just behind the town. The second order was held by Felix Wakefield, who selected his land at Sumner; he had not yet arrived in the colony. Not till the twenty-second order was produced did any land-purchaser select as his town section a site which afterwards became a valuable city-freehold in Christchurch. The interest of the day, as the founders desired, was agricultural and not speculative; purchasers selected land to cultivate, not land to sell again. FitzGerald selected a fertile valley running down from the Port Hills to the plain. When the second day ended, 106 selections had been made and the settlers could move on to the land with a secure tenure. Canterbury was founded.

The summer ended with dust-storms turning to torrents of cold rain from the sou'west, as the settlers faced the facts of colonization in virgin soil. Carriage of goods by sea from Lyttelton was difficult, dangerous, and costly; the freight was half of that charged for the voyage out from England. Timber was scarce for building or for fuel. The mettle that was in the settlers was now put to the test, upon the plains. Godley was glad to join them there, as he wrote to his father a fortnight after the day of selection*:

* J. R. Godley. Private letter to his father. 27th February, 1851.

'You would laugh if you saw the place from which I am writing. It is a little "plank tent" or "V. hut", as a thing made of long boards leaning against each other is indiscriminately called; its locality is the side of a small wood, by which runs a clear stream, on the plain, about ten miles from Lyttelton. We have removed hither *en famille*, and given up our own house to the Jacksons, to whom my dislike makes me feel it incumbent to be doubly civil. I kept them for a fortnight, and then I could stand it no longer, so I levanted one fine morning, and don't intend to reappear till he is gone. Powles and Arthur live in another hut just like ours, and William and our Maori servant in an edifice of reeds, which serves also for a kitchen. About two miles from us is the nascent capital, which is very curious to see (as the French phrase it) as it is "wisibly swellin afore our wery eyes". Two months ago it was a grassy plain unmarked by any sign of human footstep or handiwork. Now, it is covered by at least 80 habitations, of every variety in form and material. Tents, houses of reeds, grass, sods, lath and plaster, boards, mud, and dry clay, besides a few that are merely pits scooped in the bank of the river, and one or two consisting of sheets and blankets hung on poles. In these nearly 400 human beings are collected, and all sorts of business goes on, from the choosing of land, to the milking of cows. There are two "general stores", three butchers, two bakers, etc. Meat is 5d. per lb. milk 3d. per quart. One extraordinary looking edifice, composed of a huge studding sail from one of the ships, bears upon its entrance a brass plate, with "Barker, Surgeon" inscribed thereon. Then the "streets" are so busy with bullock drays, and young horses unaccustomed to struggling against the yoke, and Maories putting up houses, and innumerable dogs of every conceivable breed. We have a church consisting of a V. hut, with a flagstaff, and we have a daily post from Lyttelton to Ch.Ch. (I hope my old college is much obliged to me for naming the future capital of New Zealand after it) and beautiful offices for our survey and land-disposal, and I cannot tell you how many other symptoms of civilization. More than 100 landed properties have been chosen, and it is a good sign that every man thinks his own choice the best.'

A glance at the Canterbury Plain was sufficient to show that it was pastoral country. While the Pilgrims, of whom few were experienced farmers and still fewer practised pioneers, had their minds turned towards agriculture, the squatters and the keen-eyed speculators who were drawn by the Canterbury publicity talked of nothing but cattle and sheep. In a few months they knew they had found the best sheep-country in the world. Clifford and Weld, two young gentlemen of family—whom Godley had met in Wellington—but Roman Catholics, and therefore not land-purchasers, had come overland from Nelson to 'squat' on sheep-runs just beyond the northern boundary of the Canterbury block. Rhodes and Deans had their eye on sheep-runs, and soon a Mr Aitken arrived from Melbourne with stock, and what mattered more, with experience. Godley made friends with him but could not, if he observed the terms of his instructions, give him a pasturage licence in Canterbury. The right to pasture sheep on unappropriated land was restricted, by the Charter and by the Land Act, to original land-purchasers. Only the Association in London could authorize sales and even it could not vary the terms of sale without amending the Act. At once, even before selection day, Godley was confronted with a fatal flaw in the Association's plan. He wrote at once to Governor Grey asking for some limitations to be put upon pasturage licences outside Canterbury, but without effect.

The Deans brothers, also, had applied to Godley for a pasturage licence which he was obliged to refuse, reluctantly, since he had no authority to grant it. They appealed to Governor Grey whose Attorney-general gave an opinion in their favour. Godley promptly challenged it on grounds of law, whereupon the Attorney-general (one of Wakefield's brothers) thought better of his opinion. Having established his point of law, Godley proposed that the Governor should be asked to arbitrate, and meanwhile invited the Deans brothers to 'squat' on the run they had chosen where, he promised, they should be undisturbed so far as he could manage it.

The Deans's claim led to a breach with the Governor

who had, a second time, been overcome by Godley. Having
invited William Deans to take a seat at his nominated
Legislative Council, Grey prudently declined to commit
himself as arbitrator. William Deans refused for his part,
to go to Wellington to assist in what he and everyone else
in Canterbury regarded as a mere substitute for self-
government, but sailed for Sydney to buy stock for his new
'run'. In his absence his brother, John Deans, dined with
the Godleys at Lyttelton and regaled them with news from
New South Wales where gold had been discovered and all
the Sydney people were flocking to the Turon gold-field.
Whatever their disagreements about land-titles Godley and
John Deans had become fast friends, when in August came
the sad news that William, the elder brother, was lost at
sea. At the end of the year John Deans went home to Scotland to bring out a bride and, by the same ship, Godley
was pleased to report to the Association that coal of good
quality had been discovered on the 'run' which he had
provisionally granted to the Deans family. The formal
approval of this special concession, for the family to whom
the Canterbury settlers owed so much, had already been
given by the Association and was on its way to New Zealand in the same month, January, 1852.

The Deans affair was a test-case in Godley's relations
both with the Government at Wellington and with the
Association in London; it dragged on through the first year
at Canterbury while scores of other less personal difficulties
arose from day to day. For two or three months after the
selection there was endless work to be done in adjudicating
claims. It was one thing to allot native reserves in principle
in a treaty with Maori chiefs and another to persuade
illiterate tribesmen to accept restrictive landmarks on the
ground. The old-established homesteads of squatters in
the bays of Banks Peninsula might each have proved as
troublesome as the Deans's sheep-run. 'Turn me out if you
can,' said Mr Hay of Pigeon Bay, with a truculent grin,
when Godley arrived by boat to visit him. He took some

persuading that Godley had no such intention but only wished to check and register and admit his claim. A strict Presbyterian, he had resisted the advances of Bishop Selwyn who wanted to baptize his baby, and had the deepest suspicion of the Canterbury High-Churchmen. Like so many others, he soon succumbed to Godley's transparent candour.

A visit to Akaroa, on which he was accompanied by Charlotte and Arthur, was a pleasure to all three. The autumn weather, the winding blue bays, the bush-clad valleys were more beautiful than anything they had yet seen. The handful of French peasants were the oldest white inhabitants of Canterbury, in a settlement of ten years standing, one which might remind Godley of some Acadian village in Nova Scotia. Yet, after ten years on Banks Peninsula, the Government had done nothing to survey their holdings or to legalize their position. All this was left to Godley, and much trouble it gave him. When they had come under the British flag, a resident magistrate had been sent to Akaroa, this office being held in 1851 by a Protestant Irishman with whom the Godleys found many links of friendship. The settlers also had a *curé* of their own, whose heart leaped up when he found Godley ready and able to converse with him in French, with news from Paris, where the Godleys had spent their last holiday together before leaving Europe. Officially, Godley's adjudication of claims at Akaroa was the subject of bitter complaints by the French bishop at Wellington, and long correspondence ensued with the Colonial Office.

Churchman though he was, and leader of a Church settlement, Godley showed no trace of exclusiveness. At an early stage he received deputations of Roman Catholics and Nonconformists at Lyttelton, asking him to allot them ground for their chapels and cemetery, which he promptly granted, and was censured by Sewell in London, six months later, for doing so.

It was the religious question that caused the breach with Governor Grey. On his two visits to Canterbury in Godley's

PART OF THE TOWN OF CHRISTCHURCH, 16 JUNE, 1851

Pen and ink sketch by Dr A. C. Barker.

time, he was, as Charlotte wrote, 'quite irresistibly gracious and good-humoured'. He even allowed Canterbury a sum of £2000 for road-making, which he could hardly deny since the customs at Port Lyttelton were bringing in much more than that as revenue; he was always helpful on minor matters of administration.

In affairs of greater moment the Canterbury settlers soon formed the impression, which became an unshakeable article of belief, that the Governor's good-humour was always a sign of mischief coming. In April, 1851, he made another attempt to form a Legislative Council, which again was denounced as a sham by the settlers' associations in each of the centres. On 19th June Godley forwarded a petition asking for a real measure of provincial self-government for Canterbury. Grey replied with an extraordinary outburst in his Council, declaring that the Canterbury project was locking up the land against genuine settlers in favour of an exclusive and sectarian body. Even the downtrodden Lieutenant-Governor Eyre made bold to tell the Governor to his face that he was moved by mere personal dislike of Godley. Again Godley addressed a public meeting with explicit and reasoned arguments to which no response was possible. Grey made no further reply but found means of venting his spite on Canterbury.

Godley began by protesting that he agreed with Sir George Grey in disapproving of colonizing by means of chartered associations.

'I have been an active promoter of the Canterbury Association, and I now stand here to defend it on this ground alone, that it is better than the Government. If we had a government able and willing to make its waste territory available for British immigration, and to give facilities to intending colonists for managing their own affairs and colonizing on their own principles from the first, I should be prepared to admit that an amateur association like ours was an intruder.

'For twelve years . . . Sir George Grey and his predecessors have had nearly the whole of New Zealand under their control and in their hands. They have had every conceivable advantage and facility at their command, funds, troops, steamers, civil administration, surveyors. They have spent more money in one year than we are likely to have at our disposal in five; and what have they done? They have founded one seaport and garrison town (Auckland) to which I do not believe 500 actual settlers have ever gone . . . and yet Sir George Grey gravely complains that the Canterbury Association are keeping Her Majesty's subjects from colonizing this district under the auspices of the Government—he taunts us in fact with being an obstacle to colonization. . . . We have done more for colonization in a month than they have done in twelve years; ay, and more, as every man in New Zealand knows, than they are likely to do in twelve years to come.'

Sir George Grey's assertion that the Pilgrims 'violated conscience' by charging part of the cost of land to the Ecclesiastical Fund was very quickly demolished. Were the old settlers in Canterbury really being made martyrs for conscience sake?

'I think my friend, Mr Deans, is not very likely to complain that we have injured him by planting the future capital of New Zealand within two miles of his homestead. My friend Mr Rhodes is sometimes a little inclined to grumble and complain, but I don't think even he will join Sir George Grey in voting for the relief of his conscience by the annihilation of Lyttelton.'

He then spoke at length about a separate provincial government.

'I wish it to be understood that I advocate it only with this distinct qualification—that it be a reality, not a sham. . . . The Provincial Government of New Munster is an expensive nonentity, and I protest against the introduction of anything like it here. It is necessary to say this very distinctly, lest Sir George Grey should find in anything we do an excuse for saddling us with a costly provincial government, and giving it, when constituted, nothing to do. . . . We are very busy, and not very rich just now, and what we want is a homely government, of which the members may take their share in public business, without neglecting their own. . . . If we only try, we shall find that a few gentlemen can meet in a small room, and despatch public business very efficiently, without calling themselves by fine names or drawing high salaries.'

And in conclusion:

'If you have the courage to ask for this measure, and after having obtained it to resist manfully any delusions and abuses which may be imposed on you under its cover, I believe you may, through its means, set a fruitful example to the British Empire and to the world, the example of a people contented and loyal, yet independent and free—of an educated people fearing God, and a self-governed people honouring the King.'

Governor Grey was not much encouraged by such a declaration, to proceed with his makeshift constitution. To do him justice it should be said that he had already forwarded to Downing Street a new draft of a really liberal constitution, for which Lord Grey could not find parliamentary time in the session of 1851. The New Zealand settlers must be patient a little longer. But the Governor's favour was withdrawn altogether from Canterbury and he appointed another Commissioner of Lands, with an office at Christchurch, expressly for the purpose of granting for a nominal fee pasturage licences for the land north and south of the Canterbury boundaries. Between the Governor and the Association, Godley would have been crushed had he not the resolution to override his instructions. He demanded a real unfettered measure of self-government for Canterbury from his principals in London also, using even plainer terms to them than to the Governor. 'The business of the Association,' he said, 'was to found Canterbury not to govern it.'

As early as June, 1851, six months after the coming of the First Four Ships, Godley had decided to override the Association or break with it. He now received despatches by every ship overwhelming him with detailed instructions, many of which were quite irrelevant, and denying him any authority to adjust their plans to local conditions. They saddled him with the Bishop-designate; they seemed to suppose that he could do with a little money what he had hoped to do with a great deal; they still wrote glibly about the professors for the college, the Dean and Chapter for the cathedral; they forbade him to sell land or admit pastoral tenants in the colony; and they showed not the slightest disposition to resign their authority to the actual colonists.

He was in the incongruous position of being the chief agent in Canterbury at once of Grey's despotic government, and of the Association which now appeared as a sort of absentee landlord. All executive powers were concentrated in his hands, though he was the leader of the opposition to both of the rival authorities, and the admitted champion of self-government. He had been successful in flouting Governor Grey and knew that his friends of the Colonial Reform Society were fighting his battles on another front. But what could he do when those same friends, in their other capacity as members of the Canterbury Association denied self-government to their own settlement? It was at this time that he began to use his most celebrated aphorism; it appears in several versions in letters to his friends: 'the form of a constitution,' he said, 'might be a question for discussion, but it must be *localized*. I would rather be governed by a Nero on the spot than by a board of Angels in London, because we could, if the worst came to the worst, cut off Nero's head, but we could not get at the Board in London at all.'

With the full approval of the Land-purchasers' Council he issued a conditional pasturage licence to Aitken the Australian, in flat defiance of his instructions and of the Canterbury Land Act. In the opinion of John Deans, by so doing he saved the colony. The original settlers had mostly sunk their small capital in buying and cultivating their sections and building their homes. New land-purchasers were not as yet coming in sufficient numbers to keep up the rate of development. What the colony needed just then was stock and stockmen, and he let them in.

The last straw was a despatch from the Association informing him, in May, 1851, that they proposed to nominate a council of land-purchasers to whom they would eventually resign their powers. This seems to have been

Wakefield's plan, judging by the fury he displayed in denouncing Godley for rejecting it. Godley now made up his mind that he must return to London to force the Association to transfer its powers freely. He had never intended to stay long in New Zealand and, in June, gave notice to the Association that he should resign in the following March or April. 'I have advised them in very plain terms to abdicate altogether,' he wrote to his father with the news that he was coming home to 'agitate'. It was not a question of abandoning his task, but of fighting for self-government in London, which he always thought the decisive front.

CHAPTER IX

Godley's Last Year in Canterbury

JUST as Godley in New Zealand had known nothing of
the birth pangs of the first expedition in 1850, so in
1851 he knew little of the difficulties which confronted
the Association in London. News, when it arrived, was
four or five months stale; the answers to letters written
eight or ten months earlier were rarely helpful; instructions
were no longer relevant when they were received. Correspondence with Governor Grey in the North Island was
almost as uncertain as the English mail. Sometimes the
quickest way from Lyttelton to Auckland was to travel
via Sydney.

Most of the time and in most respects, Godley's authority
was unquestioned; in all but name he was for two years
the governor of Canterbury Colony; his three assistants
were Cass the chief surveyor, Brittan the land officer, and
FitzGerald the immigration officer. By the end of 1851,
3000 immigrants had been received, the survey was completed, 25,000 acres of freehold land had been taken up
and occupied, 400,000 acres of pasturage had been leased
and stocked with 30,000 sheep. Crops were harvested on
about 500 acres in the first season. There was a made road
from the landing stage in the river-mouth to Christchurch;
north, south, and west roads branched out from the centre
to the most settled districts. While Lyttelton was already a
town, Christchurch was still a waste of tussock and fern-

scrub with some scores of huts and sheds scattered along the lines of pegs that marked out the future streets. A new-comer lost his way one evening among the reeds and bracken of 'Cathedral Square'. Squatters' claims, pasturage leases, licences and rents, selection of lands purchased for the Association; contracts for roads and public buildings; the opening of elementary schools, a hospital, a library, the grammar school; provision of temporary churches for each township, stipends for clergymen and schoolmasters; reports and accounts; law and order: all were Godley's business.

When the colony settled down to the hard task of pioneering the settlers had less time for complaints or politics, they were content to leave everything for Godley's decision. He became conscious that he was the only man in the settlement with a sound training in law and adminis-tration. While work and responsibility stimulated and delighted him he realized that he had not come to Canter-bury to play the autocrat but to set up organs of self-government. As he well knew, and admitted with humility in his private letters, he was sometimes hasty and over-bearing, sometimes remote and unbending. If so, he never bore malice, or nursed a grudge, or spoke ill of his opponents, or was unconscious of his own faults. 'I am a little afraid,' he wrote to his father, 'that I am none the better for being such a complete despot, as I am here, and for never meeting with contradiction from anyone. It is enough to spoil one and I really need a good snubbing.'

It was not to be supposed that the servant of an absentee Association could please everybody, though he never failed through lack of taking trouble. FitzGerald has preserved a story of his overhearing two settlers in his office point out that Godley had made an error in allotting a land-claim. At once Godley mounted his horse, rode over the hills to Christchurch to fetch a document, returned within three hours and set himself to right the wrong. It cost him in the end a special journey by sea to Akaroa. A shrewd criticism of Godley's character was sent home by young Torlesse, Wakefield's nephew, and was passed round among the members of the Association. 'Mr Godley is very high-principled and conscientious, with some true Irish hastiness of decision and most obstinate adherence to first intentions. With many he is unpopular, but I see great cause of thankfulness for his presence here.'

Even his opponents admitted his superiority. Conway Rose, a Canterbury Pilgrim of good family, wrote home denouncing Godley as a dictator, but added that the little pioneer settlement was not large enough to hold him: 'he was like a whale in a duck-pond.' In spite of his opposition to Godley on many issues Rose still found him as a private companion 'quite delightful', and sincerely admired his character: 'for unflinching discharge of duties he was beyond all praise.'

Brittan was disposed to be jealous of Godley, and of Godley's aristocratic friends, FitzGerald, Stuart-Wortley, Bowen and others, whom he called the 'Right Honourable Privy Council.' In August, 1852, Brittan wrote a letter to Wakefield (which cannot have reached him before he left England), venturing the opinion that Godley was 'an ardent politician, led away by theory, heady and indiscreet, with an overweening opinion of his own superior judgment'. This was the worst said of Godley in Canterbury. Fitz-Gerald, knowing of course that Brittan was critical but not what he had written, repeated more than once in his letters home that Brittan was a 'snob' and Godley head and shoulders over any other man in Canterbury both in character and talent.

Could not Lyttelton use his influence, wrote FitzGerald, to get Godley appointed Governor instead of Sir George Grey? But that was beyond Lyttelton's powers when Godley's friends, the Peel-ites, were in opposition.

*   *   *   *   *

How, in New Zealand, did Godley spend his day? 'We

keep up our old habits,' he wrote to his father, 'getting up long before sunrise. I go to church every morning at eight for the daily service, dine at two, and drink tea at seven, with company—more or less—every night, almost. I cannot conceive it possible that I should ever again wear a chimney-pot hat or Wellington boots. My regular costume is a broad-brimmed straw and jack-boots. I never wear flannel or greatcoat, and sleep with windows open in the coldest weather.'

'The account of the general election (1852) and of my losing a chance of being returned for Leitrim would be provoking were it not that I am convinced my health would never stand the excitement and long hours of Parliament. I feel quite plainly that my old complaint is scotched not killed. There it lies, ready to be called into action at a moment's warning if I don't take care of myself.'

Every morning he read *The Times* at breakfast, the top copy from the pile that had come by the last ship. On most days he was busy for long hours in the office at Lyttelton, a few yards away from his house. Two or three times a week he rode over the hills to the land office at Christchurch and sometimes escaped on longer journeys, by sea to the bays of Banks Peninsula or on horseback to the sheep-runs on the plain. There was quail-shooting and duck-shooting to be had in plenty and, until the wild pig were driven off the plains into the hills, there was pig-sticking in Indian style. Young Arthur Godley's one clear childhood memory of his father in New Zealand was a scene at Riccarton. 'I can see my father on his horse, with a long spear resting in a socket behind his stirrup, after a day at pig-sticking.'

The first anniversary of the landing, 16th December, 1851, was celebrated as a festival which may be taken as concluding the heroic age. The day commenced with cricket between 'eleven of the Christchurch Cricket Club and eleven working men, upon the excellently prepared ground of the Club,' in Hagley Park. Brittan (26) and Godley (24) were the leading batsmen on the winning side. 'On Tuesday we had a great rejoicing in honour of our anniversary,' he wrote, 'amongst other things a cricket-match, at which I was lucky enough to distinguish myself, to the great surprise of the people here, especially the working-men, who look on me as a sort of official machine; an impersonation of pens, ink, paper, and red tape. We had horse-racing, too, of a very mild and indifferent kind, and they persuaded me to enter "Lady Nugent", Charlotte's mare, in a match against Mr Watts Russell's "Stationer". The mare won in a canter, hard-held. I am obliged to confess that I had much the best jockey. Does not all this sound very advanced for so young a colony as Canterbury, and very lively for so old a man as J.R.G.?'

He was thirty-seven years old and it is revealing to note that he was known in the settlement as 'Old Jack'. When the four public men who held most authority in Canterbury met at Lyttelton in 1851, FitzGerald was aged thirty-two, Godley thirty-five, Grey thirty-eight and already nine years a governor, Selwyn forty-one and already nine years a bishop. How old would their successors be in a similar enterprise, a hundred years later?

*   *   *   *   *

Godley's last year in Canterbury, 1852, was less exacting and, therefore, increased his anxiety to be gone. Since the colony was founded, the age of improvisation ended, and the system of land settlement and immigration working smoothly—if slowly, his own duties were lighter. As for his administrative duties, his one wish was to abdicate them in favour of a popularly elected government. The only misfortune about which he ever allowed himself to grumble, 'not enough to do', was once or twice mentioned in his letters home. His conviction that the Association had done its work and ought to vanish, or, at least, maintain its existence only in the settlement, grew stronger, and implied that his own office was superfluous. He must go, and let the settlers stand upon their own feet; but he could not go until New Zealand should have a free constitution. He would not abandon Canterbury to control by an expensive, irresponsible, bureaucratic government, situated six hundred miles away among the Maoris, at Auckland.

In March he received private letters from Adderley and Lyttelton persuading him to remain at his post until the new constitution should go through. In May he received from the Association a formal request to withhold his resignation until the constitution should be proclaimed; to this he agreed and published his reasons for doing so in the *Lyttelton Times*. In June he was still writing despondently, with doubts whether the Bill would pass in that session. In July he heard of the fall of the Whig Government and, while regarding Lord Derby's stop-gap administration with contempt he supposed, rightly, that it would accelerate his departure. The news that Sir John Pakington was appointed Colonial Secretary provoked merely the comment, in a letter to his father, '*parmi les aveugles un borgne est roi*'. Fortunately, the enactment of the New Zealand Constitution was known in the colony in good time. The Bill passed in June and was to hand at Lyttelton in mid-September. Though there were features in it that Godley disliked, he decided that it would serve its turn, and made up his mind to return to England in December.

These were the public events which directed his action. His anxiety over the timing of his departure was affected, too, by domestic considerations. Old John Godley at Killegar, in his 77th year, showed signs of failing, and urged him to return. Since it was evident that he must come soon he must arrange the dates of his voyage so as to arrive in England in late spring. He felt sure that to plunge into an English winter would destroy his hard-won health and strength. Yet he could not go too soon because Charlotte was expecting another child; her eldest daughter was born at Lyttelton in June, 1852. Public and private affairs thus combined to fix his time-table, he would reach England in the spring of 1853, just when self-government was to be established in Canterbury. As the time drew near, husband and wife both discovered that they would not leave Canterbury without a pang of regret.

They had spent the early part of the year 1852 on the plains, in the house of John Deans, who was away visiting Scotland. While the sea passage round by Godley Head and over the Sumner Bar was dangerous, it was less tiring than the scramble over the bridle-path. Charlotte made the trip on horseback, rather unwillingly as she had no nerve with horses, holding the little boy Arthur before her on the saddle. Powles preferred to walk, and she reached Riccarton first. Once over the hills and across the Heathcote river by the ferry, it was easy going to Christchurch along five miles of straight hard road.

Charlotte never forgot this journey and her parting gift to her friends in Canterbury was a wayside cross and a drinking-fountain placed where the ascent of the bridle-path was steepest. Though the house at Riccarton was more primitive than their own at Lyttelton, the invigorating air, the spacious landscape with its views of distant mountains, the tall trees, festooned with creeping plants and loud with bird-song, and the clear river running by the homestead, pleased them as the cramped and dusty little port of Lyttelton did not. There was now congenial company at Christchurch; St. Michael's Church, a temporary wooden shed, but still a church with an organ and a deep-toned bell in a tall detached belfry; a road-bridge and two foot-bridges over the Avon; some genteel houses, one of them with plate-glass windows; a cricket club and a jockey club; and a literary society known as the Athenaeum.

As for all new colonists the English mail, irregularly though it came and went, marked the periods in the passage of time. Husband and wife were copious letter-writers after the fashion of their day; he wrote thirty or forty long letters by every ship, in his neat, scholarly hand, mostly on public affairs; she maintained a current flow of conversation for her mother, including messages to all her friends, chopping it off short when a ship was ready to sail. Her letters are full of vivacious phrases, his of pregnant comments. Both waited anxiously for the replies that were so long in coming and that seemed, in 1851, to be overloaded with raptures about the Great Exhibition in Hyde Park.

The Godleys now had many friends among the settlers, a number of them, FitzGeralds, Wards, Bowens, Gressons, Westenras, Hamiltons, Irish protestant gentry of their own class. By contrast with these colonists of the best sort there were others who took up too much of the Godleys' time. No new colony ever escaped an influx of immigrants of another type, the scapegraces and the ne'er-do-wells hopefully packed off by their relatives in the hope that they might turn over a new leaf in a new society. Often, of course, they did but, if not, Mr Godley was expected to provide for them and Mrs Godley to mother them. His letters to the Association abounded with objections against these optimists. What was he to do with distressed, elderly governesses in a pioneering settlement, with unemployed seamstresses from London slums, with young gentlemen who had no capital and were too proud to work, with sprigs of the aristocracy who could not keep straight? A duke's son arrived by the same ship as the Bishop-designate, bearing letters of introduction from one of the Godleys' oldest family friends. By the same ship arrived a letter from Wakefield warning Godley against him. The Jacksons announced that they had refused to sit at the same table in the cabin with him because he used such bad language, and in a short time Godley forbade him the house at Lyttelton because he was never sober. Godley hated drunkenness. The young lord drifted away to Sydney where soon he was reported to be living on credit in the worst company. Letters continued to arrive from his distinguished friends at home commending him to Godley, who knew well that the young man's elder brother was one of the most influential members of the Association.

Young gentlemen with education, a little capital and a readiness to work were welcome enough. In almost every letter home Godley urged upon his younger brother Denis the advantages to be gained if he would emigrate and settle down in Canterbury.

*   *   *   *   *

In his last few months there Godley found a new form of activity. The Land-purchasers' Council, which, in the first days of the settlement, had expressed the nascent public opinion of the Pilgrims, faded out of existence in 1852. Its original members were too busy, up-country, to attend meetings and no longer represented the views of the settlers. With Godley's encouragement two new colonists' societies were formed at the townships, with open membership. At Christchurch political differences sprang up between two groups who founded rival associations; at Lyttelton Godley's personal influence was still supreme. The Lyttelton association became a mutual improvement society at which lectures were given and debates held upon all matters of public interest. Godley inaugurated the first session with a series of lectures upon the short history of New Zealand, a chapter in the story of colonial reform.

When copies of the new constitution arrived at Lyttelton he prepared a long and careful criticism of its features and probable effects, commending it to the colonists as an instrument by which they might attain the ideals of the Founders of Canterbury. He spoke favourably of the new constitution, on the whole, if only because it would enable the people of New Zealand to demand ('as of course you will demand') further, in fact, complete self-government. Reverting to his favourite topic, the freedom enjoyed by the American colonies under their seventeenth-century charter, he denounced the reservations of power always withheld by Downing Street in the new colonial constitutions, the fixed civil list, the control of relations with the natives, the powers of veto and disallowance in legislation. Quoting a recent speech of Adderley in the House of Commons he demanded that the only reservations of power should be in respect of a definite list of Imperial interests: allegiance to the Crown, naturalization of aliens, treaties and negotiation with foreign powers, the command of Imperial troops, and the crime of high treason. 'For these restrictions the honours and advantages of British citizenship and the protection by Great Britain against foreign enemies will be an ample compensation; nor do I think they would be felt by a single colonist as practical grievances.'

The real grievance of the colonies, in his view, was the anomalous position of the Governor, the servant of the Colonial Office and therefore unable, even if he were willing, to act always on the advice of his colonial ministers. 'It would be more convenient,' said Godley, 'that the Governor himself should be chosen by the people for a fixed term, and be responsible to them, and that his ministers should be appointed by him and responsible to him only.' In such a colony, he suggested, there might be a Royal Commissioner whose functions would be 'absolutely restricted to those matters which the constitutional law would have excluded from the jurisdiction of the local government, as matters of Imperial interest.' But here he pulled himself up, realizing that he was moving too fast for his contemporaries. On the whole and for the present the New Zealanders should make the best of responsible government as it had recently been instituted in Canada and Nova Scotia.

There was one feature of the new constitution which he regarded with distrust: it allowed a wide franchise on the basis of household suffrage. As in Ireland, so in the colonies he believed that education was a proper condition of political enfranchisement. So far as possible literates had been selected as assisted emigrants to Canterbury, and, within the first few months, elementary schools had been opened at Lyttelton and Christchurch with endowments—limited at first by the poverty of its resources—from the

Land Fund. Yet about one third of the English working-class was still illiterate a hundred years ago, and the whalers and beachcombers who frequented the bays of Banks Peninsula were drawn from the most ignorant and lawless classes. 'It appears to me,' he wrote in a formal despatch to the Association, 'that in a country like this, which on the one hand is frequented by some of the very worst kind of population in the world, and where, on the other hand, every man who exercises ordinary industry and intelligence may acquire property in a very short time, a moderate property qualification is peculiarly applicable as a test of fitness to possess political privileges.'

Godley's work in the world, to put it shortly, was to plant Canterbury with some of the very best kind of population in the world, to instil in them the doctrine of entire self-reliance, and to secure for them an absolute grant of self-government.

A few weeks earlier he had delivered another address at Lyttelton upon the constitution of the New Zealand Church, a subject which was no less urgent in the minds of the Canterbury Pilgrims. In matters of Church government as in politics he had placed himself at the head of the opposition to Sir George Grey. When the Godleys were at Wellington in June, 1850, Grey had prepared a draft constitution for the New Zealand Church, and had obtained for it the support of the Chief Justice and many leading townsmen of Auckland. It was, of course, in his private capacity as a Churchman, not in his official capacity, that he laid this plan before Bishop Selwyn. At Wellington, where any proposal emanating from the Governor was suspect, he got little support. Godley was invited by his missionary friend, Archdeacon Hadfield, to propose an alternative plan which won the support of Churchmen belonging to all political parties in the southern settlements. No legal action was taken, however, until the political constitution was promulgated in 1852. Selwyn then put forward Grey's scheme in a pastoral letter appealing to Churchmen in New Zealand for their assistance in giving it legal form, whereupon Godley summoned a public meeting at Lyttelton to discuss the particular problems of the Church in Canterbury. Unlike the other settlements, Canterbury was inhabited almost entirely by Churchmen and, unlike them again, Canterbury had provided itself with Church endowments of great potential value. He therefore claimed for the Church in Canterbury settlement a firmer organization and greater powers of self-government, than Grey intended for his fellow-Churchmen in Auckland.

Godley's speech was printed and widely circulated. Gladstone in England took notice of it and, during the next few years, when the release of the Colonial and Irish Churches from state control was a matter of high politics, it had no small effect in moulding public opinion.

His opening sentences expressed the dominant motive in his social philosophy. 'The Church in New Zealand, as elsewhere,' he said, 'is a society having a definite mission and certain practical ends to accomplish. Its essential principle, the very condition of its existence is work. To my mind, the notion of an inactive or passive Church is an absurdity. But a society, in order to work, must have an organization and a government; it must have forms, laws, qualifications, executive instruments; it must have a head and hands.'

He proceeded to explain that the Church of England at home, since the Reformation, had lost these faculties and could do nothing in its corporate capacity, it must passively accept what the State chose to do for it, whereas, in independent America, the Protestant Episcopal Church had set up a self-governing organization which should be a model to the Anglican churches in the colonies. So far he was on common ground with Sir George Grey whose memorandum to Bishop Selwyn was inspired by just the same considerations. Godley's plan, however, differed from Grey's in two important particulars; he would have restricted Church membership more closely and he would have given the self-governing Church greater power. He poured scorn on the

lawyers' fiction that all Englishmen enjoyed full membership in the Church of England by right, whether they did
their duty as Church members or not. Other churches had
no such nullifying conditions. 'Go and subscribe to a
Wesleyan meeting-house or a Presbyterian church, and see
whether your doing so will get you a vote for members of
the next Conference or the next Assembly! After much and
anxious reflection, I can see no proper qualification for a
Church franchise but that of full communion; and I say this
quite irrespectively of any doctrinal opinion about the
nature and effect of that Holy Sacrament.'

Grey would have allowed a broad franchise to nominal
adherents of the New Zealand Church, but would have
restricted its authority in matters of doctrine, ritual, and
public worship to conformity with the Mother Church in
England. Godley would have no such limitation. 'I would
claim,' he said, 'on the part of the New Zealand Church,
the right of managing to the fullest extent its own affairs,
including of course the regulation of worship, and the control over formularies. While it is necessary and right that
the formularies of the Church of England should be the
basis of union among those who combine to form a constitution for a Colonial Church, I think it would be
unworthy of our position as a national church to bind ourselves to those formularies for ever.' As an immediate
measure he proposed that the meeting should approve of
Selwyn's efforts to give the Church a constitution, in general
terms. The proposal was seconded by Mr. Jacobs of the
grammar school and carried by acclamation.

Before the end of the year he had left New Zealand and,
so far as New Zealand Church organization was concerned,
it seemed that his scheme had vanished with its author.
Owing to legal formalities in England, the 'Church of the
Province of New Zealand' was not properly constituted
until five years later and, before these problems were
resolved, the foresight of the founders of Canterbury in
endowing their diocese with land was fully justified. It was

one of Sewell's successes to create a Church Property Trust, largely under lay control, for administering these endowments and, as Canterbury progressed, the value of this property increased to a figure approaching the bold forecasts made by the Association in 1849. After a long seedtime, the Church in Canterbury began to flourish, but not until the bishopric was at last established, in 1856. Something more will be said of that in another chapter. When Bishop Harper, the first bishop of Christchurch, arrived in New Zealand, one of his first duties was to attend a Church Convention at Auckland for devising a constitution. Again, the points at issue were those which had been at issue between Grey and Godley seven years earlier. The Canterbury delegation, Bishop, clergy, and laity, while preferring Godley's policy agreed to accept a compromise on which the Church of New Zealand was then constituted and incorporated by law. The Aucklanders were successful in establishing a wide and comprehensive rule of church membership; they succeeded also in retaining the supremacy of the Mother Church over questions of ritual and doctrine. The Canterbury delegates insisted on unhampered control of their own Church property and won another concession by which Godley set great store. He had insisted that clergy and laity should sit and vote together in Church synods, and this ruling was adopted.

*   *   *   *   *

The people of Canterbury did not let their founder go without a struggle. On 10th November a deputation waited upon him at Lyttelton to present a petition, 'signed with scarce an exception by every individual who had access to it,' asking him to stand for election as first Superintendent of the Province of Canterbury; for so the executive officer under the new constitution was to be described. Among those who appeared with the deputation were FitzGerald, young Wakefield, and Charles Simeon (John Simeon's brother), who succeeded Godley as Resident Magistrate.

Godley courteously declined; he would not stand for election unless prepared to remain in New Zealand for the full term of four years, and that, for private reasons, was out of the question. If he remained, he must make a career in New Zealand politics. He believed that his duty lay in England and Ireland. There is evidence enough in his letters that he often regretted this decision. The greater loss was New Zealand's.

When the time came to say farewell, Godley found it hard to go; it had become 'his second home, dearer if possible than the first'. An opportunity of opening his heart about his dreams, his achievement, and his hope, came on 18th December when a large body of the people of Christchurch 'of all classes of the community' entertained him at a luncheon, in a marquee erected in Hagley Park for the festivities to celebrate the second anniversary of Canterbury. Two days earlier Godley had entered a horse for the Christchurch Cup, but the last day's racing was postponed because the principal settlers were assembled to do him honour. Among these speakers was young Wakefield who rose, unbidden, to assure the company that his father, if he were present, would join in their good wishes to their guest. Edward Gibbon Wakefield was then on the high seas. Godley spoke at length and with feeling.

'For the last five years, ever since the plan of founding a settlement of Church People in New Zealand was first suggested to me . . . the thought of it has hardly been for a moment out of my mind; I have become, for the time at least, a man of one idea, to which everything else, public and private, has been made subordinate. Almost every intimate friend I have in the world has been induced by me to take a part in this enterprise; whatever reputation I may enjoy, or look to enjoying, is bound up with its success; indeed I have often felt as though, if this colony had proved a failure, I could never again have had the heart and courage to engage in any public enterprise.

'All former local ties—the ties of patriotism, of hereditary attachment, of early association, appear weak in comparison with those which bind Canterbury and myself together. No

other country can ever be to me what this country is; no other
people can be to me what you are.

'The duties which I have had to perform have been in many
respects of a very invidious character. Having the whole responsibility of the public service on my shoulders, a great deal has
been expected of me; more perhaps than under any circumstances one individual could have done; more certainly than
under the actual circumstances I had the means of doing. Those
who came to me with requests, suggestions, claims, seldom were
fully aware of the difficulties which I had to contend with, and
the restricted nature of my powers, so that I feel as if for the
last two years I had been perpetually saying *no*, to people who
thought they had a right to *yes*. I know I have many short-
comings and faults to plead guilty to.

'Looking back on the enterprise as a whole, I am prepared
to maintain not only that it was a great and noble enterprise,
but that it has been successfully carried out . . . we have, to
the best of my belief, a more concentrated population, a larger
proportion of resident proprietors, and consequently a greater
demand over the appliances and civilities of society, than has
been attained before, under similar circumstances, by agricultural colonists. At the same time that we enjoy these special
advantages, there has not been any deficiency in opportunities
of profitable investment for capital, and of profitable employment for labour. . . . Though there have been cruel and
undeserved disappointments, there have been also many which
were caused by people's expecting impossibilities. I don't blame
them for it; for to a great extent I did so myself, but such is
the fact.

'No man in this world can go through any enterprise that
has greatness in it without being often and sorely disappointed,
because nothing great is ever done without enthusiasm, and
enthusiasts are often over-sanguine. When I first adopted, and
made my own, the idea of this colony, it pictured itself in my
mind in the colours of a Utopia. Now that I have been a
practical colonizer, and have seen how these things are managed
in fact, I often smile when I think of the ideal Canterbury of
which our imagination dreamed. Yet I see nothing in the dream
to regret or to be ashamed of, and I am quite sure that without
the enthusiasm, the poetry, the unreality (if you will), with

which our scheme was overlaid, it would never have been accomplished. This colony, full of life and vigour and promise, as it is, would never have been founded, and these plains, if colonized at all, would have fallen into the hands of a very different set of people from those whom I see around me. Besides, I am not at all sure that the reality, though less showy, is not, in many respects, sounder and better than the dream.

'We all know now that when men colonize, more perhaps than in any other walk of life, they have to eat their bread in the sweat of their face. But this is the advantage and pride and glory of colonization. It is the corroding evil of old and highly-peopled countries, that in them whole classes, from the Sybaritic peer to the work-house pauper have this curse hanging heavy on their lives, that they have nothing to do; and this it is that justifies us in urging men to emigrate, that in new countries every man must do something, and every man finds something to do. I have seen here clergymen ploughing, and barristers digging, and officers of the army and navy "riding-in" stock, and no one thought the worse of them, but the contrary. The principle then which it is the business of colonizers to assert, is the nobleness of work.

'I must just say one word about your new constitution. I clearly foresee that a great many of you, probably the best people among you, will be disgusted with the turmoil and agitation and strife inseparable from the working of a popular constitution. But you must fight against this feeling. You must remember that we were never meant to enjoy quiet lives. Quiet lives are for beings of a higher or a lower nature than man's; for beatified spirits or the brute creation. It is the business of man to work, to struggle, and to strive. Life is a battle not a feast.'

CHAPTER X

Australia and Home

ON 22nd December, 1852, the Godleys took leave of their friends at Lyttelton and went abroad the *Hashemy,* an old teak-built Indiaman, a celebrated ship which three years earlier had sailed from colony to colony with a load of convicts who were nowhere permitted to disembark.

During the whole day after the leave-takings she lay becalmed in harbour, and then, for four days more, idled in calms and light winds, not common in that sea, between Lyttelton and Wellington. Godley's impatience was somewhat consoled by watching the changing prospect of the Kaikouras, the snowy peaks which the whalers called the Lookers-on. It was difficult to settle down in idleness after three years of unwonted health and continuous duty. He made a regular study of the *Vicar of Wakefield,* 'read for the first time these twenty years', found Basil Hall's *Voyages* prosy, and settled down to Prescott's *History of Ferdinand and Isabella.* At Wellington came news that the old Duke, after whom the settlement was named, had died at last, news at which all the colonial newspapers 'appeared in mourning'. Otherwise the settlement seethed with political agitation over the new constitution. It was generally believed, wrote Godley to his father, that Governor Grey had no intention of working it in good faith. 'Sir George will do his best to outwit the colonists, and the colonists to thwart Sir George.' He would probably escape the ordeal of facing a popular assembly by postponing its convocation until he could obtain his own recall, 'which he is known to have asked for'. In the meantime the Godleys were 'very happy, walked and drove and rode about, our satisfaction only damped by the reflexion that we were so soon to leave a country and people that we loved so much'.

On 12th January, 1853 the *Hashemy* again set sail and made Sydney heads on the 23rd. It was a calm passage when not even Charlotte was sea-sick, or not for long. Godley attacked a new work by his favourite Washington Irving which he voted dull, and one by Emerson which was 'extravagant and affected'. It was a more useful occupation to talk shop with the captain, a Scotchman who knew the herring-fisheries at Wick and Peterhead and could prime Godley with statistics upon the herring trade with Ireland. The voyage was enlivened also by an additional passenger, a sickly young nobleman travelling round the world for his health. This Lord Robert Cecil, wrote Godley, is 'intelligent and well-disposed, anxious for information, and inclined to think for himself, but he has all the crudeness of a very young man in his political opinions, and (naturally) a good deal of the prejudices of his class and party'. Five and twenty years after Godley was laid in his grave, this youngster was to become, as Marquess of Salisbury, the Prime Minister of Great Britain.

The Godleys spent about six weeks in New South Wales in the southern summer of 1853, and disliked it. Their impressions were unusually well-preserved, in his letters to his father, hers to her mother (all of which are extant), and in two long articles on Australia which he published in *Fraser's Magazine*. They immediately felt the distinction between their dear New Zealand, systematically colonized by settlers whose tastes and needs and habits were like their own, and Sydney which had been a convict settlement and had become the site of a gold-rush. A society given over to getting-rich-quick, where wealth won without effort by the luck of the gold-fields, was the only criterion of social eminence, appeared as a monstrosity in Godley's eyes. The nobleness of work, the respect due to moral qualities, the desire for education were all forgotten. Prices, of course, were soaring and labour could not be hired. For the first time in history, the class of domestic servants had disappeared and with that disappearance went the amenities of social life. The Godleys could find no merit in cleaning their own shoes and 'answering the door' for themselves, when social equality meant only a vulgar display of prodigality by the ill-bred and un-educated. 'Masters and servants have changed places and hospitality is at an end in Sydney.'

After a hundred years, society—even genteel society—has adjusted itself to this social revolution, startling as it seemed to those who felt the first impact of it. While Godley disliked the change and dreaded the materialism which seemed the only creed of the new egalitarian world, this did not imply that he was a reactionary in politics. The squatters were not, and could not be, the real leaders of the people; they were 'an unpopular aristocracy maintaining a prescriptive and legal ascendancy against a vigorous and progressive democracy'. Nor were the politics of the squatters consistent in themselves: they demanded freedom from control by the Colonial Office while taking refuge behind the fixed civil list and nominated upper house which the Colonial Office had imposed upon the country. The gold-fields set the tone of the country and the gold-fields he must see for himself.

Godley went up to the Turon field by stage coach, over the Blue Mountains and through Bathurst, while Charlotte with her two young children struggled with the heat, the dust, the mosquitoes, and the vermin of a Sydney February. After a long search they had found lodgings near Macquarie Street at four pounds a week. The children had influenza, they could not sleep for mosquito-bites, there were bed-bugs everywhere, even, they were told, in the new Government House. There was no ice, no cold water. Yet Charlotte kept pretty cheerful, strolling in the Domain to hear the band play and watch the ships, though it was a long, hot walk for the children and, at Sydney prices, she could not afford a cab. She had her own resources and never complained. After three years in the wilds she took infinite delight in the rows of shops, the gardens, the flowering trees, and not least in the regular services at St James's which so resembled a London parish church, with its regency porch and steeple.

Across the Blue Mountains, at the Turon, Godley found life at the diggings very different from what he would have supposed from the vulgarities of Sydney during a boom. The diggers were 'a quiet well-conducted set of men'. Turon itself was a respectable village, a long straggling street of wooden houses with a church, a school, and a population of 2,000 including many women and children. In spite of these reassuring circumstances, the gold-field was in a high state of political excitement, ready to break out violently against the miners' licensing regulations, which they regarded as an oppressive tax put upon them by the squatter aristocracy. Two factors restrained the miners from violence, the influence of the Wesleyan minister, and the presence of a detachment of British soldiers, 40 men of the 11th Regiment and a troop of mounted police, 'moustached, soldierly-looking men, wearing a blue uniform, and armed like Light Cavalry'. Since Godley was travelling as a distinguished visitor, with introductions from the Governor, he was received by the Commissioner of the gold-field who surprised him by saying that he and his garrison lived 'in a state of siege'. Decidedly the politics and economics and social system of a gold-mining colony could not commend themselves to a colonial reformer.

What made the worst impression on Godley was the bad manners of the new rich class, the stage-drivers and publicans, and store-keepers who profited by the careless prodigality of those who struck gold. 'Everybody you came in contact with, drivers, passengers, ostlers, chamber-maids, seemed to take a sort of pride in being rude and insolent. I have learned in knocking about the world not to be very squeamish . . . it made my blood run cold to hear the drivers blaspheme at their horses, each other, their passengers, everything and everybody, nor could anything exceed the barbarity with which they treated their horses. I have seen the public carriages of a good many countries, some of them not very far advanced in civilization; but for discomfort, insecurity, unpunctuality, and general barbarism, the mail between Bathurst and Sydney far surpasses them all.' The driver stopped to drink at every public-house and finished the journey in a drunken sleep.

After all there were compensations in Sydney, not least the beauty of the trees and gardens. Sir Charles Fitzroy, the Governor, treated the Godleys hospitably, though they did not think that his raffish family of dependents showed the English gentry at their best. Godley enjoyed visiting his country house at Paramatta, and the neighbouring King's School, and appreciated still more a visit to Colonel Macarthur, whom he had known long since in Ireland. There were blood horses, fine-woolled sheep, vineyards and well-cultivated land to be seen at the Macarthur's place at Camden, even some prosperous farms let out to good tenants on the English leasehold system.

The Godleys left Sydney in the clipper, *Anglesey,* on 2nd March, 1853, and, after an uneventful run, far to the southward round Cape Horn, anchored at Gravesend on 16th June.

CHAPTER XI

The End of the Canterbury Association

DURING Godley's last year in New Zealand the Managing Committee in London had been embarrassed by financial difficulties which, on two or three occasions, almost reduced them to bankruptcy. Sewell, who took offence easily and was thinner-skinned than solicitors are generally reputed to be, was hurt by Godley's pointed despatches. His precise and legal mind, so apt at finding expedients within the letter of the regulations, was revolted by Godley's defiant way of overriding them. He soon convinced himself that Godley was acting very unreasonably. Godley repeatedly complained that the Association rendered no account of the way in which it spent the land-purchasers' money. Their first year's accounts, published in the *Canterbury Papers* were so scanty as to be worthless; their second year's accounts did not appear until long after he had left New Zealand; and the fact that the accounts could not be made presentable added to Sewell's exasperation.

As soon as Godley's letters began to reveal a critical attitude, even to propose some flexibility in the Association's plans, all was over between him and Wakefield. Resentment against criticism was Wakefield's foible.

The Bishop-designate had just reached England when Godley's first letter of resignation came. He fell into Wakefield's clutches and provided Wakefield with gossip about Godley. The old schemer was nearing the end of his career.

Godley had escaped from his control, as all Wakefield's young men escaped sooner or later, and, with less than his usual shrewdness, Wakefield set himself to discredit and overthrow him. He wrote angrily to Godley suggesting that his health must be giving way, and maliciously to Lyttelton hinting that Godley was out of his mind.

> Canterbury Association
> 9 Adelphi Terrace
> 7th August, 1851

MY DEAR LORD,

Being here again to-day, in order to watch proceedings *in re* Jackson, I have had talks with Mr Sewell, which induce me to say again that I think he would not be disturbed by seeing Godley's letter, but the contrary. For he fancies quite as much as the letter exhibits; and yet the uncertainty greatly disturbs him. He knows that you have a letter, and he is fretting to see it, because, of course, he knows that it contains something disagreeable. In conversation with me, he speaks of Godley's state of mind being fully as bad as it appears from the letter.

I am seriously and painfully afraid that Godley's mind *has* got into a bad state. The inconsistencies which his despatches and letters exhibit are curiously manifest. It is really very difficult for me to think in disparagement of anybody whom I have once got to admire and like, so that I shut my eyes to their unfavourable aspects: but at last, of course, the truth prevails. At last, in this case, I cannot help admitting that Godley's mind seems to me to be in a very unwholesome state. I think he is ill and longing to get home, and disgusted with his position of burthensome work and responsibility. If so, it seems most expedient that he should be set free as soon as possible by the sending out of a successor. I am bound to confess that I have lost confidence in his judgment. It is very distressing. But I do not faint at all. On the contrary; for the new difficulty calls for more pertinacity of effort from those who do not mean to break down as so many have done.

> I am, my dear Lord
> Very faithfully yours
> E. G. WAKEFIELD.

Lyttelton's response to this innuendo has not survived. But his view of Wakefield's judgment is recorded in a pencilled note at the foot of a further letter from Wakefield on Canterbury affairs, dated 29th November, 1851. 'One of his queer delusions' he writes against an emphatic statement by Wakefield, and against another simply the word, 'falsehood'.

Sewell was also an opponent of Godley's in the Association, naturally enough since the long, verbose despatches to which Godley replied so scornfully were his handiwork; and it was Sewell who had to devise ways out of every difficulty. He could not transfer the Land Fund and the chartered rights to New Zealand because the Association was bound to comply with its undertakings, which since the demise of the New Zealand Company, had lapsed to the Crown. In 1851 Lord Grey was as pressing in his demand for one-sixth of the purchase-money as the directors of the Company had been in 1850, and again the land-sales fell far short of £50,000. Land-orders were still being sold, ships were still being despatched, Godley was still receiving shiploads of settlers at Lyttelton but the flow of emigration to Canterbury was diminishing, not growing. In the three years of its activity the Association despatched to Canterbury 22 ships carrying 3,247 settlers, all of them selected with the same care as the original pilgrims; but in those three years more than 300,000 emigrants left Great Britain (and more than twice as many left Ireland), to go to America and Australia. 1851 and 1852 were the booming years of the Australian gold-rush, which drew off the adventurous. Gold lured away the crowds and perhaps increased the selective character of the Canterbury colony, while it restricted the number of settlers. Sewell still hoped to launch another expedition to Canterbury in 1852 and would not 'abdicate' till it was organized. He could not abdicate until he could find a way of paying the Association's debts.

As for self-government, that was a question rather for

Adderley and the Colonial Reform Society. In 1849 they
had concentrated on abolishing the transportation of convicts, in 1850 on the Australian Constitution Act, in 1851
they were busy over the Cape colonists and the Kaffir war.
When at the end of the session William Fox arrived from
Wellington, primed with news of Godley's defiance of
Sir George Grey, they turned their attention to a constitution for New Zealand. In July there was a house-party at
Hams Hall, where, as Adderley proudly recorded, Sewell,
Wakefield, Fox, and he drafted a constitution, sitting on
the terrace. It seems that he over-stated his claim, since
Professor Morrell, after examining both documents, has
demonstrated that the constitution actually adopted is not
based upon this draft, but upon the draft sent home by
Sir George Grey.

More vital was the question whether Lord Grey could
be induced to get it through Parliament. Instead of inducing
him, they got rid of him at last. As a result of the quarrel
between Palmerston and Russell in December, 1851, the
Government was tottering and would plainly fall. According
to Palmerston's account it was the attacks of the Colonial
Reformers that brought it down. Adderley gave notice of
a vote of censure on its South African policy and, in the
words of *The Times,* the Government 'stooped to avoid the
blow.' Lord John Russell resigned and with him went the
unpopular Lord Grey, who had done so much for the
colonies without a word of thanks from any one of them.

A stopgap administration, one of the weakest ever known
in England, was formed by Lord Derby, with no help from
the Peel-ites. It was plain that he could not long survive
without appealing to the country and might well appeal in
vain. For the time being, he patched up a Cabinet of
unknown men and gave the seals for the colonies to a
respectable Tory squire from Worcestershire, Sir John
Pakington, who was as astonished as the rest of the world
at his own promotion. When he took over Lord Grey's draft
of a New Zealand Bill, there was a change that the world

did not observe in the relation of the Colonial Office to the Colonial Reformers. Pakington was a country neighbour of Lord Lyttelton and Adderley, and was willing to take their advice on matters with which he was quite unfamiliar. Adderley claimed that he induced Pakington to press forward with the New Zealand Constitution Bill.

Unlike Wakefield and Sewell, Adderley and Lyttelton were delighted with Canterbury's early screams for self-government. 'They say it's lucky,' Adderley wrote, 'for an infant to squall as soon as it is born.' They were able to assure Godley that a constitution would shortly be granted to New Zealand and that the Association would then bequeath its functions to the Provincial Government of Canterbury. With this assurance, they persuaded Godley to remain in New Zealand until the constitution should be proclaimed. In his last nine months in Canterbury Godley took pains to bring expenses within the limits of actual revenue, making the best of such resources as the settlement possessed and eschewing the ambitious schemes of capital development with which the settlers had once deluded themselves. Characteristically he had begun his work at Lyttelton by reducing his own salary from £800 to £600 a year and, when the Association would not countenance this reduction, he charged himself rent for his official house, at the rate of £200 a year, which had the same effect.

A true Gladstonian, Godley had no doubts about the proper course for the Association to pursue. They should live within their income and, if they could not afford a cathedral and a college, they should forgo these advantages until they had earned enough money to pay for them. He had no doubt that with hard work and strict frugality the real resources of the country would soon provide a surplus of revenue over expenditure.

Sewell in London was in a different plight. Again in 1851 the land-sales had failed to reach the amount prescribed in the charter and again the first charge on their expenditure was the unproductive payment of one-sixth of the receipts

TOWN OF LYTTELTON AND HARBOUR, 1852
Engraving by R. Norman.

to the Crown. Furthermore, the representatives of the Company, who were engaged in winding up its affairs, still had claims outstanding against the Association. They had waived these claims in 1850, on consideration of Lord Lyttelton's guarantee, and were now pressing for a settlement. Throughout 1852 Sewell held off his two creditors, the Crown and the Company's representatives, by a series of expedients in which he showed extraordinary ingenuity.

The first guarantee was cancelled and bank loans were raised on a second guarantee of a larger amount, for which it was necessary to find security. The guarantors were invited to advance £10,000 against a mortgage raised upon lands held by the Association. But the Association was not proprietor of the Canterbury block, it merely enjoyed a pre-emptive right. It was therefore necessary for the Association in its corporate capacity to exercise the pre-emptive right for its own advantage. The only asset which could be realized and converted into land was the sum deposited with trustees for founding a bishopric. Accordingly, with Lord Grey's permission shortly before his fall, a part of this fund was invested in Canterbury land, a dubious device, but one which had three advantages. It secured the loan, it inflated the nominal figure of the land-sales, and it enabled a little money to go a long way. One-third of the sum received from land-sales was automatically placed to the credit of the Ecclesiastical Fund and was at once invested in more land, whereupon a third of the sum received for the second purchase was placed to the credit of the Ecclesiastical Fund, and so on *ad infinitum*. In short, by transferring £6,500 from the Bishopric Fund to the Land Fund, Sewell acquired land nominally worth £10,200, and immediately raised a loan of £10,000 on his new asset.

This device brought him a long way forward but not far enough. The Company and the Crown clamoured for further repayments. Some members of the Association proposed that they should agree severally to purchase land as absentees, a proposal which was quickly rejected when it

G

was realized that the first effect would be a further liability
to the Crown of one-sixth of the purchase-money. The more
land they bought, the more they would be embarrassed,
unless they could stimulate the real growth of the colony.
The plan for a second settlement to be called 'Gladstone',
in South Canterbury, lapsed for lack of support. One way
out of the difficulty that would naturally occur to-day, the
floating of a large loan with some official backing, was
frowned upon by authority. There is even, in Sewell's
correspondence, an allusion to using the influence of the
University of Oxford for extracting some help from the
Government—the name of Mr. Jowett of Balliol was mentioned as a likely intermediary—a counsel of despair. Only
one way out of the impasse remained; the members of the
Association must put their hands in their pockets and find
the money to pay the debts for which, perhaps imprudently,
they had made themselves jointly and severally responsible.
Many members of the Association were by this time as
anxious to shake off their obligations as Godley in New
Zealand was to shake off their authority.

In June, 1852, the New Zealand Constitution Bill was
passed, with powerful support from Gladstone in the House
of Commons. It authorized the foundation of a federal system in New Zealand with wide powers of provincial self-
government. At once the Association petitioned the Government for leave to transfer its assets, liabilities, and functions
to the Province of Canterbury. Perhaps the Colonial Office
might have been gracious, had not the Law Officers of the
Crown been watching the interests of the Treasury. There
was an outstanding debt of £4,215 which they had no
intention of remitting. There were also persistent critics of
Canterbury who wrote abusive letters in the press. Lord
Lyttelton was very roughly handled in correspondence with
a Mr Serjeant Adams who did not mince words in alluding
to the financial methods of the Association. In his view the
shuffling of assets backwards and forwards between the
Ecclesiastical Fund and the Land Fund was barely honest.

It seems to have been Adderley who first accepted the inevitable conclusion. He circularized the members of the Association, excluding the four guarantors who, he said had done enough already, and called for subscriptions, after putting himself down for five hundred guineas. The members came forward, handsomely on the whole, though not without some complaints and conditions. It is not easy to distinguish the precise sums paid; the contributions, called up in two instalments, in 1852 and 1853, amounted to about £16,000. Lyttelton, in spite of Adderley's exception, was the largest contributor. The Duke of Newcastle (who had joined the Managing Committee soon after succeeding to his father's title in 1851) paid Sewell's subscription of £250, as well as his own. Godley, after his return to England, subscribed £100. On 7th October, 1852, Lyttelton informed the Colonial Office that the Association had ceased to exist.

Much, however, remained to be done. For more than a year there had been talk of sending Sewell to New Zealand as Godley's successor. He was now despatched with instructions to wind up the affairs of the Association, to transfer its secular funds to the Provincial Government, and to make provision for an educational and ecclesiastical trust. Wakefield, too, had always said that he would emigrate as soon as the work of founding Canterbury was complete. The two men sailed for New Zealand, in September, 1852, leaving H. S. Selfe as 'honorary secretary to the shade of the Association.'

John Deans of Riccarton, a man of no illusions, travelled back to New Zealand in the same ship as Wakefield, with whom he quarrelled about choice of berths. 'Wakefield and Sewell are by no means favourites,' he wrote in a family letter. 'I do not think him [Wakefield] the clever man that I have often heard him called. He has an excellent memory and a large stock of brass and impudence, and these seem to carry him through.'

Lyttelton's correspondence during the three years of active colonization, and for many years thereafter, reveals the extent of the obligation owed to him by the Canterbury settlers. Not only did he bear the brunt of the guarantee, which, on two occasions at least, saved the undertaking from total collapse, not only did he subscribe £2,000 to the repayment of the Association's debts, it was he who took final responsibility in all emergencies at home as did Godley in the colony. Sewell referred almost every detail of administration for Lyttelton's decision, writing him scores of long, verbose, and meticulous letters, in a very crabbed handwriting. (It is fair to say that Lyttelton's own handwriting was worse and Adderley's worst of the three.) In addition to the despatches which he sent to the Association, Godley wrote at length by every ship, usually a 'triangular' missive, designed for Lyttelton and Adderley. Wakefield (whose handwriting was worst of all), wrote Lyttelton frequent insinuating letters beginning, soon after Godley's departure, to decry Godley, to abuse FitzGerald, and to build up Sewell's reputation. It is evident that Lyttelton knew well how to discount the old schemer's crotchets. When Sewell took offence at Wakefield's violence of temper ('unrestrained even by the presence of the Duke of Newcastle'), it was Lyttelton who had to mollify Sewell. When Selfe complained that he was held responsible for £250 while Sewell was subsidized, it was Lyttelton who talked Selfe round. Lyttelton felt the weight of Selwyn's anger over the case of the Bishop-designate, Lyttelton replied to the searching questions of Serjeant Adams, Lyttelton wrote to *The Times* defending the Association against calumny. It was Lyttelton to whom settlers in New Zealand expressed their gratitude, their anxieties or their complaints. Yeomen farmers from his own estates wrote with delight of their success in Canterbury, clergymen asked pointedly what had become of the church endowments, a maiden lady reported with dismay that her observations led her to believe that Canterbury was rank with 'irreligion and immorality'.

Brittan wrote smooth and suave letters assuring his lordship that he had other friends in Canterbury as well as Fitz-Gerald. FitzGerald wrote with enthusiasm, warning Lyttelton not to believe a word of Wakefield's abuse of Godley. Many of these letter-writers urged him to visit the colony in which he had so large a stake and when, in 1868, Lyttelton visited New Zealand he was received with the honours due to a founder and a benefactor.

It will not be necessary here to recount in any detail the difficulties which Sewell encountered when winding up the affairs of the Association in Canterbury. He arrived in New Zealand with the fixed opinion that the Association had behaved well and Godley badly, and almost got himself tarred and feathered for saying so. He was a timid and sensitive but pertinacious man soon at cross-purposes with almost everyone in the colony. 'I am sorry that Mr Godley had left before we arrived,' wrote John Deans to his friends in Scotland, 'as he would have been the colonists' best champion. Wakefield and Sewell take every opportunity of damaging his reputation.' Sewell improved his position by challenging in the courts a sudden decision of Sir George Grey to overrule the statutory price of land in the southern settlements, and won his case. That victory put him on a better footing with the Canterbury people. Almost inevitably he fell foul of FitzGerald by criticizing Godley's actions adversely in a statement to the *Lyttelton Times*; and Brittan fell foul of him by taking entire charge of the Land Office with the books and the common seal of the Association. There was no outlet for Sewell's troubles but to write, publicly and privately, at enormous length, to Lord Lyttelton by every mail. At first he disliked Canterbury, where everyone seemed hostile to his employers and his mission, but succumbed to its spell and even succeeded in persuading the larger-minded among the settlers that the Association had, however imprudently, acted with the best intentions. He discovered, too, that the same excuse could be offered for Godley. Sewell's journal is the fullest and most candid account of life in early Canterbury.

The Provincial Government was brought into existence before the end of 1853, with elections for the Superintendency and for the Provincial Council. Sewell expressed alarm at the candidature of FitzGerald, whom he still regarded as the enemy to all good management, but FitzGerald was elected Superintendent. A government candidate, adopting Sir George Grey's policy of selling land cheap, was handsomely defeated, even though the vote of the orthodox Canterbury settlers, for maintaining a high price, was divided between FitzGerald and another candidate.

There was much heartburning and loud complaint over Sir George Grey's next move. Having inaugurated the Provincial Governments he retained his own authority over the central executive, by delaying to summon the Legislative Assembly for a full year; then confounded his critics by departing—on furlough—and by leaving a deputy-governor to meet the first New Zealand Parliament. When at last it was summoned, in 1854, FitzGerald was elected for Lyttelton, and Sewell had so far overcome his unpopularity as to secure election for Christchurch. He was then a happier man. 'You in England,' he wrote to his brother, 'believe that we are in a state of ruin and misery. Nothing can be more absurdly mistaken. This is the finest colony, I believe, in the world, and the Association scheme is a perfect success. The feeling about the Association and its affairs is greatly changed.'

Wakefield, also, was elected to the first New Zealand Parliament, for a Wellington constituency. To him was accorded the honour of moving the formal resolution that responsible government should be established; it was his last achievement. Within a few weeks his intrigues had so disgusted his fellow-members that all combined against him. After an illness in 1856 he withdrew into retirement and died, six years later, at Wellington, almost a forgotten man, and quite unhonoured in the country he had founded. His last word on Canterbury was that he would have 'fancied himself in England but for the hard-working industry of the upper classes and the luxurious independence of the common people'.

FitzGerald, as well as being first Superintendent of Canterbury, is usually described as first premier of New Zealand on account of his attempts to form a government in the session of 1854. His vivid talents did not shine in parliamentary management. Sewell formed a government in 1855 which lasted for several months; he was a useful member of several later administrations. Both these men did their best work in provincial affairs, the real centres of social life in New Zealand's early days. Much as they differed, they agreed on one general principle, that the ideals of the founders of Canterbury must be carried out, so far as the realities of colonial life permitted. Sewell invested the remaining funds of the Association in land which he selected with prudence. He formed the Church Property Trust, and obtained an act of incorporation for the College, a corporation consisting of a Warden and Fellows who, in the primitive age of Canterbury, were responsible for the hospital, the library, and the parish elementary schools, as well as for the grammar school and the 'upper department', which was to have been the nucleus of a university. FitzGerald, as superintendent, followed Godley's traditions in all particulars except one; he named the college after his own *alma mater* at Cambridge instead of after Godley's at Oxford, and Christ's College it remains.

Sewell and FitzGerald together, after a long political struggle, persuaded the Provincial Council to accept responsibility for the debts of the Association in 1855.

CHAPTER XII

Godley in London: Canterbury and the Empire

THE Godleys arrived in England in June, 1853, to find that, since they left Canterbury, there had been another change of Government. The Peel-ites had taken office in Lord Aberdeen's coalition ministry, with Gladstone at the Exchequer and Newcastle at the Colonial Office. Godley's first official visit was to dine with his former patron, Newcastle. There seems, however, to have been some coolness in their relations, probably because Newcastle, then and thereafter, supported Sir George Grey's policies through thick and thin. At least, with the patronage of the Empire at his disposal, he found no place for Godley, who would dearly have loved a place in the Colonial Office. Before many weeks had passed, Gladstone offered him an appointment as a Commissioner of Inland Revenue for Ireland, a post which he was glad to accept since he lacked a livelihood. In his celebrated budget for the year 1853, Gladstone had extended the income tax to Ireland, at seven-pence in the pound, and needed a staff to organize it. Godley was to travel about Ireland hearing appeals, and soon complained that he had not enough work to do. Many times did he admit that he regretted leaving Canterbury. After about six months, in March, 1854, Gladstone transferred him to a better post in the Inland Revenue Department, with his headquarters in London.

At this time Godley also acted as an honorary agent in London for the Canterbury colonists. Since emigration was at a standstill until the new Provincial Government should take charge, there was little to be done in that capacity either, except to keep up the spirits of the crestfallen friends of Canterbury in England*.

Godley's first opportunity of serving his fellow-settlers was by speaking at the complimentary banquet which Adderley arranged in his honour. It was held at Greenwich in August, 1853. Many of Godley's other friends were there, as well as former members of the Association. Lord Monteagle, William Monsell, W. H. Gregory and R. S. Rintoul came and so did Sir John Pakington, recently relieved from the cares of office. It was Godley's first task to assure his hearers that the Canterbury settlement was not a failure, even though the Canterbury Association had got into financial trouble. It had developed and was developing more rapidly than any other agricultural settlement in British history. Whereas New South Wales did not feed itself in twenty years nor Wellington in twelve, Canterbury in its fourth year would be self-supporting. It was already exporting food to the gold-fields at Melbourne, and the export of wool would inevitably surpass that of the Cape in a few years. Already the exports per head of the population were three times greater in proportion to numbers than the exports of the United Kingdom. He was able, by reading extracts from the *Lyttelton Times* to demonstrate that Canterbury was at least as civilized a place as any large English country parish with a similar population.

If there was as yet no cathedral there were four churches in the settlement, if no college yet there was as large a grammar school as the community needed, and an elementary school in each town. The fault of the Association was

---

* He was also invited by the Wellington settlers to become their salaried agent, but declined, on the advice of Gladstone who thought the post incongruous with Godley's official duties. The Wellington settlers thereupon transferred the invitation to Adderley.

not in failing to build a college in three years, but that they so positively announced that there would be one. 'To that criticism,' he said, 'there is no answer, save that we were over-sanguine.'

He defended the part he had taken against Sir George Grey in politics on the grounds that it forced Grey to demand the more liberal constitution which Sir John Pakington had granted; and completed his political summary by an appeal for a new approach to the problems of empire, stating in its extremest form his doctrine of self-reliance.

'The one great fundamental maxim of sound colonial policy is to let your colonies alone. They will never do anything, or be fit for anything great, so long as their chief political business is to complain of you, to fight with you, and to lean upon you, so long as they consider you as responsible for their welfare, and can look to you for assistance in their difficulties. I protest quite as much against subsidies and subscriptions as against vetoes and restraints; indeed more, for the poison is more subtle, and the chance of resistance less. I want you neither to subsidize their treasuries, nor to support their clergy, nor to do their police duty with your soldiers, because they ought to do these things for themselves, and, by your doing it all, you contribute to making them effeminate, degenerate, and helpless. Do not be afraid to leave them to themselves; throw them into the water and they will swim. Depend upon it, the greatest boon you can bestow upon colonies is what Burke calls "a wise and salutary neglect".'

At this period, when Colonial Reform was occupying so much parliamentary time, Godley's advanced views on colonial 'independence' had an effect upon his political friends which was of lasting importance. While the Peel-ites were inclined to take up colonial self-government as a party doctrine, the Derby-ites dallied with alternative plans for strengthening the bonds of Empire. When Lord Derby had been at the Colonial Office his notions of colonial reform had tended that way and, in the debates of 1849, 1850, and 1851, his support had been given to measures which maintained the Imperial authority rather than to the decentralizing measures of the Colonial Reformers. He and Disraeli refused to join Adderley's Society for the Reform of Colonial Government, and, in this context, Disraeli made the only allusion to Godley which has survived in his printed correspondence. 'I apprehend,' he wrote to Derby, 'that all these colonial motions and manoeuvres, in whatever form and by whomsoever proposed, are, in fact, the stir of Wakefield, in whom I have little confidence. One Godley, in whom I have less, is the instrument.' There is no record that Godley and Disraeli were ever acquainted, though both were members of the Carlton Club.

Derby and Disraeli proceeded to discuss the possibility of a federal union of the Empire, to be achieved by admitting some colonial members to the British House of Commons and, though nothing came of it, the topic attracted some attention in the eighteen-fifties. To Disraeli (who at as late a date as 1852 made his celebrated blunder in describing the colonies as 'mill-stones round our neck') colonial self-government was a small matter and colonial nationalism quite incomprehensible. While it does not appear from the correspondence that Disraeli ever considered his proposed legislative union in any other light than its effect upon the balance of parties in the House of Commons, there was some real interest in the subject among loyalists in the colonies. In June and July, 1854, the *Spectator* published an article commenting on a recent speech delivered in England by an ex-viceroy of India, Lord Ellenborough, and a speech in North America by Joseph Howe, the Premier of the loyalist province of Nova Scotia.

Joseph Howe had spoken enthusiastically, if rather loosely, proposing a simple legislative union of the empire; the colonies should simply be 'incorporated' with the mother-country. On the other side, Lord Ellenborough, a Peel-ite, advocated the common belief of the age, that the ultimate destiny of the colonies was separation and total independence. The editor was inclined to support Howe.

Godley entered the arena with two uncompromising letters published in the *Spectator*.* He demolished Howe's proposals as merely visionary. They would involve one of two alternatives, either the colonial parliaments must be suppressed and the Imperial Parliament must transact the whole business of the Empire, or 'an Imperial Congress must be constituted to manage the affairs of the Empire at large, and the parliaments of the component provinces—including that of the United Kingdom—would be restricted to local or municipal concerns'. Did Joseph Howe suppose that the people of Nova Scotia would abdicate their hard-won self-government to a legislature in London even if it should contain a handful of colonial members, or that the people of England would overthrow their ancient parliamentary system? 'It is hard enough to get the smallest and most necessary constitutional changes carried in this country; and I am inclined to think that if a Minister came down to the House with a proposal for abolishing Parliament and issuing writs for a Federal Congress, the result would be his immediate consignment to Bedlam.'

In his second letter he returned to the prospect of colonial 'independence' with an allusion to the similar case of Greek colonization, an analogy to which he often recurred. The Greeks 'considered that the business of a colonizing country was to found not to govern colonies. From the very day on which the band of emigrants left their native shores, they possessed not merely complete autonomy but every other attribute of a nation. It does not appear that the feeling which prevailed between the metropolis and the colony was the less cordial and affectionate from their political independence. Rather the more, perhaps. Corinth held herself morally bound to succour Syracuse against the Carthaginians, and Athens Ionia against the Persians, as we should to succour Canada against the Yankees. The colony too,

* *The Spectator*, 1st and 15th July, 1854.

possessing a national organization of its own, was able to return the obligation. There was, in fact, as a general rule, a perpetual offensive and defensive alliance between them, supported, not by formal stipulations, but by mutual affection, habitual intercourse, community of race, language, historical traditions and religious rites. It appears to me that this was a better political arrangement than that which has prevailed in later times.'

Godley's use of the stark, forbidding word 'independence' when speaking of the future of the British colonies, is somewhat softened by this paragraph. It is independence in partnership, not separation with unkindness, that he has in mind. England would never be 'so base as to cast off the colonies against their will,' he thought*, and if she did she would 'deserve the decline and fall which her cowardice would prognosticate'. Yet, she should face the fact that at some future date subordination of any kind would be impossible. 'A nation of three millions of Englishmen is really master of its own destinies. Whenever, therefore, the colonists shall, with anything like unanimity, demand independence, we should give it them at once, even joyfully, and without one *arrière-pensée* of ill-feeling.'

In this letter, and repeatedly in his later correspondence, Godley urged that colonial nationalism was something which the English should encourage by all means, and most of all by throwing the colonies upon their own responsibility. 'When British America has an army and navy proportioned to its population and resources, it will, I hope, be equivalent to a corresponding augmentation of our own forces.'

A few days later he wrote to Adderley: 'I met Gladstone riding in the Park yesterday, and rode for some time with him. He said he had read my letters in the *Spectator* with great pleasure. "Indeed," he added, "I often wish I had you to speak my sentiments on colonial affairs, for I know no one with whom I so entirely agree." ' Long afterwards, in

---

* Yet, only six months previously, he had deplored the weak withdrawal from the Orange Free State.

1869, when Gladstone was Prime Minister and Godley in his grave, the imperialists of that age denounced the Liberals for their supposed intention of disintegrating the Empire. Gladstone replied in the House with a speech that echoed Godley's letters to the *Spectator*.

There followed, in 1854, a triangular correspondence between Godley, Adderley, and Joseph Howe upon Imperial organization, with interventions by Francis Hincks of Lower Canada and W. H. Prescott the American historian. Howe wrote a long rhetorical appeal to Adderley enlarging upon the sentimental attachment of Canadians to Britain, and urging the British to respond. Godley dismissed this rambling letter as 'unstatesmanlike and illogical'. Adderley proposed that they should work for an Imperial Council of Delegates on the model of the old Spanish Council of the Indies, but Prescott said that the Council of the Indies was nothing of the kind. Hincks was for letting things alone; he did not believe that to demand a federation of the Empire or even a federation of the British North American provinces was good political tactics. Godley seized upon the one limb of these general conversations that was relevant to current affairs and tried to concentrate attention on that.

Throughout the eighteen forties and fifties, the United States was expanding in numbers, wealth, and territory, at a rate that defied all computation. Shortly she would be more populous even than the Empire of Russia and a far more dangerous rival to the British Empire. Her press was bitterly anti-British; every American election in those decades was fought on the issue of an aggressive foreign policy. In Central America, in Oregon, in New Brunswick, on the Newfoundland Coast, American filibusters threatened British territorial rights. Each of the petty struggling provinces of British North America was in danger of absorption. The real need of British colonial policy, the practicable task, for statesmen with their feet on the ground, was to federate Canada not to federate the Empire, even if, in the distant future, Canada were destined to become

England's independent ally, not England's colony. Godley drew Adderley's attention to the matter. 'Any movement in this direction should originate in the colonies. . . . Suppose you write to Hincks and Howe, both of whom you know, and find out whether there is any tendency that way among influential people out there. You should see what Lord Durham says about the matter . . . . and refer to the first steps taken by the Provinces towards federation, previously to the Declaration of Independence.' Adderley pegged away and, twelve years later, conducted the British North America Act through the House of Commons.

* * * * *

When the Canterbury dinner was again held at Greenwich, on 9th July, 1856, the need for apologies had passed away. About thirty members of the Association, the Bishops of Oxford and St Davids, Lords Lyttelton and Courtenay, Adderley, Simeon, McGeachy, James, Cocks, Halswell, Selfe and others met to hear a speech from Godley in very different vein. The news had reached England that the Canterbury Provincial Government had accepted entire responsibility for the debts of the Association, and had undertaken to repay the sums advanced by its members, between 1850 and 1853, with accrued interest. The sum so repaid was £28,935. Many of the members had lost faith in the ability of the Province and most of them in its willingness to accept responsibility for this debt of honour. It was a triumph for the administrative skill of Sewell and Fitz-Gerald in Canterbury and no less for the credit of Godley who had never ceased to sustain the flagging confidence of his friends. The debt to the Crown had been met in 1853, the debt to the Company was borne by the settlers as part of the funded debt of New Zealand, the debt to the members of the Association was now liquidated. Every penny of the cost of founding Canterbury thus came out of the pockets of the settlers, and the Canterbury contribution to the revenue of New Zealand already far exceeded any receipts from the New Zealand Treasury for provincial purposes.

An Australian named Alfred Cox, somewhat awed by the grandeur of the company he was keeping, recorded his impressions of this Canterbury dinner. Though Lord Lyttelton and Bishop Wilberforce spoke, it was not they who made a lasting impression on him. 'Mr Godley was the chief speaker,' he said, 'and perhaps the only one who conveyed any solid information as to the actual condition of the province. He appeared to have at the tip of his tongue, and ready to be spouted forth at a moment's notice, all matters financial, political, and social that could possibly interest his hearers.'

Lord Lyttelton's correspondence in 1855-56 is rich in expressions of delight from contributors who had written off their subsidies or loans as dead loss and who, perhaps, had sometimes regretted their earlier enthusiasm for Church colonization. The Duke of Newcastle wrote on 13th December, 1855: 'I am truly glad to receive your report of the highly honorable conduct of our thriving children in Canterbury—not so much because I am glad to receive back money which I never expected to see again (though the unusual nature of that sensation makes it decidedly pleasant), as because it is a proof that, in spite of much obloquy, the colony has been attended with a fair measure of success.'

*   *   *   *   *

At this point it will be convenient to give a summary of the accounts of the Association. Published early in 1853, when the reputation of the settlement was low, they were received by the press with a chorus of abuse. They were late, they were obscure, they showed evidence of financial trickery, and they proved only too plainly that the great Canterbury bubble was burst. The Canterbury Association had not escaped what Godley said was the ordinary fate of colonizing bodies: 'it has exceeded its means, and it has incurred considerable unpopularity in the Settlement it has founded'.

The general view of the Association, in Canterbury, was

that it had squandered in England the money that should have been spent for endowing schools and churches in New Zealand. The Association, said FitzGerald, had been 'plundered in the City' over its shipping contracts. Bowler, the shipping agent, arrived in New Zealand a wealthy man, by virtue of his commissions, and Felix Wakefield, the agent for land-sales, was thought even worse when it was found in Christchurch how careless he was over small debts of honour.

When the accounts reached Canterbury they were referred to a sub-committee of the Provincial Council which spent more than a year in investigating them, without coming to the bottom of every entanglement. Selfe in England and Sewell in New Zealand, the two lawyers who were winding up the Association's affairs, were not on good terms with each other and did not put the same construction on the evidence. It was impossible to reduce the Bishop-designate's accounts to order, and almost impossible to give due credit to the benefactors who had contributed to the assets of the Association, by gift, loan, mortgage or guarantee. Sewell made out the sum total of these benefactions as £16,279, in addition to the outstanding guarantee for £12,000 given by Lord Lyttelton and three others on the security of the church lands; Selfe made out the sum to be £17,519.

The audited accounts as presented to the Provincial Council in February, 1855, uncertain as they are in these particulars, give a fair account of the very modest cost of founding Canterbury. The sums received from genuine land-purchasers, during the three years of the Association's activity, appear to have been £79,484 in England and £7,963 in the colony. No more explanation is required of Godley's difficulties than this. The Association had undertaken to sell land to the value of £150,000 in this period and had hoped to sell land to the value of £300,000. Their error lay solely in the estimate of the time required. Their objective could not be attained in three years though it was attained with great ease and far surpassed in five-and-twenty years. £79,484 was not enough for a commencement but, by the device of transferring assets from the Ecclesiastical Fund to the Land Fund, and borrowing on the security thus created, they increased the nominal value of the land-sales to £112,453 4s. 5d. (including some sundries); with this sum they managed to proceed on a reduced scale.

Their revenue was increased by subsidies of various kinds, by an advance of cash to the amount of £28,958 from the New Zealand Company, by the sum of £31,604 contributed by settlers in passage-money, by £16,279 (on Sewell's reckoning) in benefactions, by £10,000 advanced on the Lyttelton mortgage, by £2,691 advanced by Governor Grey for road-making, by £2,362 in subscriptions which the Bishop-designate collected, and by miscellaneous items of which one is a loan of £133 3s. which Godley advanced to the Ecclesiastical Fund. The grand total of revenue from all sources amounted to £213,566 17s. 7d., and this sum may be taken as the cost of founding Canterbury. The Land Fund, which, according to the theory of the founders, should have provided the whole of it, did not in fact provide much more than one-third of this sum, during the first three years.

Of the sums nominally paid into the Land Fund, one-sixth, that is to say £18,742 was appropriated by the Crown and the New Zealand Company, according to the terms of the Canterbury Settlement Land Act. If the whole revenue had consisted of the return from land-sales, one-third of the total should have been placed to the credit of the Ecclesiastical Fund, one-third to the credit of the Emigration Fund, and the remaining sixth part should have been spent on survey and public works in the colony. Inevitably the practical requirements of the three departments worked out in a different ratio.

The actual expenses of the emigration department, in transferring 3,247 settlers to Canterbury in 22 ships, were

£85,012. Of this sum £37,484 was drawn from the Land Fund, £31,604 was contributed by those settlers who paid the whole or a part of their own fares, and the remainder was drawn from the subsidies. The Emigration Fund was heavily loaded with incidental expenses to which the critics took exception. £2,524 was paid in commissions to Bowler, the shipping agent, £1,382 (two-fifths of his total earnings) to Felix Wakefield the agent for land-sales, £3,405 in berths for ships' surgeons, £2,709 in berths for ships' chaplains, £742 for festivities at London docks, and there were many other items. The net cost of ships' charters was £44,956.

The sums expended on survey and preparation of the site had amounted to £41,264, a much larger proportion of the whole revenue than the sixth part which had been estimated, and yet not nearly enough; for the road from the port to the plains was still unfinished in 1855. In addition, about £17,000 had been spent on administration and publicity in England, for which no adequate provision had been made in the estimates. After taking some sundries into account the expenses of the Miscellaneous Fund reached the total of £67,165. Though Godley had been responsible for the prospectus, he went abroad before any large expenditure was incurred in England. His comment on the unforeseen charge of £17,000 would have been that it was largely unnecessary. The Association should have begun its work economically in a small way and, at an early stage, should have transferred itself, with its officers, its charter, and its accounts, to the colony, as the Massachusetts Company did, two hundred years earlier.

Since emigration and miscellaneous expenses had swallowed up more than their share before the colony was founded, there was not much left for those functions of the Ecclesiastical Fund which were to appear at a later stage. Of the total sum, £42,646, allotted to the Ecclesiastical Fund, two-thirds, £24,816, were locked up in the land-purchases which Sewell had devised to save the Association from bankruptcy. The episode of the Bishop-designate had swallowed up £1,882, of which £628 consisted of 'sundries, particulars not given'. On the other side of the account was the equally vague item of subscriptions collected by the Bishop-designate, to the amount of £2,362. Chaplains and schoolmasters sent out with the ships had been remunerated to the amount of £3,438, which left no more than £8,696 12s. 7d. for the working capital of the churches and schools in Canterbury. To this small sum had the lavish endowments promised by the Association dwindled. Godley had somehow contrived to build two temporary churches and a schoolroom, but was not yet able to contemplate a college or cathedral. The unanswerable objection to Sewell's policy was that he had invested and mortgaged the funds which should have provided stipends for the resident clergy and schoolmasters of the first four parishes in Canterbury. It was a poor consolation to them to be assured—and rightly—that the Church in Canterbury would be handsomely endowed a generation later.

Godley had not been many days in England before he wrote to Lord Lyttelton, enclosing subscriptions from himself and Sir W. Farquhar to make up the deficiency, since the guaranteed stipends of the parish clergy had not been paid.

Sir Cracroft Wilson, an Indian civilian who visited Canterbury in 1854, and made up his mind to settle there, described the Pilgrims as 'poor, proud, pious, and without servants'. In the year 1856 their affairs took a turn for the better. Sewell's work was done, the debts of the Association were paid off, the College was founded, and an actual Bishop appeared upon the scene. The long deadlock over the subdivision of Selwyn's diocese was broken by Selwyn himself, who visited England in 1854, and quickly made up his quarrel with the friends of the Canterbury settlement. He proposed that Dr H. J. C. Harper should be the first Bishop of Christchurch, obtained the approval of the Archbishop of Canterbury, and reported his action to the clergy in Canterbury settlement. A petition was then sent to the Queen signed by all the leading Canterbury Pilgrims asking that the royal letters-patent should be issued to Dr Harper. Delighted as Godley was to hear of this development, he was disgusted to consider that the actual appointment must be made by the Secretary of State, just then Sir William Molesworth, a Colonial Reformer but a professed atheist. His own part in the proceedings was to reassure Harper that a colonial bishop might live simply on a modest stipend. Harper was consecrated by Archbishop Sumner at Lambeth, in August, 1856, in the presence of Lyttelton, Godley, and others of their circle, and immediately set sail for New Zealand. FitzGerald, as Superintendent of the Province of Canterbury, received him at Lyttelton on 23rd December, 1856. Bishop Harper proved to be the very man whom they had desired and under his rule the Church in Canterbury became what the founders had wished it to be.

In 1857, when FitzGerald completed his term of office as Superintendent, he returned to England for a few years as the salaried agent of Canterbury Province. Land-sales, now fixed at the standard price of £2 an acre (£1 less than formerly, since the Church had been endowed and the schools had been taken over by the Provincial Government) were going briskly and the despatch of selected emigrants was renewed. In his time the new settlers of Canterbury, gentle and simple, were men and women of the same stamp as the original 'Pilgrims'. He kept up a correspondence on these matters with Lyttelton and the others of their set, and he also made it his business to collect subscriptions for the College and the Cathedral. There was no accomplishment to which FitzGerald could not turn his hand, and one of his last acts before leaving the colony had been to design a plain and spacious school hall, the old 'Big School' of Christ's College, to be built in local stone with an open timbered roof of original design. He wanted funds for the Cathedral, and he wanted books for the College library, and his plan was to appeal to fresh benefactors since the former members of the Association had done all that could be decently asked. He got some new subscribers, including Molesworth and the University of Oxford, but from Godley he got a typical letter of disapproval. 'Godley says,' wrote FitzGerald to Lyttelton, 'he will do exactly the opposite of what I asked him. He will give me £50 but will be no party to asking anyone else who has no connexion with the place.' This was a contribution to the Cathedral Fund; on another occasion Godley gave £100 to the College Fund with an equal generosity in act and an equal parsimony on principle. He was at this time a salaried civil servant with a growing family and very modest means.

The Cathedral was taken as the criterion of success in Canterbury. In 1861 sufficient funds were in hand to obtain a plan from Sir Gilbert Scott, to prepare the site, to lay the foundation stone, and to appoint a resident architect, and so the matter stood for about twenty years. When Samuel Butler settled in Canterbury in 1863, when Lord Lyttelton paid his promised visit in 1868, when Trollope wrote the account of his globe-trotting tour in 1873, the Cathedral site stood bare as a mockery of high endeavour. It was not built up until 1884. Yet considering that Wren took longer to build St. Paul's, four and thirty years does not seem long for a little community in the wilderness. A pity that they boasted too much of their intention before they set sail!

Trollope's account of Canterbury was accepted as authoritative by the small part of the English world that took an interest in the colonies. 'The scheme,' he wrote, 'had all the merits and all the faults which have attended the fabrication of Utopias, since the benevolence of men has taken that direction.' Then turning from the settlement to its founder, Trollope changed his tune. 'Mr Godley, whom I remember as a boy at school thoroughly respected by all his schoolfellows, seems early in life to have been taught by the Tractarian movement at Oxford that the religion of a community should be its most important consideration.

. . . His letters have recently been published . . . . and no volume of correspondence ever fell into my hands which left upon my mind a higher impression of the purity, piety, philanthropy, truth, and high-minded thoughtfulness of the writer.' This was praise, indeed, out of the mouth of the Philistines. Godley's statue in Christchurch was very noble, so Trollope went on to say. 'Among modern statues, I know no head that stands better on its shoulders.'

* * * * *

It may be symptomatic of the changing values in Victorian England, between the 'forties and the 'sixties, that the Canterbury Pilgrims built themselves a railway with a celebrated tunnel before they built their cathedral. Fitz-Gerald's successor as Superintendent, W. S. Moorhouse, taking his cue from Wakefield, was determined to boost Canterbury by a policy of bold borrowing. So thriving a settlement had no difficulty in raising loans, even though the strict economists, above all Godley, deplored any such endeavour. A nation, like a man, he thought, should live within its income. The Sumner road, on which so large a part of the preliminary expenses had been lavished, was hardly opened when it fell into disuse. Before he left for England FitzGerald, to the great risk of his life, had driven a tandem over the road, but the settlers were already talking of tunnelling the hills. They took a pride in doing so before the Simplon tunnel through the Alps should be completed. Until then the Lyttelton tunnel would be the longest in the world.

Though Godley advised caution, and even the mercurial FitzGerald favoured a less ambitious railway plan, the scheme for tunnelling the hills was being hotly canvassed when, for the last time, Godley spoke at the annual Canterbury dinner, held at the Albion Tavern, on 23rd November, 1858. Since there was now no doubt that Canterbury settlement was flourishing, Godley was able to trounce his critics. 'I stand here,' he said ironically, 'as the notorious author of the Great Canterbury Failure. And yet Canterbury is now selling as much land at forty shillings an acre as Auckland is giving away for nothing.' There was no previous example in the history of the British Empire of an agricultural colony that was self-supporting in its third year, free of debt in its sixth year, and which enjoyed a favourable balance of trade in its eighth year. Even the gold-rush to Melbourne had drawn away only about 500 of the Canterbury settlers, mostly unmarried wage-labourers. For the year 1857 the public revenue had been authorized by universal suffrage and collected at the rate of £14 per head of the population per annum, 'more than double the amount of revenue any community had to dispose of since the world began,' in proportion to the population. This was Godley's last speech on Canterbury and he did not let the occasion pass without a word of warning.

'There is no position on earth where men can exercise such immense influence, and acquire such immense power as that in which those who first go out to a new colony, and become the seed-plot and nursery of a new nation, find themselves; and unless we keep continually before their eyes the power, and the deep responsibility that ought always to be connected with that power, there is a danger of the whole course of the growing nation being turned into degeneracy. If the founders of the American Republic had been formed of the same materials as the settlers of California, the genius and liberties of America would have been lost in anarchy or absorbed in an inevitable despotism. It was because . . . they were senators and soldiers, impressed with the due sense of the heavy responsibility that rested upon them, and not mere money-getters, that they succeeded in laying the foundations of the greatest republic in the world.'

The census of December, 1858, returned the population of Canterbury as 8,967, of whom 545 were Maoris. The proportion of females to males, always the test of civilization in a new community, was high, 3,666 to 5,301. Sixty per cent of the population were English by birth, twenty per cent were born in the colony, fourteen per cent were

Irish, Scottish or Welsh, and six per cent Maori. Seventy-two per cent were members of the Church of England. About one in eight of the Europeans was illiterate. 22,900 acres of land were fenced, and 13,900 acres under cultivation. The province contained 2,700 horses, 20,000 cattle, 495,000 sheep. In the first stage of its development the colony grew rich on wool. The back-blocks were quickly taken up by runholders but, as the founders had foretold, close settlement around Christchurch gave a home market for foodstuffs and provided the amenities of civilized life. With its churches and its College; markets, clubs, and sports; and its lively local politics, Canterbury already had a name for social pre-eminence among the southern colonies in the eighteen-sixties and deserved it in the eighteen-eighties.

The gold-rush to the West Coast in 1864 brought a wave of prosperity which did not submerge the character of the little colony. When the fortune-hunters passed on to other eldorados Canterbury survived, richer, but as English and Anglican as before the boom. The opening of the Lyttelton railway, through its long tunnel, at the end of 1867, brought solider gains. Canterbury was by far the richest of the provinces when, in 1876, the provincial system was replaced by a single unitary constitution for New Zealand. Unlike all other provinces, Canterbury handed over to the central government a balance-sheet free from debt, since the value of her railways offset her liabilities. More than two-thirds of the whole land-revenue of New Zealand, in the last year of provincial government, was derived from the high-priced Canterbury land. The comment of Rusden, the first historian of New Zealand, on the effect of the system of Wakefield and Godley was that 'out of 11,915,393 acres sold from the foundation of the colony till 31st October, 1876, for £8,101,859, the enormous proportion of £5,395,000 had been received by Canterbury and Otago for less than 4,500,000 acres. For about the same amount of land as that sold by Auckland, Canterbury had received thirteen times

as much money.' It had been spent on systematic colonization with selected immigrants, on public works such as no
other settlement could boast, on building Christchurch out
of lasting stone, and in creating funds which were used for
the benefit of less prudent provinces. Hardly was the new
constitution established when the use of refrigeration
brought a new and still greater prosperity to the province
from the export of 'Canterbury lamb'. To visitors at the end
of the nineteenth century, Christchurch, in appearance and
in character, was the decent, thriving, Anglican, cathedral
town that its founders had meant it to be, burdened neither
with a class of idle rich, nor with a class of hopeless paupers;
it had attained this happy state, in spite of some initial set-
backs, by pursuing the aims and maintaining the principles
of its founders. The population of Canterbury, when Godley
died in 1861, was 16,000; in 1878, at the abolition of the
provincial system, it was about 70,000; at the end of the
century about 130,000, and it is now about a quarter of
a million.

Soon after Godley's death, his former secretary, Charles
Bowen, wrote to Lord Lyttelton: 'I know you will be angry
with my talking in this way of Canterbury. But if your lordship were to land, I fear that, while you admired the
material progress of the Settlement, you would share the
heart-sickness of those who remember the aspirations of
Mr Godley's time and who have learned that a colony *must*
go through all the phases of a new country in modern times.'

It would, of course, be absurd to allege that Canterbury
became—or could have become—the early-Victorian
utopia that the Rev. Thomas Jackson had so fervently
envisaged. Godley's farewell speech dispelled any lingering
dreams of such a consummation. Yet there was scholarship
and science and piety in Canterbury settlement, even in an
age of growing materialism and under circumstances which
favoured its growth. If Samuel Butler found that men in
Canterbury talked of nothing but sheep and 'scab', he found
there, too, a publisher for his philosophy. Bishop Harper

sitting in his stall, as Warden of Christ's College, in extreme old age, might look about him at the chapel walls, and back upon a well-spent life without disdain. Was it not inevitable that the demands of pioneering life should seem to pre-dominate? The 'seed-plot and nursery of a new nation' would need time to bring forth fruit; it was the quality of the seed that counted.

CHAPTER XIII

Godley at the War Office

DURING the years when Canterbury was making quiet progress which its friends watched with growing pleasure, and which passed unnoticed by the rest of the world, Godley was employed as a civil servant, at first in the Inland Revenue Department, and later in the War Office. He lived again at the London house which he had let furnished while he was in New Zealand. Some years later, in 1859, the requirements of a growing family, a boy and four girls, obliged him to move from Number 69 Gloucester Place to a larger house, Number 11, a few doors away. In Number 11 Godley spent the remainder of his life and there his widow dwelt after his death.

In summer they took a villa in some country retreat, Hanwell or Streatham, rural in those days but near enough for Godley to ride into the War Office each day, and in the evening 'gallop back to play cricket with Arthur'. No autumn passed in which he did not get some shooting with Sir Charles Taylor, or Sir Walter James, or with Adderley at Hams Hall whom he could visit on his way to Ireland. Once or twice the Godleys went to Killegar for Christmas and, three times, at least, they went abroad: to Paris, in 1856 after the Peace; to Switzerland in 1857; to Italy in 1860. After visiting Lucerne Godley wrote loyally to Adderley comparing it unfavourably with Killarney.

Though he was not wealthy, Godley's earnings, his allowance from his father, and some small investments enabled him to live at the rate of about £1500 to £2000 a year, a substantial income in those days. The Godleys were sociable and dined out frequently with political and civil service friends. When some visitor from Canterbury was in London he was welcome, and Godley maintained his friendships also with men he had met in Canada and the United States. Chief Justice Robinson came to Gloucester Place, as did S. G. Hillard, a lawyer from Boston. For many years Hillard wrote regularly to Godley on American politics, and gave him news of literary New England. 'Your friends here are all well,' he wrote. 'Ticknor has just published his work on Spanish literature which will take a permanent place in our own. Prescott is at work on the history of Philip II but makes slow progress on account of his failing eyes. Longfellow is just publishing another volume of poems and Sumner is making a collection of his addresses.' In London, too, Godley had literary connexions, with Rintoul of the *Spectator* and Cook of the *Morning Chronicle,* with John Murray the publisher, with Thackeray and with Tennyson. Presumably it was through Simeon, now Sir John Simeon of Swainston, Tennyson's close friend and neighbour, that Godley came to know the poet.

War was declared against Russia in January, and in February an expeditionary force was despatched to the Black Sea. The situation developed slowly, and it was September before the allies landed in the Crimea. Then, indeed, there was dramatic news; before the winter set in, the three great battles of the Alma, Inkerman, and Balaclava had been fought, and the armies had closed in to besiege Sebastopol. William Godley was in the trenches with his regiment; Charlotte's brother was killed leading a company at Inkerman. In such times John Robert Godley was not the man to be content with a leisurely round of income-tax appeals. He was invited, with Lyttelton, to visit the Gladstones at Hawarden Castle and wrote to Adderley, on 16th October, 'It is rather irksome to feel that in the enjoyment of good health, and with a considerable capacity for work, I am employed about work which the most uneducated man, if he have only commonsense and integrity, could do as well, and which, except during the three months a year which I have to spend in travelling, does not take half an hour a day. I took heart the other day, and in spite of my reluctance to "ask for things", which I have never done yet in my life, got Lyttelton to express to Gladstone my wish, not for more pay, but more work. He replied very kindly, that he fully entered into my feelings, and would promote my wishes if he had an opportunity, but that it is difficult, *etc.* . . . I am very uneasy about the army in the Crimea. Their position seems to me ticklish and difficult in the extreme. It is difficult to think of anything else.'

Before Gladstone had an opportunity of finding him a more exacting post, *The Times* newspaper thundered out its denunciation of the Government. As the winter deepened, worse news came from the Crimea, week by week, and in January, 1855, Roebuck's motion for a committee of enquiry overthrew the Government. Newcastle bore the brunt, though the historians have on the whole credited him with doing his best. Sidney Herbert, another Peel-ite, remained in office a short time longer. For a few weeks he held the seals of the Colonial Office and Godley seized the opportunity of appealing to him.

'My dear Mr Godley,' wrote Herbert on 27th February, 1855, 'I would have jumped at your offer to take colonial service, had I remained in office and had any vacancy at my disposal which had been worthy of your acceptance.' But, in March, Palmerston emerged from the political struggle at the head of a new Whig administration from which most of the Peel-ites were dropped. Lord John Russell, who was most unlikely to employ Godley, took the Colonial Office.

Godley did, however, find an opportunity of serving his country in a department where there was scope for unlimited energy. One of his oldest friends, William Monsell, a Liberal

M.P., held the high appointment of Clerk of the Ordnance and he, on 8th March, wrote to Godley: 'I think that I have made out an appointment for you which you will like and the duties of which you are admirably fitted to discharge. Those duties will be laborious but highly honourable, and I know that you are a glutton for work.' He was to be Director-General of Stores in the Ordnance Department at a salary of £1000 a year, and to wrestle with the simultaneous problems of reorganizing a chaotic department and of shipping to the Crimea stores which should have been provided six months earlier. There was not much time for private correspondence that summer. On 21st August he wrote to Adderley: 'I have been terribly busy of late, or I would have written to you before. We are engaged in sending out mortars and shells enough to bury Sebastopol under solid iron, and huts enough to shelter the whole population of Southern Russia, and the worst of it is that we have to find *steamers* for them all. We shall despatch some *forty* steamers, for the Crimea alone, within six weeks. Heaven help those who will have to pay the bill.'

Every schoolboy knows of the confusion which had overwhelmed the British effort in the first campaign of the Crimean War. To find out what was at fault and what part Godley played in setting our military administration on a better footing it will be necessary to glance back at the earlier history of the War Office. Originally the Army had been under immediate command of the Sovereign and had been paid from his privy purse. That command had devolved upon the Commander-in-chief, a soldier, who was responsible directly to the Queen and not to Parliament. But when Parliament took over the finances of the Army an official known as the Secretary-at-War had been appointed to present the estimates to the House of Commons. The Secretary-at-War paid the piper and the Commander-in-chief called the tune. This confusion was worse confounded in 1801 when one of the Secretaries of State was given special charge of 'War and the Colonies'. Between Waterloo and the Crimea these topics naturally fell together because the Army was largely dispersed in colonial garrisons and employed on colonial campaigns. The Secretary of State for War and the Colonies laid down lines of general policy, but could give no orders to the troops, for that was the Commander-in-chief's privilege, and had no control over finances, which were the affair of the Secretary-at-War. Furthermore, the artillery, the engineers, the royal munition factories, and all the organization for supplying arms and ammunition, were controlled by an entirely distinct department, the Ordnance, and the Master-general of the Ordnance often had a seat in the Cabinet. In 1854 the post was held by Lord Raglan who was away, commanding the troops in the Crimea, and his civil assistant, Monsell, acted for him. The Commissariat Department and the Medical Department, again, were quite separate bodies.

Newcastle, as Secretary of State for War, had devised the strategic plan for invading the Crimea, in consultation with the Commander-in-chief, and it has generally been approved by military critics as a sound plan. When the Army was launched, it was soon discovered that there was no cohesion, no co-operation between the other administrative offices; they were quite unable to conduct the campaign which Newcastle had initiated. Hence the shocking chaos of the first Crimean winter, and the necessity to reorganize the departments while the war was being fought.

The first step had been taken in June, 1854, when the Colonial Office was separated from the War Office. Gladstone said that Newcastle made his first mistake, at that point, by giving up the Colonies and retaining the War Office for himself. He should have retained the Colonial Office which he thoroughly understood, and let the War Office go to some other statesman who was familiar with its problems, which, as we have seen, were appallingly complicated. When the chaos in the Crimea was laid bare in the newspapers, many reforms, long overdue, were improvised by the departments. The most celebrated is the reform of the Hospitals and Nursing Service by Florence

PART OF THE CITY OF CHRISTCHURCH, 1950

Air photograph by V. C. Browne.

Nightingale who was sent to the Crimea in October, 1854. This was done on the initiative of Sidney Herbert, then Secretary-at-War, who held the purse-strings. By the end of the winter, the whole resources of Victorian enterprise and industry were deployed. The campaign of 1855 was the first in which full use was made of the steamship, the light railway, the submarine telegraph cable, and the rifled gun. By the end of the summer the British troops were much better equipped than their French allies and, in this achievement the Stores Department of the Ordnance was the focal point. Supply and Transport was the limiting factor in the campaign and, as Director-general, Godley held the key to the problem.

While stores were being obtained and despatched to the Crimea it was necessary for the heads of departments, at the same time, to reorganize their relations with one another, a task of great administrative complexity, always obscured and confused by personal factors. The wars of 1914 and 1939 have familiarized thousands of staff officers and civil servants with these difficulties. It will be sufficient to say that, in August, 1855, the Ordnance Department was incorporated into the War Office, and Godley thus came under the authority of Lord Panmure, who had succeeded Newcastle as Secretary of State for War. After the bloody battles for the Redan and the Malakoff forts, in September, the Russians evacuated Sebastopol and the campaign drew to a close. Through a second winter, of comparative comfort, the troops remained in the Crimea and, in March, 1856, peace was signed at Paris. Just at this time the friends of Canterbury were congratulating one another on the repayment of the Association's debts.

With the return of the Army, demobilization, and the inevitable cry for economy in the Army estimates, Godley soon found himself again suffering from the old complaint. At the War Office, in time of peace, there was not enough to do. He made one more effort to exchange into the Colonial Department but without much hope, for the

H

Whigs were firmly entrenched there, under Labouchere, who had been Chief Secretary for Ireland in 1847. Again, Gladstone's good offices were invoked but without success. Labouchere wrote, on 8th April, 1856, 'My dear sir, I should be very glad to be able to offer you a colonial appointment, but you would hardly be willing to exchange your present place except for one of real interest and importance. I will bear in mind what you say.' This was civil but no more; we know from other letters that Labouchere was one of those who still thought of Godley as 'the author of the Great Canterbury Failure'. No suitable vacancy appeared, or none was offered to Godley, and, in the Army estimates of 1857, he was established by Panmure as Assistant Under-Secretary of State for War, at £1200 a year. He held this appointment until his death.

A further step in Army reorganization was then taken by the abolition of the redundant office of Secretary-at-War, with the effect of releasing some senior officials who must be provided for. One of them was Sir Benjamin Hawes who had been comfortably ensconced there for some years. An able, well-meaning, elderly, public servant, temperamentally hostile to innovations, he had formerly been Under-Secretary for the Colonies and, in that capacity, had furiously opposed Godley's scheme for Irish emigration. Later, as Deputy Secretary-at-War, he had been the *bête noire* of Florence Nightingale. In 1857 he was appointed permanent Under-Secretary at the War Office and, thus, was Godley's immediate superior. Godley bore with him patiently, and laid before him a series of plans for the better management of the Army, which were unlikely to have much effect so long as Hawes was alive.

Much of his energy in the summer of 1856 was taken up with an absurd quarrel on a point of honour. Godley had solved some practical problem of transporting stores, by simple exchange of notes with a junior officer of the Admiralty, thus arousing the ire of a brassbound admiral who complained, in terms that Godley thought insulting, against action outside the proper channels. Godley excused himself for what he had done and demanded an apology for the insult. He got it, but only after a spate of letters at all levels of correspondence; the First Lord and the Secretary for War were drawn in on behalf of their clients. Godley's point of honour pursued Lord Panmure to Balmoral where he was attending the Queen. This storm in a teacup was one lesson on the difficulties of the higher control of the fighting services.

Though committed to his work at the War Office, Godley did not lose interest in the colonies, nor his reputation as a colonial expert. News from Canterbury, especially, was always a delight to him and his annual appearances at the Canterbury dinner gave him opportunities of proclaiming his faith in its prosperity. When a change of government came, at the end of 1857, the new Colonial Secretary, Bulwer Lytton the novelist, wrote to make Godley's acquaintance and amused him by addressing him as 'Colonel' Godley, assuming that he must be a military man. He went to visit Lytton at Knebworth, in August, 1858. A bloody campaign was then raging in India but the war of the Indian Mutiny seems to have been taken in its stride by Godley's department. Presumably the lessons of the Crimea had been well learned. At least the despatch and equipment of troops for India are not much discussed in Godley's papers. Most of the responsibility fell on the East India Company, not the War Office.

'Lytton talked incessantly, and charmingly,' wrote Godley to Adderley, 'quite realizing my ideas of an illogical, eloquent, man of genius. The house is not in good taste, but picturesque, and full of all sorts of articles of vertu, paintings, books, old furniture, etc. After dinner the first day, he lionized me round his historical portraits, discoursing most admirably on each. Sunday he spent entirely in the house, dressed in a black and red slashed dressing-gown, unshaven, and with his hair unbrushed, looking like a wizard, and smoking the whole time a long cherry-stick pipe. He is (literally) half-mad with his responsibilities, and fancies he is going to reform the whole colonial empire. He gets up in the middle of the night to write despatches, and is furious if they don't actually *go* in twelve hours.' It was part of Disraeli's romantic notion of empire to promote this strange talented aristocrat to high office where he remained for the twelve months of Lord Derby's second administration (in which Disraeli was the dominant figure). In that short time Lytton inaugurated the colony of British Columbia and quarrelled with Sir George Grey (Governor, at that time, of the Cape) over federating the South African colonies, but whether these actions were taken on Godley's advice is not known. Godley was an enthusiast for confederation in Canada and would, probably, have agreed with his old opponent, Sir George Grey, that confederation would benefit South Africa also.

In June, 1859, Palmerston returned to power after a general election which went against the Conservatives. He now incorporated the leaders of the dwindling Peel-ite group in his administration, and their conversion to the new Liberal Party may be described as complete. Godley's three friends and patrons held the ministries which affected his work and interest, Gladstone at the Exchequer, Newcastle at the Colonial Office, Herbert at the head of Godley's own department, the War Office. He was at last able to bring some of his plans into being.

From his first days at the War Office he had given his mind to general schemes of reorganization, which carried to much greater lengths the movement towards unity of control and simplicity of administration begun during the Crimean War. With his usual impatience of the obstructiveness that comes from lethargy and lack of imagination, he brought forward proposals that had no chance of acceptance until some great emergency should prove them inevitable. It was vain to suppose that permanent officials would reform themselves out of their comfortable existence in time of peace.

As Assistant Secretary of State, Godley's time was largely taken up with problems of man-power, and, among his papers, there are several estimates of the actual distribution of the troops during the war. He became obsessed with the waste of men and money in colonial garrisons. This is his note of the position on 1st January, 1856.

Guards, cavalry, and infantry in the Crimea . . . 49,600
Guards, cavalry, and infantry in India 25,500
Guards, cavalry, and infantry in Great Britain . . . 33,500
Guards, cavalry, and infantry in Ireland 15,400
Guards, cavalry, and infantry in the colonies dispersed
   in twelve small garrisons 29,650
                                 153,650

Fifty-one battalions of the precious infantry of the line, the best troops in the world, never reached the Crimea. Even before he entered the War Office Godley had been deeply concerned about the part played by the colonies in the War. Several of the self-governing colonies presented loyal addresses and made grants of money to Imperial funds. Canada went further and offered, or intimated that she might offer a contingent of troops, an offer which the War Office met with a snub. Newcastle 'did not think it expedient to make such a demand on the labour market of the province'. The War Office did not want colonial volunteers, would not even withdraw the colonial garrisons, and, during the first Crimean winter, came news that British regular infantry, instead of fighting the Russians, had been employed to put down a miners' insurrection in Australia, at the Eureka Stockade. 'It was monstrous,' said Godley, 'a startling illustration of the necessity for some change in a system by which our troops are made to do the duty of colonial police'; he had foreseen in New South Wales that some such blundering outbreak must occur. He noted, too, that scattered detachments of troops, mis-employed in this way, would be useless to defend Victoria if the Russian naval squadron in the Far East were to attempt a raid upon a gold-producing colony. It was not as if soldiers were plentiful; they were exceedingly scarce, and about a quarter of them deserted after receiving the bounty paid them on enlistment.

No remedy was found for the shortage of good troops but the bad old remedy of hiring German mercenaries. It was Godley's duty to inspect the quarters they occupied at Portsmouth after the war. 'Nice fellows, these Germans are! For two days they have been in open mutiny at Portsmouth, broken open the gaol at Gosport, and committed all manner of excesses. Fortunately these loyal defenders had not been entrusted with ball-cartridges, or they would have murdered their officers.' He was furious with anger at the offer of Sir George Grey to receive eight thousand of them, still on full pay, as 'military colonists' in South Africa. 'Why, they will cost the country more than half a million before you've done with them,' he wrote to Adderley, 'and then not be half as useful as ordinary labourers. You *can't* combine the colonist and the soldier, and as they become the former they will cease to be available as the latter, except in the way of isolated riflemen. . . . I can't write openly against Government—but I wish you would consider how one can protest against this iniquity. I think I will write to Gladstone about it.'

Half a million to settle German mercenaries rankled when the Government had refused to advance a penny towards Canterbury settlement. That job had been done for an initial cost of £23,000 subscribed by the settlers and another £29,000 borrowed from Lyttelton and his friends.

Godley spent much of the year 1856 travelling about the British Isles from Jersey to Fort Augustus, inspecting military stores, and, according to his custom, observed many other things on his way. He was particularly interested that year in the contrast between the frugal well-cultivated small-holdings of the Channel Islands and the large lease-hold farms of the Scottish lowlands, perhaps the best-managed land in the world: and wrote an article for the *Economist* on this topic.

At the War Office, he next set himself to study recruiting. Bounties on enlistment, low rates of pay, and long service with a pension only after 21 years had made the army, for a century, the last refuge of the unemployable. The bounty was no more than a premium on desertion. He prepared a memorandum on 'the Means of Recruiting the Army and on an Army of Reserve', beginning with a careful study of the methods employed by other countries. He had no hesitation in rejecting conscription. 'At first sight and superficially a cheap mode of recruiting armies, it is, in reality, the most expensive that can be adopted.' Godley proposed, as an alternative, to abolish the bounty on enlistment; to recruit volunteers for seven or ten years at a much higher rate of pay than formerly, making it comparable with the market rate of wages; and to pass the time-expired men into an Army of Reserve which would be paid a small retaining fee and be called up for annual training. This plan was printed, circulated, and highly commended by Sir Charles Trevelyan of the Treasury since, on the figures presented, it would lead to a considerable economy. But nothing was done for about ten years until Gladstone became Prime Minister, and Cardwell Secretary of State for War. The name of Cardwell is to be found once or twice in Godley's correspondence and Cardwell was one of Gladstone's Oxford friends, a Peel-ite. It does not appear that he had more than a slight acquaintance with Godley.

Another abuse hotly attacked by Godley, but not abolished until Cardwell came to the War Office, was the purchase of officers' commissions. Much correspondence survives on this subject between Godley and his military colleagues who clung to their superstition that it was the means of attracting men of substance and social position into the service. Godley had little difficulty in demolishing their arguments though not their prejudices. In his eyes the system was condemned, if only because under the system of purchase young officers were under no obligation to work hard. 'You have only to dine at any regimental mess, and you will see at a glance that you are not among soldiers, but among young gentlemen playing at soldiers.'

These were but small matters and he was not deterred from considering reforms of larger scope. Before he had been two months in the War Office he prepared a draft plan, dated 20th September, 1855, for a single Ministry of Defence. Here he was about eighty years ahead of the official outlook and it is hardly surprising that no more was heard of it, though, again, he got some support from Trevelyan at the Treasury. He was so bold as to suggest that the Secretary of State for War should actually be what his name implies, that is, that he should exercise supreme authority over both services. The executive control should be committed to a General commanding-in-chief and an Admiral commanding-in-chief, both subordinate to the Secretary of State; and that a Deputy-Secretary should answer for each service in Parliament. The administrative details were elaborated at some length.

Godley's fault was always impetuosity. Four years later, when his friends came into office, he put forward a more modest scheme for reorganizing the War Office alone, on the same principles, and won the support of Gladstone, who minuted on it: 'I return Mr Godley's admirable paper. He is a perfect master of the subject, and has made it as clear as day. I cannot say how strongly I agree with him. This paper, I conclude, has been submitted to the Duke of Newcastle? On hearing that it has, I shall suggest its being printed for the Cabinet. Hawarden. Oct. 13th [1859?]'

The new plan had three main objects: 'a more complete control by the Secretary of State over the whole administration of the army, a more complete co-operation between the separate departments, and a larger infusion of the military element into the War Office.' The system of administration was to borrow several features from the Admiralty. A War Department, said Godley, should consist of 'a statesmen assisted and advised by soldiers'. There should be four comprehensive departments: *'Personnel* at the head of which should be the Commander-in-chief, *Material* at the head of which should be another military officer (usually of Artillery), *Constructions,* including fortifications and barracks with a third military officer (of Engineers) at the head of it, *Finance and Supply* at the head of which should be a civilian.' These four heads of Departments should be immediately responsible to the Secretary of State.

This was far too simple and forthright to succeed; even the Cardwell reforms of the eighteen-seventies came nowhere near it. Forty years after Godley's death his plan was brought to the notice of the officials, who held an inquest over the administrative weaknesses revealed by the Boer War, and was still ahead of the times.

If Godley's career at the War Office had seen nothing but these ambitious failures it would not have been worth much. It is a sterile victory to be approved by posterity for having been always right but always ineffective. These were the unfulfilled aspirations of a valued civil servant who carried out his duties with the approbation of his superiors and distressed them only by attempting too much. There was, however, one field in which Godley was an unrivalled authority, the field of colonial defence; and since his proposals on this head all tended towards economy in men and money they were welcomed by the other Departments.

On 14th March, 1859, Sir Benjamin Hawes wrote to the Colonial Office proposing a conference on 'the numerous questions of military expenditure which are continually arising in most of the colonies'. A committee was soon appointed, consisting of three under-secretaries, G. A. Hamilton for the Treasury, T. F. Elliott for the Colonial Office, and J. R. Godley for the War Office. Godley wrote the report; Hamilton approved it after inserting a few amendments in the vain hope of satisfying Elliott who, however, presented a minority report expressing his disagreement with his two colleagues. The Colonial Office, true to precedent, obstructed any innovation.

By the time the report was ready Palmerston and the Peel-ite leaders were in power. The years 1859 to 1861 were characterized by alarm about a possible war with France and the beginnings of the volunteer movement in England. Palmerston as Prime Minister put himself at the head of the patriotic forces and strove to fortify the coasts and modernize the navy. He was for expenditure on defence while his colleague, Gladstone, at the Exchequer, was—as always—for peace and retrenchment. Behind the scenes a struggle raged in the Cabinet where Gladstone urged on the adoption of Godley's report as a measure of economy while Palmerston thought the time unripe for economy in defence. Godley's motives were different, he wished to throw the colonies upon their own resources, obliging them to be self-reliant for their own benefit and honour, while concentrating the striking forces of the Empire at the decisive point.

Godley's report began by pointing out that military expenditure in the colonies amounted to £3,900,000 a year, and that less than one-tenth of this sum was contributed by the colonists themselves. The Cape, which swallowed up £800,000 contributed no more than £34,000. Twenty-six garrisons amounting to 47,000 men were maintained in various colonies and the rates of contribution—if any—bore no relation to the number of troops retained. It could not even be alleged that these garrisons served any strategic purpose. They were rarely large enough to resist a raid and could never hold out if the Royal Navy lost command of the sea. The Navy and the Navy alone was the real protector of the colonies.

But the gravest objection to the colonial garrisons was the 'tendency which this system must necessarily have to prevent the development of a proper spirit of self-reliance amongst our colonists, and to enfeeble their national

character. By the gift of political self-government, we have
bestowed on our colonies a most important element of
national education; but the habit of self-defence constitutes
a part hardly less important of the training of a free people,
and it will never be acquired by our colonists if we assume
exclusively the task of defending them.'

The solution was easy, to distinguish the 'Imperial posts',
such as Malta and Gibraltar, from the self-governing
colonies, to make special provision for the garrisons of the
former; and to offer the latter a system of defence upon the
principles of 'Colonial management and joint contribution
at a uniform rate'. Each colony should 'decide on the
nature of its own defences' and the Imperial Government
should offer to undertake a fixed proportion of the cost.

Such a plan as this was not quite new. Lord Grey had
adopted the excellent principle some years earlier that 'self-
government begets self-defence', and had begun to withdraw some superfluous garrisons. What was new was to
make it systematic. The report of the committee was at first
secret and was the subject of Cabinet discussions during the
session of 1860. Its ventilation was managed by one of those
devices which the Colonial Reformers often employed.
Adderley who, of course, was privy to the whole affair,
asked a question in the House and moved for a committee
of enquiry. This took time and the committee did not
actually meet until the session of 1861. Its membership was
hand-picked and included Adderley and other Colonial
Reformers. Godley himself was consulted about the choice
of a chairman and recommended Arthur Mills, a member
of the group. In the interval between the sitting of the two
committees, the inter-departmental committee of 1859 and
the Parliamentary Committee of 1861 Godley's health
broke down and when he appeared before the latter as a
witness, on 2nd May, 1861, he was a dying man. Nevertheless he answered firmly and resolutely to a long cross-
examination on problems in particular colonies. He strongly
condemned the policy of Sir George Grey, who maintained

his troops at the Cape by grants from the British exchequer. He read extracts of letters from FitzGerald in New Zealand complaining that the Governor would not call up colonial volunteers but insisted on using British regulars for the Maori War.

Unfortunately for Godley's plan 1861 was a year of colonial troubles. A far more serious matter than the Maori War was the threat of war with the United States and the necessity of sending 12,000 British soldiers to the Canadian frontier. There was no doubt of England's willingness to defend a colony in so fearful an Imperial crisis. Frontier campaigns against uncivilized tribes were another matter, and the Maori War was to be the test case for the self-reliant policy.

In March, 1862, Mills moved a resolution in the Commons 'that the self-governing colonies ought to bear the main responsibility for their own internal order and defence.' Newcastle made this the rule of the Colonial Office in 1863, and during the next seven years the garrisons were withdrawn from all except Imperial posts.

CHAPTER XIV

Last Years and Death

INSTEAD of going to Killegar for Christmas, after the busy autumn of 1859, Godley went to Scarborough where, it was thought, the climate would favour his throat. He was again in poor health and losing weight. The holiday proved insufficient and, after a short spell of work in London, he spent the Easter of 1860 in Rome, with Charlotte and her sister Frances, on medical advice. Much as he had travelled, it was his first view of Italy, and stirred him into writing to his father quite in the old vein. Soon tiring of the picture galleries, he delighted in the landscape which he found far more beautiful than his expectation, and having exhausted the landscape he turned to politics, among a population 'mainly composed of foreigners, beggars, and priests, with French soldiers to take care of them'. 'The sight of those everlasting "pantalons rouges",' he wrote, 'would drive me mad if I were a Roman.' This was Garibaldi's year, and the Godleys who had come by sea, touching at Genoa and Leghorn, noticed the 'resolute, unscrupulous, aggressiveness of the Northern Italians' and watched, open-eyed, for the coming revolution which, in fact, broke out, six months later.

One experience in Rome, unusual indeed for an Irish Protestant and Tory, came to Godley as a complete surprise. The party went, as tourists do, to have an audience with the Pope, regarding it merely as a sight-seer's visit. The Pope came down the line with his retinue and, on their approaching the Godleys, Frances Wynne observed that the chaplain 'nudged' the Pope and indicated John Robert Godley. The Pope stopped and before giving a general benediction said to him: 'To you belongs the special blessing!' He had been informed that Godley was responsible for appointing Roman Catholic chaplains to the Irish regiments of the British Army.

His throat still disqualified him for work, and, returning to England, he spent the summer at Malvern, exchanging political letters with Adderley. The outlook at the office was less pleasant when Sidney Herbert was raised to the peerage. According to custom he then required a parliamentary under-secretary in the House of Commons, to replace young Lord de Grey, a friend of Godley's who had worked well with him in the War Office. Letters from New Zealand also brought disquieting news since a dispute over the Waitara land, between a native tribe and the New Plymouth settlers, was hardening into war. Godley thought it a test-case for the self-reliant policy. He blamed the colonists, not for oppressing the natives but for lack of an independent spirit. 'Their only notion, on the approach of danger, was to shriek for troops and abuse the imperial government.' He inquired anxiously for news of his favourite Canterbury settlers. Were they volunteering to assist their fellow-colonists in the North Island? Fox and Weld, leaders of the self-reliant party in New Zealand, wrote asking for advice which he gave, through Adderley, with his usual firmness. They should claim full responsibility for native affairs, and protest against interference by the Colonial Office. He wrote to Gladstone to that effect.

But now there was little that he could do for the colonies. Though in July he was able to climb the Malvern Beacon, no inconsiderable hill, he was obliged to write to Adderley after doing so: 'I can't get my throat better, and suffer acute pain from it, especially in swallowing. I don't want you to come and see me just now. My voice is so much affected that I am forbidden to talk, so that it would only tantalize me to have you with me.' A few days later he removed to Scarborough. At the end of the year, most of which had been spent in a vain search for health he noticed sadly that it was the first year since he was fourteen years old in which he had not taken out a game-licence. 'I wonder whether I shall ever take out another.'

Urgent business made it essential for him to return to London in January, 1861. He was to be examined before the Select Committee of the House of Commons on Imperial Defence. His friend Arthur Mills was in the chair, and the whole proceedings of the committee had been arranged to ventilate Godley's views.

The work of the committee was hardly over when Sidney Herbert's health suddenly collapsed. He resigned in July, and died in August, 1861. Godley was deeply affected, not only because Herbert was his friend and patron but also because he felt his own death very near. After writing at length to Adderley on the calm piety of Herbert's death-bed, he added: 'It appears to me that death should by no means be made purposely and (as it were) artificially religious: I dislike therefore the custom of sending for a clergyman, and all that sort of thing. Passing out of life should be neither more nor less religious than passing through it.' Then after alluding to other matters, he wrote on: 'my own opinion is that I shall not recover: according to all rule, indeed, I ought to have died long ago; but I have a peculiar elasticity or toughness, combined with debility of constitution, which seems able to keep me hanging on.' He then turned briskly to business: 'Hawes [the Under-Secretary] is away, which gives me a little more to do just now; not half enough, though.' It was one of his sayings that he would 'rather wear out than rust out'.

London, in those unhygienic days, was shockingly unhealthy in August, and the old War Office in Pall Mall a notably insanitary building. It was afterwards remarked that the mortal illness of the Secretary of State for War was followed in a few months by that of his two chief assistants, for Hawes, too, was sinking.

Godley again spent the summer vacation in Yorkshire, at Whitby. At first he wrote cheerfully to Adderley, taking great delight in the appointment, by his friend Newcastle, of his friend Charles Monck as Governor-general of Canada. Monck had been one of his associates on the land-lords' committee in Dublin, fifteen years earlier. He now carried off Godley's younger brother, Denis, to Canada as his private secretary. But the air of Whitby brought no relief and Godley was visibly dying. In October, feeling stronger for a moment, he returned to London and to the War Office, at the urgent desire of Hawes who wanted help, which he could give for a few weeks only. Until the last day of his life his work was brought from the War Office to his bedroom. Some impurity in the water-supply had given him diarrhoea which, in his weak state, he was unable to shake off. He began to set his affairs in final order, writing to his father to unburden his conscience of a debt of honour. There was a sum of £1,500 outstanding which he had borrowed, on his expectations, at the time of his marriage. He wished to assure his father that he had funds to meet the obligation, which would not be a charge on the family property. At last, on 16th November he wrote to his youngest brother, then at Killegar:

'Dearest Archie, give my father the enclosed when he is alone. It is to tell him I am dying. God bless you and goodbye, my dear brother. Do not think of coming over. I hate last interviews and they only do harm. I need not tell you to prohibit positively anything so insane as my father and mother coming. You and Denis are my executors. Write a line to James and Harriet. Ever your most affectionate, J. R. GODLEY.'

The last word was for his son, Arthur. In his reminis-cences Lord Kilbracken wrote fifty-five years later, of his schoolboy reverence for his austere, reserved father. No parent could have been kinder or more just, though he rarely unbent and had no knack of being easy with children.

Arthur had given his father some concern that summer, by his precocity at his studies. He had been sent to Radley, the new school founded by William Sewell, their old family friend and, at fourteen years old, had exhausted its resources; he was already at the top of the highest form. The intention had been to send him on to Harrow, his father's school, but now, at short notice, there was no vacancy. The next best thing was to get him into Rugby, which was arranged through the influence of Adderley and Selfe, as governors of the school. Arthur was no sooner put down for Rugby than it became necessary to bring him home to recuperate after some childish ailment. He found his father ill but had no suspicion that the illness was mortal. 'I had been at home for a week or more,' he wrote, 'when one morning I was told that he wished to see me. I went cheerfully into his room, bidding him good-morning, as usual, when, to my amazement, he told me that he was going to die, spoke his last words to me, and dismissed me: and in the afternoon he died.'

Only Adderley was sent for, and he arrived too late. It was 17th November, 1861.

* * * * *

Old John Godley was 'quite felled to the ground' by the premature death of his talented eldest son, but lingered two years more. He died in 1863. Charlotte Godley lived on at Gloucester Place with her son and her four daughters; her widowhood was longer than that of Queen Victoria.

* * * * *

The news of Godley's death reached New Zealand in 70 days, since by that time steamships plied to Australia. The Provincial Council of Canterbury, as was due to their founder, resolved to erect a statue of Godley in the principal public square at Christchurch. Woolner, the Pre-Raphaelite sculptor, was commissioned by Lord Lyttelton to execute it and, when it was erected in 1867, Godley's friends pronounced it an excellent likeness. It is the most revealing portrait of him that survives. The first public monument erected in New Zealand, it stood for some years in a waste space of hutments, horse-standings, and empty sites over-grown with weeds, a symbol of faith that the cathedral, college, and civil offices which he had planned would yet arise in decent masonry around it, a faith that was not belied.

FitzGerald wrote a memoir of his friend and prefixed it to a volume of his public speeches and official despatches, which were published in Christchurch. These tributes to their founder were paid in the colony, as duty required; but, for a man whose name was unknown to the English public, whose death passed unnoticed by the London newspapers, the tribute paid by his English friends was remarkable. Adderley prepared a volume of Godley's personal letters for private circulation among his friends, dedicating it to Lyttelton as a memorial of 'one of the most leading minds, and soundest judgments, and most uncompromising con-sciences' they knew. This volume, said Gladstone, was Godley's best monument. In old age, Adderley used to say that he wished to be judged by Godley's letters to him.

No man is upon his oath when composing an epitaph, and Lyttelton, who was celebrated for his skill in such com-positions, may be thought to have written too warmly of Godley's merits in the Latin eulogy which he wrote for a memorial tablet in Harrow School Chapel. Its validity is, however, endorsed by a Prime Minister, a Lord Chancellor, a Secretary of State, a Viceroy of India, a Governor-general of Canada, a Minister to the United States, and a Prime Minister of New Zealand, who united with others of Godley's friends to record their names beneath Lyttelton's inscription. It runs thus in translation:—

'John Robert Godley, a steadfast and great-hearted man if ever one lived, born to control affairs and manage men. As a young man he travelled, observantly, through his native land and parts of America. He was among the first to recall the attention of his contemporaries to the precepts of our forefathers, by which colonies should be not so much ruled as founded. He planned, led and established the flourishing settlement at Canterbury, and held it dear to his heart as long as he lived. On his return he accomplished tasks of outstanding merit in our military councils; but died, as is said, an untimely death, borne down by ill health which prevented him from reaching the highest rank. Here, at his old school, this memorial has been placed by those few of his friends to whom he was most strongly attached.'

Among those who combined to erect this memorial, Gladstone bore the greatest name, and Gladstone spoke of Godley as ἄναξ ἀνδρῶν, a king among men, using the phrase that Homer used of Agamemnon. Unable to do more for Godley, Gladstone transferred his affection to Godley's son, Arthur, whom he made his private secretary. Arthur Godley was sometimes astonished at the respect paid to his father's memory by his friends. In 1868, the year of Gladstone's first administration, Arthur Godley was a young undergraduate at Balliol and somewhat awed at the prospect of taking breakfast with the celebrated Dr Jowett, who usually said something unexpected. He surprised young Godley by saying 'I suppose you know that if your father were alive he would be a member of the Cabinet to-day'. Roundell Palmer described Godley as a 'born politician' whose noble life was too soon cut short. The Duke of Newcastle, Colonial Secretary at the time of Godley's death, corresponded with him regularly on political matters and treasured his letters.

FitzGerald, who had seen him at work in New Zealand, wrote some lines of high praise which reveal, nevertheless, the reason why the influence of his personality acted most strongly upon those who knew him best. He never enjoyed, nor sought, nor valued common popularity. 'There was one feature in his character which was not a popular one, and which he never cared to conceal or control, and that was his unmitigated hatred and contempt for humbug of every kind: whether it appeared in the form of dishonesty in money matters, or hypocrisy in religion, or of corruption in public life, or, what is still common enough with us, of vulgar pretension, it met with little mercy at Mr. Godley's hands. Honorable himself up to the loftiest standards of chivalry, he shrunk instinctively from anything like trickery, public or private, in other men. Such a man is sure to be hated and feared by some, so long as deceit and fraud shall find a resting-place upon earth. The example and influence of such a man in so small a community must have been great beyond measure.'

Lyttelton, who knew all the lions of Victorian society, said that Godley was 'the man of all whom I have known, the best fitted to be a leader of men in the conducting of a great enterprise'. But the faithful Adderley was the one among Godley's friends who lived to report him and his cause aright. Adderley lived to a ripe old age, was loaded with honours—he was raised to the peerage as Lord Norton —and held many high offices of state. In a long life of public service, devoted to improved housing, town-planning, the safety of shipping, reformatory schools, and countless other good causes, he never lost sight of the ideal which Godley had planted in his mind, a free, enlightened, and self-reliant spirit in the colonies. He played a great part in abolishing convict transportation, in providing Cape Colony and New Zealand with liberal constitutions; he conducted the passage of the British North America Act through the House of Commons and was thus one of the founders of the Dominion of Canada. In 1850 he admitted that he felt lost since Godley had gone to New Zealand, in 1903 he was still pamphleteering for a free and united Empire, still quoting Wakefield and Godley as its major prophets.

Appendices

APPENDIX A

Letter to Mr. Gladstone, on the Government of the Colonies

To the Right Hon. W. E. Gladstone, M.P.

MY DEAR MR GLADSTONE,

On the eve of leaving England for one of our most distant colonies, I cannot resist the desire of saying a few words before I go, to the British public, on the subject of colonial politics, under the new aspect which they have lately assumed; a subject in which I have long been speculatively interested, and in which I am now about to acquire a deep and immediate personal concern. And I have ventured, with your kind permission, to prefix your name to my observations; not from any presumed accordance between your views and my own, but simply because, as you seem to me to be the one among our leading statesmen who has most fully considered the question of colonial reform, so you are the one most likely to appreciate and encourage the humblest effort to advance that cause.

Judging, indeed, from the speeches which you have made during the last two sessions, and from the line of conduct which you think it right to adopt with reference to this question, I infer that you do not agree with me; that is, that you are far from estimating so highly as I do the danger which threatens our colonial empire, and the necessity of meeting it promptly by measures of thorough reform. If you did, I feel sure (from my faith in your patriotism and public spirit) that, waiving all considerations of a personal and party nature, you would stand forth as the active champion of those searching remedies by which alone the disease which is consuming our greatness can now be cured. I speak confidently, perhaps presumptuously, but my convictions have at least not been formed without much thought and observation. My occupations have for some time past thrown me into habitual intercourse with colonists personally, and acquaintance with the various organs of colonial opinion. No one has had better opportunities of appreciating the immense change which has lately come over the colonial mind, and the utter hopelessness of satisfying it *now* with 'gradual instalments' of freedom. A year or two ago I thought, as perhaps you think now, that, though a system so absurd in theory, and so unsuccessful in practice as that by which our colonies are ruled, must break down sooner or later, still it might last indefinitely—for ten years to come, or perhaps for twenty; and that our efforts might safely be directed to a *gradual* amelioration of it. I am now convinced that I was wrong: the real danger is, not that the despotism of the Colonial Office will last ten or twenty years—not that the colonists will be oppressed by it for an indefinite time to come—but that it may last just long enough to break up the British Empire; a consummation which, at the present rate of progress, will not perhaps take a great deal more than ten or twenty *months*. I should be very glad now to be as sure that the flag of my country will not be hauled down during my lifetime in any part of the Queen's dominions, as I am that the hours of 'Mr Mother-country's' reign are numbered. The point, therefore, which I am most anxious to urge upon you, as upon all Colonial reformers, is, that whereas they have hitherto pleaded in the interests, as they thought, of suffering colonies alone, they must now plead in the interests of British honour and British supremacy; that whereas the alternative has hitherto appeared to lie between local self-government and the centralism of Downing Street, now it is between local self-government and national independence. Many causes have contributed to this change in the aspect of the question; but the chief of them are these—first, the increased strength of the colonies, or rather (perhaps) their increased consciousness of strength; and secondly, the growth in England of a political school holding the doctrine that the colonies ought to be abandoned. As I am anxious to avoid even the semblance of writing in a party spirit, I forbear to enlarge on the stimulus imparted to the operation of both these causes by the persevering mismanagement to which the colonies have been of late subjected; but it would be mere affectation to ignore altogether an influence so undeniable and so important.

On the one hand, I say, the colonists have acquired an increased confidence in their own strength; a confidence derived not only from the knowledge that their material resources are yearly increasing, but also from the moral power which is imparted by the experience of successful conflicts. Not only has the Colonial Office received many damaging defeats of late, but it has so timed its resistance and its concessions as to give precisely the utmost possible encouragement to colonial revolt. Canada, for example, gained by rebellion nearly all for the sake of which she rebelled, and which during years of peaceful agitation she had been refused; and she is now given to understand very plainly by official people, that the rest of her demands will be similarly granted, if she apply in a similar way. New South Wales, too, has more than once within the last two years repulsed the aggressions of the colonial minister. But the turning point of the conflict I consider to be the successful resistance of the Cape of Good Hope. It is morally impossible that the authority of Downing Street over the colonies can long survive the shock which it has just received in South Africa. That small and feeble but high-minded dependency has taught a lesson which others, more powerful at once and more aggrieved, will not be slow to learn. The machinery which she has employed for her special purpose may be employed by any other colony for any other purpose with respect to which the colonists shall be at issue with the Imperial Government; and, if equal energy and unanimity be displayed, with equal success. It will be used to obtain immunity from convict emigration in every shape; to acquire local self-government, or even to assert independence. Fortified places we may continue to hold, and naval stations: but I think it is henceforth established that we cannot govern, or even occupy, a distant colony permanently without the consent of its population. It would be useless to deny that these facts, and the knowledge of them prevailing among colonists, are very dangerous under present circumstances to the stability of the Empire.

On the other hand, a political school has grown up in this country which is supposed to advocate the abandonment of

colonies, on the ground that they do not 'pay'. I say supposed
to advocate, because I do not know that the doctrine has yet
been distinctly stated and fairly *avowed*. Still, there is no moral
doubt of its being in fact held, or of its being in accordance with
the general tone and views proclaimed by a powerful and
increasing class of English politicians. With those who enter-
tain this anti-Imperial doctrine, I need hardly tell you that I feel
no sympathy; but I cannot help perceiving how formidable it is,
because it falls in with the positive and material character of
the age, and especially with the habits of thought prevailing
among the now very powerful middle classes of this country.
Moreover, I see manifold grounds for believing that statesmen
of far higher position and greater mark (some from spite, and
more from indolence) regard the possibility of a separation
between England and her colonies without any kind of dissatisfaction. 'Mr Mothercountry' is of opinion, no doubt, that
if our colonial empire is not to be kept as a toy for *him* to play
with, it is not worth keeping at all. On the whole, then, it
appears to me that we are on the eve of what may truly be
called a revolution in our Colonial relations; and that during
the next year or two, in all probability, it will be decided whether
'the British Empire' is to endure and to grow, as it has hitherto
grown, for an indefinite time to come, or whether it is to shrink
by a rapid progress of disintegration into the dimensions of two
small islands. Now, although to me, an intending colonist, this
consideration is one of deep and momentous import, it will
appear, I fear, to a large portion of my countrymen a matter of
comparative indifference. There are powerful and popular
reasoners who will soon inquire openly, as they now do by
implication, 'What shall we lose by separation? If, as you say,
colonies are no longer to be used as fields of official patronage
—no longer to be debarred, for our profit, from the commerce
of the world—no longer to be made receptacles for the surplus
population of our gaols—if, in short, their proper functions are
to be henceforth undischarged, what, we beg leave to ask, is
the good of colonies?' This will soon become the question of the
day; and it is one for which it behoves us to prepare betimes an
answer.

The best argument, perhaps, against separation, is to be
found in the strength and prevalence of a moral instinct which

separatists do not recognize, and which they hardly understand, though they bear a strong testimony to its truth in the remarkable reluctance which they manifest to *avow* their doctrines. A true patriot personifies and idealizes his country, and rejoices in her greatness, her glory, and her pre-eminence, as a loving son would exult in the triumphs of a parent. Doubtless such greatness and glory may be too dearly bought; but that is not the question. I say that, independently of reasoning they are *felt* to possess a great and real although an immaterial value, and that they are the more keenly so felt in the most heroic periods of a nation's history, and by the best and noblest of its sons. Nay, I maintain, that the love of empire, properly understood—that is, the instinct of self-development and expansion—is an unfailing symptom of lusty and vigorous life in a people; and that, subject to the conditions of justice and humanity, it is not only legitimate, but most laudable. Certain I am, that the decline of such a feeling is always the result, not of matured wisdom or enlarged philanthropy, but of luxurious imbecility and selfish sloth. When the Roman eagles retreated across the Danube, not the loss of Dacia, but the satisfaction of the Roman people at the loss, was the omen of the Empire's fall. Or, to take an illustration nearer home, it is unquestionable that, notwithstanding the disgraceful circumstances under which America was torn from the grasp of England, we suffered less in prestige and in strength by that obstinate and disastrous struggle, than if, like the soft Triumvir, we had 'lost a world, and been content to lose it'. Depend upon it, the instinct of national pride is sound and true; and it is no foolish vanity which makes Englishmen shrink from the idea of seeing their country diminished and humbled in the eyes of the world.

But the case of those who defend the preservation of our colonies does not rest on any such instinct alone; it rests also on perfectly tangible and material grounds. I will admit, for the sake of argument, that our trade with the colonies *might* not suffer by separation, though I have little doubt in fact that it *would*. A certain kind of emigration, too, such as that which now proceeds to the United States, would of course go on. But there would be no good colonization: no English gentlemen—indeed few Englishmen of any class who were not bad specimens of it—would deliberately renounce their allegiance, and place themselves in a position where they might be called upon, by their duty to their adopted country, to fight against the country which gave them birth. They would not consent to stand towards their friends and kindred in the relation of 'foreigners'; they would never give up the name, the rights, and the privileges of Englishmen. This may be a very foolish and unphilosophical feeling; but experience as well as theory shows that it is entertained: and consequently, by making 'foreign countries' of our colonies, we should cut off on the one hand the best part of the British nation from colonization, and on the other we should abandon the plain duty of building up society *in its best form* throughout those wide regions which are destined to be peopled by our descendants. We should deliberately provide for the construction of hostile democracies out of the worst of the materials which compose the British people. Again, the union of the provinces which make up the British Empire constitutes a positive element of material strength. It is perhaps true, that now the value of our colonies may be counterbalanced by their cost; but such has been the case only since the invention of the Colonial Office—that is, since we have made colonies effeminate by our protection and disaffected by our tyranny. The early British colonies contributed largely, both in men and money, to the military expenses of the Imperial treasury; they fitted out privateers to destroy the commerce of the common enemy; nor did they confine themselves to the defence of their own territory against aggression, but single-handed they conquered and kept new realms for England. Why should we doubt that modern British colonies, if allowed similar liberty, would show equal loyalty? Their Imperial patriotism is a thing of which we at home have but a faint idea. Until they are spoiled by bad government, they delight in their connexion with England, they worship the British flag, their eyes fill with tears at the thought of 'home', and their highest boast is the share they claim in the triumphs of English literature, arts, and arms.

But, notwithstanding their good natural dispositions towards us, there is one thing which colonists will not endure at our hands—and that is, being governed from Downing Street. They would not be Englishmen if they did. By a steady and persevering course of distant government, we *do* succeed in destroying, to a very great extent, the love of mother-country, and implanting in its place a feeling which is peculiar to colonies governed from home, a feeling made up of jealous dislike and cowardly dependence. But this is factitiously engendered, and would disappear with the causes that produced it. The normal sentiment of colonists towards England greatly resembles that felt by ourselves towards our Sovereigns. We should not like them to *govern* us; but so long as they abstain from that, our affection of them is not only enthusiastic, but deep and real. We rejoice in their joys, and sympathize with their sorrows, as matters in which we have a personal interest; nay, I fully believe that there are not many individuals in this island who would hesitate to sacrifice property and life in order to save the Queen from indignity or danger. Of a like nature is the feeling which colonists cherish for an ideal England; and I would ask those who hold that its existence and maintenance are of no importance, whether loyalty such as I have described (and such as is perfectly consistent with a determination to be self-governed) does not exercise a powerful and ennobling influence on the national character and national history of England?

It may seem that I have unnecessarily insisted on the desirableness of the colonial connexion, and that I should have better employed my time in explaining and defending the practical means which I would propose for preserving it. I do not think so, however; and I am sure time will show that I am right. I am not going to waste arguments in support of the Municipal system as applied to colonial government, because, in fact, everything has been said that can be said on that side of the question, whilst, literally, nothing worth notice has been said on the other. Besides, we really have passed the argumentative stage in this part of the business. That the Central system, whether right or wrong, will be speedily abolished, no man with a grain of political foresight can doubt. I repeat, that the only question which remains to be settled is, whether its abolition shall be the result of a dissolution of our colonial empire or not. I have therefore confined myself to urging a proposition which will be much more seriously debated—namely, that such a dissolution is neither unavoidable nor desirable, but pre-eminently the reverse.

But it is necessary for me to state what I mean by local self-government; as the phrase, though hackneyed, has been much abused. I do *not* mean, then, mere powers of paving and lighting and road-making; nor the privilege of initiatory legislation; nor the liberty of making subordinate official appointments; I do not mean a regimen involving the reservation of civil lists, or the interposition of vetoes, or any other of those provisions in virtue of which Ministers in Downing Street are in the habit of interfering with the internal concerns of colonies. I mean by local self-government, the right and power to do, within the limits of each colony respectively, without check, control, or intervention of any kind, everything that the supreme Government of this country can do within the limits of the British Islands—*with one exception.* I allude to the prerogative of regulating relations with foreign powers. This one prerogative, the concentration of which is essential to Imperial unity, the colonists themselves would gladly see reserved, in exchange for the privilege and the security of being identified with the Empire: but more than this it is neither beneficial nor possible for us to retain. I need hardly say that my idea of self-government includes the power of making and altering local constitutions. We ought not, I am sure, to impose upon the colonists any form of government whatever, even to start with. When we shall have duly authorized them to act for themselves, our function with regard to their internal affairs should end. Paper constitutions, drawn up by amateurs without personal interest in the subject, never answer. All the best of the old colonial constitutions were framed by the colonists; and while many of them have endured, with hardly an alteration, for more than two hundred years, all of them, whether altered from the originals or not, give (being home-made) perfect satisfaction to those who live under them. I have yet to hear of a Colonial Office constitution which has lasted ten years, or given a moment's satisfaction to any one but the doctrinaires who drew it. I define, then, the proper conditions (as they appear to me) of a colonial relation to the Mother-country in three terms—1, an acknowledged allegiance; 2, a common citizenship; 3, an offensive and defensive alliance. Less than these it is idle to offer, because to these, after whatever struggles, we shall come at last; only that if granted after struggles, and not freely, they will perhaps lose all their efficacy.

As a matter of course, colonies enjoying, as those of New England did, the perfect administration of their own affairs, ought not to cost the Mother-country a shilling for their government; and I am confident that, like Massachusetts and Pennsylvania of old, they would regard total pecuniary independence of the Mother-country as an important means of preserving their municipal privileges.

There is, I suppose, little doubt that even the Colonial Office will think it necessary to 'do something' in the way of colonial reform next year; nay, that what they do will be in advance on the absurd measures proposed last session; but I cannot bring myself to believe that they will do anything 'thorough', and I most earnestly hope that the friends of the colonies will not be satisfied with anything less. We must hear no more of 'gradual ameliorations'; things have gone much too far for experiments and instalments; and the session after next it may be too late for *reform*. I conclude by repeating, that if to you at home the issue of this impending struggle be a matter of comparative indifference, I can answer for it that to British colonists it will appear one of absolutely vital moment. For my own part, I can only say, that though I might consent, in spite of reason and experience to live in a colony permanently governed by a Minister in London, I would neither do so myself, nor ask others to do so, if the colony we founded were destined during our lifetime to be separated from the Mother-country. It is in the hope of seeing the only means adopted by which you can avert such a consummation that I now leave England.

Believe me, my dear Mr Gladstone,

Yours very faithfully,

JOHN ROBERT GODLEY.

Plymouth, Dec. 12, 1849.

APPENDIX B

List of Members of the Canterbury Association as published in May 1848, with biographical notes.*

PRESIDENT. *Archbishop of Canterbury* (J. B. Sumner, 1780–
1862. Educ. Eton and King's Coll. Cambridge. Promoted to the Archbishopric only in Feb. 1848.)

Archbishop of Dublin (R. Whately, 1787–1863. Educ.
Oriel Coll. Oxford. Long interested in Irish emigration.)

Duke of Buccleuch (the 5th Duke, 1806–1884. Educ.
St. John's Coll. Cambridge.)

Marquess of Cholmondeley (the 3rd Marquess, 1800–
1884. Educ. Eton and Christ Church, Oxford.)

Earl of Ellesmere (F. Egerton, the 1st Earl, 1800–1857.
Educ. Eton and Christ Church, Oxford.)

Earl of Harewood (the 3rd Earl, 1797–1857, a soldier,
wounded at Waterloo.)

Earl of Lincoln (1811–1864. Educ. Eton and Christ
Church, Oxford. Succeeded his father as 5th Duke of
Newcastle, Secretary of State for War and the
Colonies, etc. Served on the Managing Committee of
the Association in 1851.)

Viscount Mandeville, M.P. (1823–1890. A soldier, had
served at the Cape. Succeeded his father as 7th Duke
of Manchester. Afterwards President of the R. Col.
Institute.)

* In this list those marked with an asterisk were original members of the
Committee of Management.

THE GODLEY STATUE, CATHEDRAL SQUARE, CHRISTCHURCH
Bronze by T. Woolner. Photograph by Dr A. C. Barker, 13 January, 1869.

Bishop of London (C. J. Blomfield, 1786–1857. Educ. Trinity Coll. Cambridge.)

Bishop of Winchester (C. R. Sumner, 1790–1874. Educ. Trinity Coll. Cambridge. Brother to the Archbishop.)

Bishop of Exeter (H. Phillpotts, 1778–1869. Educ. Corpus Christi Coll. Oxford.)

Bishop of Ripon (C. T. Longley, 1794–1868. Educ. Westminster and Christ Church, Oxford. Formerly Headmaster of Harrow and Godley's headmaster, afterwards Archbishop of Canterbury.)

Bishop of St. Davids (C. Thirlwall, 1797–1875. Educ. Trinity Coll. Cambridge.)

Bishop of Oxford (S. Wilberforce, 1805–1873. Educ. Oriel Coll. Oxford.)

Bishop W. H. Coleridge (1789–1849. Educ. Christ Church, Oxford. Retired Bishop of Barbados.)

Viscount Alford, M.P. (J. H. Cust, 1779–1853. Educ. Christ Church, Oxford, afterwards Earl Brownlow.)

Lord Ashburton (William Baring the 2nd Baron, 1799–1864. Educ. Oriel Coll. Oxford.)

*Lord Lyttelton (George William, the 4th Baron, 1817–1876. Educ. Eton and Trinity Coll. Cambridge, formerly Under-secretary for the Colonies, afterwards chairman of the Public Schools Commission.)

Lord Ashley, M.P. (1801–1885. Educ. Harrow and Christ Church, Oxford. Succeeded his father as 7th Earl of Shaftesbury. The great philanthropist.)

*Lord Courtenay, M.P. (1816–1888. Educ. Westminster and Christ Church, Oxford. Succeeded his father as 11th Earl of Devon.)

Lord Alfred Hervey, M.P. (1816–1875, son of the Marquess of Bristol. Educ. Eton and Trinity Coll. Cambridge.)

Lord John Manners, M.P. (1818–1906. Educ. Trinity Coll. Cambridge. Leader of the 'Young England' party. Succeeded his father as 7th Duke of Rutland.)

*Sir W. Farquhar, Bart. (1810–1900. Educ. Christ Church, Oxford. Barrister of Lincoln's Inn.)

Sir W. Heathcote, Bart, M.P. (1801–1881. Educ. Winchester and Oriel Coll. Oxford.)

Sir Walter James, Bart. (1816–1893. Educ. Christ Church, Oxford, afterwards Lord Northbourne. A close friend of Gladstone's. Named in Godley's will as guardian of his children in the event of Mrs Godley's death before they should come of age.)

Sir Willoughby Jones, Bart., M.P. (1820–1884. Educ. Trinity Coll. Cambridge.)

Rt. Hon. H. Goulburn, M.P. (1784–1856. Educ. Trinity Coll. Cambridge, formerly Chancellor of the Exchequer in Peel's administration.)

Rt. Hon. Sidney Herbert, M.P. (1810–1861. Educ. Harrow and Oriel Coll. Oxford. Afterwards Secretary of State for War, *etc.* Raised to the peerage as Lord Herbert of Lea.)

Hon. Sir E. Cust (1794–1878. General in the Army.)

Dean of Canterbury (W. R. Lyall, 1788–1857. Educ. Trinity Coll. Cambridge.)

*C. B. Adderley, M.P. (1814–1905. Educ. Christ Church, Oxford. Afterwards Under-secretary for the Colonies, President of the Board of Trade, K.C.M.G., 1st Lord Norton, *etc.*)

W. H. Pole-Carew, M.P. (1811–1888. Educ. Oriel Coll. Oxford. Godley stayed in his house while awaiting the departure of the *Lady Nugent*.)

*Hon. R. Cavendish, M.P. (1794–1876. Son of Lord Waterpark of Co. Cork. Served under the East India Company. A wealthy landowner, of Thornton Park, Bucks.)

*Hon. F. Charteris, M.P. (1818–1914. Educ. Christ Church, Oxford. Afterwards Lord Elcho and 10th Earl of Wemyss.)

*T. Somers Cocks, M.P. (1815–188(?). Educ. Christ Church, Oxford, Banker to J. R. Godley and to the Canterbury Association. Mrs. Godley's brother-in-law.)

*Rev. Edward Coleridge (1801–1883. Educ. at Corpus Christi Coll. Oxford. Asst. master at Eton.)

*William Forsyth, M.P. (1812–1899. Educ. Trinity Coll. Cambridge. Barrister of Lincoln's Inn. A parliamentary counsel.)

Rev. G. R. Gleig (1796–1888. Educ. Magdalen Hall, Oxford. Chaplain-general to the Forces.)

J. R. Godley (1814–1861. Educ. Harrow and Christ Church, Oxford.)

E. S. Halswell, Q.C. (d. 1874. Educ. St. John's Coll. Cambridge. Barrister of the Middle Temple. Formerly, for a short time, a government officer in New Zealand.)

Ven. Archdeacon J. C. Hare (1795–1855. Educ. Trinity Coll. Cambridge. Author of philosophical and other works.)

Rev. E. Hawkins (1802–1868. Educ. Balliol Coll. Oxford. Secretary to the Society for the Propagation of the Gospel.)

Rev. Dr S. Hinds (1793–1872. Educ. Queen's Coll. Oxford, formerly of Codrington College, Barbados, then, successively, chaplain of Abp. Whately, Dean of Carlisle, and Bp. of Norwich.)

Rev. Dr W. F. Hook (1798–1875. Educ. Winchester and Christ Church, Oxford. Afterwards Dean of Chichester.)

J. Hutt. (Governor of Western Australia, 1839–1846.)

G. K. Rickards (1812–1889. Educ. Balliol Coll. Oxford. Afterwards Professor of Political Economy at Oxford, and K.C.B. Served on the Managing Committee of the Association in 1851.)

J. Simeon, M.P. (1815–1870. Educ. Christ Church, Oxford. Barrister of Lincoln's Inn. On the death of his father, became Sir John Simeon, Bart. of Swainston. A close friend of the poet, Tennyson.)

Augustus Stafford, M.P. (1811–1857, formerly known as Stafford O'Brien. Educ. Trinity Coll. Cambridge. In politics a Derby-ite.)

Hon. J. Talbot (1806–1852. Educ. Charterhouse and Christ Church, Oxford. Barrister of Lincoln's Inn.)

Rev. C. M. Torlesse (d. 1874. Educ. Harrow and Trinity Coll. Cambridge. Vicar of Stoke-by-Nayland, Essex. A relative of E. G. Wakefield.)

Rev. R. C. Trench (1807–1886. Educ. Harrow and Trinity Coll. Cambridge. Professor of Divinity at King's Coll. London, and afterwards Abp. of Dublin.)

E. Jerningham Wakefield (1820–1879. Only son of E. G. Wakefield; an experienced colonist.)

Ven. Archdeacon R. Wilberforce (1802–1857. Brother to Bp. of Oxford. Educ. Oriel Coll. Oxford. A leading 'Tractarian' who became a Roman Catholic in 1854.)

SECRETARY. *H. F. Alston,* 41 Charing Cross.

Among those who joined the Association later, some active members were:

Sir J. T. Coleridge (1790–1876. Educ. Eton and Corpus Christi Coll. Oxford. Judge.)

J. D. Coleridge (1820–1894. Educ. Eton and Balliol Coll. Oxford. Afterwards Lord Chief Justice. Son of Sir J. T. Coleridge.)

Rev. T. Jackson (1812–1886. Educ. St. Mary Hall, Oxford. Prebendary of St. Paul's, *etc.* 'Bishop-designate of Lyttelton', 1850.)

S. Lucas (1818–1868. Educ. Queen's Coll. Oxford. Historian and journalist.)

F. A. McGeachy (1809–1887. Educ. Balliol Coll. Oxford. Barrister of Lincoln's Inn. M.P. A public-school reformer.)

H. S. Selfe (1810–1870. Educ. Glasgow University. Stipendiary magistrate in London. Legal adviser to Lyttelton.)

Henry Sewell (1807–1879. Solicitor. Deputy-chairman of the Association 1850–2, agent in New Zealand, 1853–5. Afterwards prominent in New Zealand politics.)

Lord Wodehouse (1826–1902. Educ. Eton and Christ Church, Oxford. Afterwards Earl of Kimberley and Secretary of State for the Colonies.)

C. G. Wynne (1815–1874. Educ. Eton and Christ Church, Oxford. Mrs Godley's brother. Changed his name to Wynne-Finch. M.P.)

Rev. J. C. Wynter (1807–1877. Educ. St. John's Coll. Oxford. Rector of Gatton.)

APPENDIX C

*Names of Godley's friends
inscribed on the Memorial in Harrow School Chapel*.*

*C. B. ADDERLEY	*DUKE OF NEWCASTLE
*T. SOMERS COCKS	R. PALMER
*EARL OF DEVON	SIR R. H. POLLEN
*J. E. FITZGERALD	*SIR J. SIMEON
W. E. GLADSTONE	SIR E. THORNTON
LORD DE GREY	W. P. PRENDERGAST
M. J. HIGGINS	*C. G. WYNNE
*SIR W. JAMES	ARTHUR MILLS
*LORD LYTTELTON	*H. S. SELFE
LORD MONCK	*F. A. McGEACHY
W. MONSELL	HON. E. TWISLETON

W. E. Gladstone (1808–1898) was educated at Eton and Christ Church, Oxford. In 1862 he was Chancellor of the Exchequer, and later, was Prime Minister of the United Kingdom.

George Robinson, Earl de Grey (1827–1909), educated privately. In 1862 he was Under-Secretary for War, and later, as Marquess of Ripon, was Viceroy of India.

M. J. Higgins (1810–1868), educated at Eton and University College, Oxford. Journalist, wrote under the name of 'Jacob Omnium'. An expert on Ireland and on the West Indies.

* Those marked with an asterisk appear in the list of members of the Canterbury Association (see page 224).

Charles, 4th Viscount Monck (1819–1894), educated at Trinity College, Dublin. Was Governor-general of Canada in 1862.

William Monsell (1812–1894), educated at Winchester and Oriel College, Oxford. M.P. Held high appointments in the War Office and, later, was Under-Secretary for the Colonies. Raised to the peerage as Lord Emly.

Roundell Palmer (1812–1895), educated at Winchester and Christ Church, Oxford. Afterwards Earl of Selborne and Lord Chancellor.

Sir R. H. Pollen, Bart. (1816–1881), educated at Eton and Christ Church, Oxford. Married Godley's sister.

Sir E. Thornton (1817–1906), educated at Pembroke College, Cambridge. British Minister at Washington, 1866.

W. P. Prendergast (d. 1902), educated at Harrow and Trinity College, Oxford. Barrister in Dublin.

Arthur Mills (1816–1898), educated at Rugby and Balliol College, Oxford. M.P.

Hon. E. Twisleton (1809–1874), educated at Balliol College, Oxford. Barrister. Served on several Royal Commissions.

APPENDIX D

*Very rough notes on the organization
of the War Department*

Sept. 20*th,* 1855.

The following are my ideas as to what the outline of the organization of the War Dept. should be. The details I could only fill up so far as regards what is called the Ordnance Branch of it.

The primary and essential defect of the system under which our Military administration was conducted before the late changes, was its want of unity. It may be said that all our reforms have been endeavours after unity. When I speak of unity, I mean of course unity of purpose and design, of which the proper accompaniment and accessory is separation of instruments—one head working by many hands. It is evident that this object has been very imperfectly attained, and till it shall have been attained it is to be feared that no results adequate to the inconvenience and risk of extensive change will accrue.

Our Constitution forbids, or is supposed to forbid, administrative unity in its highest phase. This can only be had, where a single man, King, Dictator, or President, is really at the head of the Executive Government. Here, unless where a high Minister, of the calibre of Pitt or Peel, exercises Dictatorial power in his Cabinet, the best we can hope for is Departmental Unity. If there be any one Department more than another where unity is required, it is the Dept. of War. This is not the place to enlarge upon or explain the advantages of unity in warlike administration—advantages which are indeed self-evident. I will confine myself to stating shortly the means by which I think they may best be secured.

In the first place at the head of the pyramid should be the Secretary of State for War. Being like other Ministers, responsible to Parliament, he may be assumed to agree with and represent the nation in sentiments and policy. When he ceases to do so, he ceases to be a Minister. He may therefore be trusted with more extensive and peculiar powers than could safely be committed to a non-political soldier. The Secretary of State for War should be supreme over all warlike operations. He should direct, administer and govern the military service, as well as those civil departments which are immediately connected with and accessory to, warlike operations. He should have, in the last resort, the supreme control of all appointments and promotions in the army. Under him, at the head of the army, should be the Commander-in-Chief; a non-political officer, holding his place by the same tenure as Military appointments are now held and acting as *adviser* of the War Minister in military matters. He should be, as the Commander-in-Chief now is, responsible for the government, discipline, distribution, and movements of the troops, and he might be practically entrusted, to a great extent, with the disposal of appointments and promotions, but only in the way of recommendation, and subject as I have before said to the paramount control of the Secretary for War. As this part of the question is sure to give rise to difference of opinion, I will dwell on it somewhat further. It is objected by many that by giving the patronage of the army to a politician we should make soldiers politicians, i.e. partisans, and consequently dangerous to order or to liberty. My reply is twofold; in the first place, it is an undeniable fact that other departments of the service, in which the patronage *is* wielded by political partisans, have not themselves become impregnated with political partisanship to any perceptible, far less to any dangerous, extent. There are as many political soldiers as political sailors. The Duke of Wellington and Lord Hardinge were more political than Nelson or Collingwood; as political as any great sailor ever was. Although for 25 years the patronage of the Navy has been almost uninterruptedly dispensed by 'Liberal' Ministers, I never heard of a Whig majority in this frigate, or of the Radicals having it all their own way in that three-decker, while on the other hand I *have* heard of messes where it was not considered very safe or pleasant to run counter to the prevalent tone of fashionable Toryism. If the servants of the Colonial Office be politicians, as in their origin they often must be, they certainly don't let their party politics affect their official conduct. Who troubles his head to remember what political party Sir Henry Ward and Sir William Denison, and Sir Henry Barkly, originally belonged to, or believes that their administration of the provinces they govern is injuriously affected by their party connexions at home?

But, in the second place, I maintain that *promotions* in the army which are the largest part of patronage, might be practically left to the Commander-in-Chief. It may even be provided by Order in Council that in all cases he shall recommend, and that in no case shall the Secretary of State overrule his recommendation, without placing his reasons for doing so on record; which would certainly provide a security against anything like frequent or undue interference. If it be said that practically a political head would manage to monopolize the patronage of the Dept., I reply by pointing to the Inland Revenue, with which I happen to be practically acquainted. It is connected with, and subordinate to, the most 'political' (in the patronage sense of the word) of all the public departments; namely, the Treasury, and all the first appointments are avowedly made on parliamentary recommendations, but *there* the interference of the Treasury stops; the more important branch of 'patronage', that is, the *promotion* of the department is left completely and exclusively in the hands of the permanent departmental head, i.e. the Board of Inland Revenue, and is disposed of without the slightest reference to political interest. Now, it will be said that (and probably necessary, however the constitution of the department in other respects be settled) to make *admission to the army* independent of the will of the head, be he 'political' or permanent, and I maintain that the example of the Inland Revenue shows that *promotion* in a department *may* be kept clear of political influences.

But it is not sufficient for the War Minister to have the control and direction of the *Army*; he should have that of the *Navy* also. Being solely responsible for the plan and conduct of the war, it seems to follow, as a matter of course, that he should wield all the weapons by which war is carried on. That two independent and equal Ministers should satisfactorily and successfully direct the operations of two departments so essentially dependent on each other as the land and sea-service are in time of war, would be impossible unless both of them were practically subject to a common head (who would then be the real War Minister as Chatham was), or unless, contrary to human nature, they were so free from departmental and personal jealousies, that they worked literally as one man. The very names and designations of *War* Minister, War Office, &c. as now applied, are absurd, because they are used as synonymous with Minister for the *Army* office for the *Army*, &c., as if the *Navy* had nothing to do with *War*!

I may observe here that no analogy applicable to England on this point is to be drawn from the practice of France, or any other despotic Government. Where there is a *real* Monarch, there may be a separation of the departments concerned with wars; because the necessary unity is furnished by the Monarchical element.

All the arguments which are strong against a division of command in the field, are far stronger against a division of supreme direction in the Cabinet. In short, I repeat, if departmental unity be an object desirable and attainable at all in this country, there is no department where unity is so desirable, no department where unity is so natural, as that which directs war-like operations, and as war-like operations involve a combination of military and naval forces, the War Minister should be supreme over army and navy. The same rule should apply to the internal management of the navy as to that of the army. The naval adviser of the War Minister should be a non-'political' sailor, an Admiral Commanding-in-Chief; that officer should be responsible for the government, discipline, distribution, and movements of the navy, and he should practically dispense as a general rule, naval appointments, and promotions.

If this were done the change which I advocate would actually *diminish* the political element in the two services, because, while it would not, as I maintain, give a mischievously 'political' character to Military patronage, it would take from naval patronage the 'political' character which now affects it. The naval member of the Cabinet, accordingly, should cease to exist; the First Lord of the Admiralty (if it were determined to maintain a Board, and not a single person, to manage naval affairs) should be a naval man, and not a 'Minister' (in the popular sense of the word).

But it would perhaps be necessary to have in Parliament a *Naval* Deputy-Secretary for War, the immediate subordinate of the War Minister who should prepare the naval estimates and represent the naval administration generally. On the other hand, there should be of course a *Military* Deputy-Secretary for War to prepare the Military estimates, and represent the Military administration in Parliament. I do not mean a soldier necessarily, but a Minister representing the military department. I use the designation of Deputy-Secretaries advisedly, not that of Under-Secretaries, because I think the latter might conveniently be confined to the permanent officers, who should in fact conduct, as they do in other departments, the routine business of the offices. I do not know how many Under-Secretaries would be required, to do the work of the consolidated War Department properly; this is a matter of detail, and comparatively unimportant. Probably one would be sufficient for the Naval branch and one for the Military branch. I do not know enough of the business of the Admiralty, to attempt to say how it ought to be divided between the Naval Commander-in-Chief and the War Department but I am quite clear about the principle of division, which is the same as that which should govern the Military arrangements, as between the War Department and the Horse Guards. That principle is I think pretty well understood, as regards military matters, at present, though it is imperfectly carried out, as indeed it must be, so long as the Horse Guards and the War Dept. are theoretically independent of each other.

The immediate and necessary consequence of departmental *independence* is a certain amount of departmental *jealousy*. In many respects greater freedom of action and more extensive jurisdiction would probably be allowed to the Commander-in-Chief within this own province, if the subordination of that province were clearly established. For example, the organization, arming, discipline and movements of foreign corps, militia, embodied or disembodied, yeomanry in short, of all the land forces, should properly be under the cognizance of the Commander-in-Chief; it should become unnecessary to maintain the existing restriction upon expenditure of money through the H.Gds. With him, too, it seems to me that the immediate super-

intendence of the Military academies should rest, although the
system on which they should be conducted, and the nature of
the relations between military education and admission to the
service, are matters of public policy which it would be for the
Minister of State to settle.

Again, such *jarrings* as necessarily take place under the
present system would be avoided. The War Minister is at present
understood to name, *in concurrence with the Commander-in-
Chief*, General officers to commands on active service. But
suppose they should irreconcilably differ, who is to decide the
question? The War Minister sent the other day for a regiment
to the Cape, and the General commanding there, not having
received orders from the Horse Guards, refused to let it go.
Now, these matters should be conducted, *always through* the
Horse Guards, and, *as a general rule*, practically *by* the Horse
Guards, but with a supreme controlling authority in the Secretary for War, without which the Military administration of the
empire must be either a mass of confusion, or a subject for
perpetual negotiation and compromise. The proper idea for a
constitution of the Military branch of the War Dept. is in my
opinion obvious. The Parliamentary *Under* Secretaryship should
be abolished. One Parliamentary representative of the Military
Administration, besides the Secretary of State, is enough. There
is not a proper province for a second. The present 'War-Office'
should be consolidated with the 'Ordnance', as there is no
logical or practical distinction between the business of the two
offices. The Chief of the 'Ordnance' is to be entrusted, I understand, with the duty of laying the estimates for the whole army
before Parliament, that is, he will be responsible for the finance
of the army. But the special and exclusive business of the 'War-
Office' is the finance of the army. It is desirable, therefore,
indeed I think it is necessary, that the Chief of the 'Ordnance'
whom I would call 'Deputy Secretary for War' should be the
head of the 'War-Office'. The present Deputy-Secretary at War
should become (what I have called, but it does not matter about
the title) Military Under-Secretary of State for War, and should
be the *permanent* chief of the Military Departments, subject of
course to the 'political' chiefs (the Secretary and Deputy-
Secretary) as the permanent Under-Secretaries for the Home
and Foreign Departments, are subordinate to the 'political'

Secretaries and Under-Secretaries who represent the Government of the day.

If the Military branch of the War Department were thoroughly amalgamated (as it ought to be) I see no reason why there should be *two* permanent Under-Secretaries in it, and many advantages in there being only one. But this, as I said before, is a matter of detail. The establishment of a permanent Under Secretary of State (say Mr Hawes) at the head of the permanent Staff of the Military Department, would supply a want now practically felt at the 'Ordnance', and which cannot, I am convinced, be otherwise supplied. Mr Monsell has now routine business to do with which he ought never to be troubled, and which a 'political' officer, who should come to his work in utter ignorance of it as politicians often necessarily come to it, *could* not do. As it is, when the Parliamentary session recommences, he will never be able to do it. Now, I am certain that defect cannot be remedied except by making an officer *whose official position should be clearly superior to that of the heads of the subordinate offices,* the centre of unity for those offices. There is such a centre in every other department of State; there is one in the Whitehall branch, and another in the 'War-Office' branch of the War Department. There *must* be one for the 'Ordnance' also; or rather the 'Ordnance' business should be placed within the circle of one of the existing centres, i.e. the 'War-Office'.

APPENDIX E

Abstract of the Passengers who sailed from Plymouth* on the 7th September, 1850, in the first four ships chartered by the Canterbury Association, viz., *Sir George Seymour*, *Charlotte Jane*, *Randolph*, and *Cressy*.

	Sir Geo. Seymour		Charlotte Jane		Randolph		Cressy		Total	
	Adults	Souls	A	S	A	S	A	S	A	S
Chief Cabins	34½	42	23½	25	25½	34	23	27	106½	128
Fore Cabins	15½	19	19½	23	14	14	20½	23	69½	79
Steerage: Assisted	105½	138	71	94	105½	148	115	164	397	544
Paying	10	14	9	9	12½	16	2	2	33½	41
	165½	213	123	151	157½	212	160½	216	606½	792

The above Steerage Adult Males and Unmarried Females consist of:

Carpenters	. . .	14	
Plumbers and Glaziers		2	
Blacksmiths	. . .	6	
Bricklayers	. . .	4	
Masons	. . . .	4	
Brick and Tile Makers		3	
Wheelwrights	. . .	1	
Gunsmiths	. . .	1	
Printers	. . . .	3	
Lightermen	. . .	2	

Cd. forward . 40

Bt. forward . 40

Millers	. . . . .	4	
Bakers	. . . . .	2	
Butchers	. . . . .	1	
Gardeners	. . . .	8	
Shepherds, Agricultural and other Labourers		111	
Stockmen, Dairymen, etc.	. . . . .	12	
Agricultural Machine Makers	. . .	1	
Domestic Servants	. .	30	

Total . . . 209

* Only 769 passengers were landed at Lyttelton. The embarkation lists appear to have included two families that were going on to other New Zealand settlements. There were also several deaths on the voyage.

Bibliographical Note

Bibliographies of the history of New Zealand may be found in *Cambridge History of the British Empire* Vol. VII (Cambridge, 1933) and in *The Colonization of New Zealand* by J. E. Marais (London, 1927).

1. Printed sources for the life of J. R. Godley:

> *A Selection from the Writings and Speeches of John Robert Godley* collected and edited by James Edward FitzGerald (Christchurch, New Zealand, 1863).
>
> The prefatory memoir of Godley, by FitzGerald, is the principal source of all the notices of Godley's life in current books of reference. This memoir was first published in *The Press* (Christchurch, New Zealand) on 29th January, 1862.
>
> *The Founders of Canterbury,* Vol. I, being letters from the late E. G. Wakefield to the late J. R. Godley, etc. (New Zealand, 1868).
>
> A selection of letters mostly written to members of the Canterbury Association between 1847 and 1850. They were collected and printed by the younger Wakefield to demonstrate the part played by his father in founding Canterbury.
>
> *Canterbury Papers,* Nos. 1–12 (London 1850–1), New Series, Nos. 1-2 (1858–9).
>
> A series of documents issued by the Canterbury Association. The first volume was issued in 1851. Two more numbers were issued in 1858 and 1859 by J. E. FitzGerald, as agent of Canterbury Province in London.
>
> *Extracts from the Letters of J. R. Godley to C. B. Adderley* (edited by C. B. Adderley, afterwards Lord Norton, and printed privately in London, 1863).
>
> Extracts from private letters written from Godley to Adderley between 1839 and 1861. Documents of the highest importance for the history of the Commonwealth.

The Life of Lord Norton (Rt. Hon. Sir Charles Adderley, K.C.M.G., M.P.) by W. S. Childe-Pemberton. (London, 1909.)

Contains numerous allusions to Godley, their joint undertakings and their mutual friends.

Reminiscences of Lord Kilbracken (Sir Arthur Godley). (London, 1931.)

The earlier chapters contain Arthur Godley's reminiscences of his father, J. R. Godley.

Letters from Early New Zealand, by Charlotte Godley with an introduction by A. P. Newton (privately printed, London, 1936; second edition, Christchurch, 1950).

Obituary notice in the *Lyttelton Times* (New Zealand), 25th January, 1862.

Obituary notice in the *Harrow Gazette,* 5th July, 1862, written by W. P. Prendergast.

Conventional notices of J. R. Godley in *Alumni Oxonienses* and *Harrow School Register,* and of the Godley Family in *Burke's Peerage* under Baron Kilbracken.

A Few Reminiscences of Killegar, County Leitrim, by Archibald Godley. (Dublin, 1906.)

A leaflet, written by Archibald, brother of J. R. Godley, and privately printed, with some memorials of the family.

A full account of the Leitrim Election was printed in the *Freeman's Journal,* under various dates in August, 1847.

2. Manuscript sources (a) in England:

Correspondence and private papers of *J. R. Godley,* in the possession of Miss Eleanor Godley. The collection includes a large number of letters written by Godley to his father, with some replies.

Correspondence and private papers of *George William, 4th Lord Lyttelton,* in the possession of the Viscount Cobham, Hagley Park, Worcestershire.

The collection includes letters from Godley, J. E. FitzGerald, E. G. Wakefield, H. Sewell, Bishop Selwyn, Sir George Grey, C. B. Adderley and many others. (While this book was in the press many of these letters were presented by Lord Cobham to the Canterbury Museum, Christchurch, New Zealand.)

Papers of *C. B. Adderley, Lord Norton*, in the Birmingham Reference Library.

A search of this collection revealed one useful document, the minute-book of the Society for the Reform of Colonial Government, 1850-1.

The Gladstone MSS in the British Museum.

A search in this gigantic collection proved disappointing. Although Godley was on terms of friendship with Gladstone from 1844 to 1861, and was a guest in his house, the written evidences of the friendship are scanty. Three letters from Gladstone to Godley ('My dear Mr Godley . . . . most sincerely yours'), and one affectionate letter from Mrs Gladstone to Mrs Godley, are in the Gladstone MSS. Another letter from Gladstone to Godley is printed in *Founders of Canterbury*. No letters to or from Godley have been traced in the Gladstone MSS. There are many friendly allusions to J. R. Godley in Gladstone's correspondence with Lyttelton, Adderley, FitzGerald, Sir W. James, and Godley's son, Arthur, Lord Kilbracken.

The Wakefield Papers in the British Museum (MS. Additional. 35261.)

The archives of the Dukes of Newcastle are not open to the inspection of scholars. It is known that the 5th Duke corresponded regularly with Godley and preserved his letters.

2. Manuscript sources (b) in New Zealand:

Correspondence of *J. R. Godley* in the Canterbury Museum, Christchurch.

Minute-books and dispatch-books of the *Canterbury Association*, in the possession of the Diocese of Christchurch.

A collection of letters, mostly to H. S. Selfe, in the Hocken Institute, Dunedin.

The Journal of *Henry Sewell* and letters from *E. G. Wakefield and others* at Canterbury College, Christchurch.

The archives of Christ's College, Christchurch.

The Foundation of Canterbury, an unpublished thesis by M. M. Hickey.

3. General works on the Canterbury Settlement:

A full bibliography may be found in *The Colonization of New Zealand* by J. E. Marais (London, 1927). I have found the following useful when writing of Godley.

T. Cholmondeley: *Letter to J. R. Godley* (Lyttelton, N.Z., 1852).

A. Cox: *Recollections of Australia and New Zealand* (Christchurch, N.Z., 1884).

(W. and J. Deans): *Pioneers of Canterbury*. Correspondence of the Deans brothers, 1840–1854. Edited by J. Deans (Dunedin, 1937).

A. J. Harrop: *England and New Zealand* (London, 1926).

A. J. Harrop: *Amazing Career of E. G. Wakefield* (London, 1928).

James Hay: *Reminiscences of Earliest Canterbury* (Christchurch, 1915).

R. Garnett: *Edward Gibbon Wakefield* (London, 1898).

W. P. Morrell: *The Provincial System in New Zealand* (London, 1932).

H. T. Purchas: *History of the English Church in New Zealand* (Christchurch, 1914).

H. T. Purchas: *Bishop Harper and Canterbury Settlement* (Christchurch, 1903).

A. Trollope: *Australia and New Zealand* (London, 1873).

H. F. Wigram: *The Story of Christchurch, New Zealand* (Christchurch, 1916). The best published account of the Canterbury Settlement.

4. Other works containing allusions to Godley, or to his concerns:

Disraeli, Life of, Vol. III by W. F. Monypenny and G. E. Buckle (London, 1920). Adverse criticism of Godley.

Gladstone, Life of, Vol. I by John Morley (London, 1903). Weak on colonial policy. Indirect allusions only.

Granville, Life of Earl, by Lord E. Fitzmaurice (London, 1905).

Gregory, Sir W. H.: *Autobiography* (London, 1894) for Godley's Irish period.

(Herbert, Sidney) *Life of Lord Herbert of Lea*, by Sir A. Gordon, Lord Stanmore (London, 1906).

History of 'The Times', Vol. II (London, 1939).

Lyttelton, George William, Lord: *Ephemera* (1st series, London, 1865, 2nd series, 1872).

Newcastle, Life of the 5th Duke of, by J. Martineau
(London, 1908).

Norton, Lord (C. B. Adderley): *Colonial Policy of Lord
John Russell* (London, 1869).

Norton, Lord (C. B. Adderley): *Imperial Fellowship*
(London, 1903).

O'Rourke, Rev. J.: *The Great Irish Famine* (Dublin,
1875). Adverse criticism of Godley's Emigration scheme.

Selborne, Memorials of R. Palmer, Lord (London, 1898).

Tennyson, Alfred, Lord. A Memoir by H., Lord Tennyson
(London, 1897).

Wakefield, E. G.: *The Art of Colonization* (London,
1849).

For a general account of the Colonial Reform move-
ment the most useful books have been:—W. P. Morrell:
British Colonial Policy in the Age of Peel and Russell
(Oxford, 1930); *Cambridge History of the British
Empire,* Vol. II, chapters 10, 19, and 22 (Cambridge,
1940); and P. Knaplund: *Gladstone and Britain's Imperial
Policy* (New York, 1927).

It is regrettable that there is no adequate biography
either of Bishop Selwyn or of Sir George Grey.

5. Godley's printed works:

Letters from America, by J. R. Godley (2 vols.) (London,
1844).

Writings and Speeches. Ed. J. E. FitzGerald. *See above.*

Letters of J. R. Godley. Ed. C. B. Adderley. *See above.*

For several years Godley was a working journalist.
From February, 1848, until December, 1849, he was
regularly employed as leader-writer for the *Morning
Chronicle.* Among his casual writings the following have
been noted:—

Dublin Evening Mail. Letter on Canada, 25th January,
1843.

A Letter on the Subject of Poor Rates (Dublin, 1843).
A pamphlet.

Observations on the Irish Poor-Law (Dublin, 1847). A pamphlet.

Spectator. Six practical letters on the state of Ireland, October-November, 1847.

Morning Chronicle (20th December, 1849), and other journals. Open letter to Mr Gladstone on the Government of Colonies, dated 12th December, 1849.

Speech on Church Government, printed at Lyttelton, 1852, reprinted in London, 1856.

Frasers' Magazine. Journal of a visit to New South Wales. Two articles, November and December, 1853.

Spectator. Two letters on federating the Empire, 1st and 15th July, 1854.

Economist. Letter on agricultural tenures. . . . 1856.

Extracts from some of these pieces are reprinted in *Writings and Speeches* or in *Letters of J. R. Godley. See above.*

6. Parliamentary Papers:

> For Godley's Irish Emigration Scheme.
>> P.P. 1847, Vol. VI; 1848, Vol. XVII.

> For the Canterbury Settlement.
>> P.P. 1847–8, Vol. XLIII; 1849, Vol. XXXV; 1850, Vol. XXXVII; 1851, Vol. XXXV; 1852–3, Vol. LXV, p. 327.

> For the Committee on Colonial Defences.
>> P.P. 1859 (Session 2), Vol. XVIII, p. 114; 1861, Vol. XIII, p. 423.

7. Colonial Office Papers in the Record Office, London:

> Those relating to Canterbury may be traced from the entry C.O. 208, 83; 114–8.

Index

First Four Ships, 94, 109, 112, 118, 131
Fitzgerald, Dr, 108
FitzGerald, James Edward, 73-4, 80, 85, 89, 92, 113, 115, 117, 122, 123, 124, 134, 135, 136, 138, 147, 164, 165, 166, 167, 175, 177, 181, 182, 204, 210, 211, 229
Fitzroy, Sir Charles, 155
Fly, H.M.S., 113
Forsyth, William, 226
Fox, William, 106, 111, 159, 206
Franklin, Sir John, 81
Fraser's Magazine, Godley's articles on Australia, 152

Garibaldi, Guiseppe, 205
Gell, Rev. J. P., 81
Gladstone, W. E., 2, 6, 27, 29, 31, 53, 55, 67, 68, 73, 74, 77, 83, 109, 145, 162, 168, 169fn., 173-4, 189, 190, 192, 194, 196, 198, 199, 200, 202, 206, 210, 211, 215, 229
Gleig, Rev. G. R., 68, 227
Glynne family, 29
Godley Archibald, 45, 208
Godley, Arthur, 45, 96, 107, 108, 125, 128, 137, 140, 208-9, 211
Godley, Charlotte, 30, 45, 63, 95-7, 107, 108, 112, 120, 121, 122-3, 128, 138, 139, 140, 141, 152, 153-4, 189, 205, 209
Godley, Denis, 15, 19, 97, 142, 208
Godley, Harriet, 208
Godley, James, 208
Godley, John Robert, *Letters from America,* 1-2, 25; birth and early education, 3; at Harrow, 4-5; at Christ Church, Oxford, 5-9; called to Irish Bar, 9; travels in Europe, 10; interest in *Tracts for the Times,* 11; law practice in Dublin, 14; travels in United States and Canada, 16-23; views on slavery, 19; Canadian constitutional problems, 20-3; the Church in America, 22; disturbances and famine in Ireland, 24-46; High Sheriff of County, 24; county magistrate, 25; support for Peel's Irish Education Bill, 27; engagement and marriage, 29-30; Dublin committee for relief of distress, 33; secretary of

new Irish Party, 34; plan for mass emigration of Irish to Canada, 35-6; evidence to Lord Devon's Commission, 37; support of Wakefield system of colonisation, 37; Lord Monteagle's Committee, 40-1; Parliamentary candidate for County Leitrim, 40-6; birth of son, 45; writing for *Spectator,* 47, 59; the Colonial Reformers, 48; first meeting with Edward Gibbon Wakefield, 48; the man in 1847, 48; persuaded by Wakefield to take leading part in plan for Church of England Settlement in N.Z., 56, 59, 60; Director of N.Z. Company, 60; settles in London, 62; success as journalist, 64; interest in Irish Catholic colonisation, 64-5; formation of Canterbury Association, 65; friendship with C. B. Adderley, 65; member managing committee of Canterbury Association, 68; health deteriorates, 75; persuaded by Wakefield to go to N.Z., 75-6; Resident Chief Agent for Canterbury Settlement, 76; negotiations concerning Canterbury bishopric, 78; plan for a college, 81; sails for Canterbury, 81; letter to Gladstone on government of colonies, 83, 215; FitzGerald's friendship, 89; voyage to N.Z., 95-7; at Otago, 97; arrival at Lyttelton and description of site, 103-6; funds overspent, stops preparatory work, 106-7; at Wellington, 107-12; hydropathic treatment, 108; opposition to Sir George Grey, 109-12; return to Lyttelton, 112; welcomes Pilgrims on arrival, 113; Resident Magistrate and Commissioner of Crown Lands, 115; difficulties about Bishop-designate, 118; getting settlers onto their land, 121-3; description of site of Christchurch, 125; difficulty over pastoral licences, 126-7, 132; visit to Akaroa, 128; further disagreement with Sir George Grey, 129; demands local self-government, 131; sends resignation to Association, 133;

opinions of Godley as administrator, 135-6; persuaded to remain temporarily, 142-4; views on Constitution of N.Z. Church, 144-7; setlers ask him to remain in Canterbury, 147; farewell speech, 148-50, in New South Wales, 152-5; Sewell suggested as successor, 163; return to London, 168; Commissioner of Inland Revenue for Ireland, 168; speech at complimentary banquet, 169-70; letters on federal union of Empire, 172-3; Canterbury Dinner of 1856, 175; speech in 1858 reviews Canterbury progress, 184; Director-General of Stores at Ordnance Department, 191; Assistant Under-Secretary of State for War, 194; proposals for administrative changes, 196, 200, 231; committee on colonial military expenditure and report, 201-4; health becomes worse, 205; last days and death, 208-9; statue in Christchurch, 209; FitzGerald's memoir, 210; Harrow School memorial, 210, 229
Godley, John (Senior), 3, 14, 25, 27, 28, 43, 45; letters from John Robert, 62-3, 125, 138; health failing, 139; effect of John Robert's death, 209; death, 209
Godley, William, 15, 189
Goulburn, Henry, 66, 226
Gregory, W. H., 36, 44, 169
Grey, Lord, 38, 39, 54-5, 57, 67, 69, 71, 72, 73, 74, 75, 77, 79, 91, 109, 111, 119, 121, 131, 158, 159, 161, 203
Grey, Sir George, 53, 55, 70, 71, 73, 75, 107, 109-12, 113-4, 126-32, 134, 136, 138, 144-7, 151-2, 159, 165, 166, 168, 170, 178, 196, 198, 203

Hadfield, Archdeacon, 108, 144
Halswell, Edmund S., 40, 67, 68, 175
Hamilton, G. A., 201
Hardinge, Lord, 232
Hare, Ven. Archdeacon J. C., 227
Harewood, Earl of, 224
Harper, Dr H. J. C., 180, 181, 186-7
Harrow School, 4-5, 10, 209-10

Hashemy, The, 151, 152
Hawes, Sir Benjamin, 39, 194, 201, 207, 208, 237
Hawkins, Rev. E., 68, 86, 227
Hay, E., 127-8
Heathcote, Sir W., 225
Herbert, Sidney, 6, 31, 64, 66, 85, 190, 193, 196, 206, 207, 226
Hervey, Lord Alfred, 225
Higgins, M. J., 229
Hildyard, Colonel, 62
Hillard, S. G., 189
Hincks, Francis, 174, 175
Hinds, Rev. Dr S., 59, 85, 92, 227
Hook, Rev. Dr W. F., 227
Howe, Joseph, 171-2, 174, 175
Hornbrook, Major A., 103
Hutt, John, 67, 68-9, 72, 83, 227

Ireland, immigrants in America, 2; Irish emigration, 2, 36-41, 71; Royal Commission on Irish distress, 2; famine and disturbances, 24-46; Irish Education Bill, 27; New Irish Party, 34; Irish election, 41-4; Godley's letters in *Spectator* on social conditions, 47-8

Jackson, Mrs, 120
Jackson, Rev. Thomas, 86-7, 90, 94, 118-21, 125, 156, 157, 164, 177, 178, 180, 186, 228
Jacobs, Rev. Henry, 116, 146
James, Sir Walter, 66, 68, 175, 188, 226, 229
Jollie, Edward, 101, 102
Jones, Sir Willoughby, 226
Jowett, Dr, 162, 211

Keble, Rev. John, 7
Kilbracken, Lord, see *Godley, Arthur*

Labouchere, Henry, 32, 194
Lady Nugent, The, 95, 97
Lafontaine, Hippolyte, 20, 21
Land-purchasers' Council, 115, 122, 132, 142
Lansdowne, Lord, 38
Leitrim, Lord, 41
Letters from Early New Zealand, 96
Lincoln, Lord, 28-9, 31, 32, 39, 64, 66, 94fn, 163, 164, 168, 176, 190, 192, 196, 197, 200, 204, 208, 211, 224, 229

Wellington, the Godleys in, 106-12, 151-2
Wellington, Duke of, 72, 151, 232
Whately, R., 36, 59, 65, 224
Wilberforce, S., 67, 68, 85, 86, 94fn, 175, 176, 225
Wilberforce, Ven. Archdeacon R., 228
Wilson, Sir Cracroft, 180

Winchester, Bishop of, see *Sumner, C. R.*
Wodehouse, Lord, 228
Woolner, T., 209
Wynne, Charles, 10, 29, 66, 84
Wynne, Charles Griffith (Senior), 30, 228, 229
Wynne, Frances, 205, 206
Wynter, Rev. J. C., 228

For EU product safety concerns, contact us at Calle de José Abascal, 56–1°,
28003 Madrid, Spain or eugpsr@cambridge.org.

www.ingramcontent.com/pod-product-compliance
Ingram Content Group UK Ltd.
Pitfield, Milton Keynes, MK11 3LW, UK
UKHW010346140625
459647UK00010B/860